FREE DVD FREE FREE DVD

From Stress to Success DVD from Trivium Test Prep

Dear Customer,

Thank you for purchasing from Trivium Test Prep! Whether you're a new teacher or looking to advance your career, we're honored to be a part of your journey.

To show our appreciation (and to help you relieve a little of that test-prep stress), we're offering a **FREE *ATI TEAS 6 Essential Test Tips DVD**** by Trivium Test Prep. Our DVD includes 35 test preparation strategies that will help keep you calm and collected before and during your big exam. All we ask is that you email us your feedback and describe your experience with our product. Amazing, awful, or just so-so: we want to hear what you have to say!

To receive your **FREE *ATI TEAS 6 Essential Test Tips DVD***, please email us at 5star@ triviumtestprep.com. Include "Free 5 Star" in the subject line and the following information in your email:

1. The title of the product you purchased.
2. Your rating from 1 – 5 (with 5 being the best).
3. Your feedback about the product, including how our materials helped you meet your goals and ways in which we can improve our products.
4. Your full name and shipping address so we can send your **FREE *ATI TEAS 6 Essential Test Tips DVD***.

If you have any questions or concerns please feel free to contact us directly at 5star@triviumtestprep.com.

Thank you, and good luck with your studies!

* Please note that the free DVD is not included with this book. To receive the free DVD, please follow the instructions above.

ATI TEAS 6 Study Guide 2018-2019

2018-2019

ATI TEAS Version 6 Study Manual
and Practice Test Questions

TABLE OF CONTENTS

ONLINE RESOURCES

To help you fully prepare for your ATI TEAS exam, Accepted includes online resources with the purchase of this study guide.

Practice Test

In addition to the practice test included in this book, we also offer an online exam. Since many exams today are computer based, getting to practice your test-taking skills on the computer is a great way to prepare.

Flash Cards

A convenient supplement to this study guide, Accepted's flash cards enable you to review important terms easily on your computer or smartphone.

Cheat Sheets

Review the core skills you need to master the exam with easy-to-read Cheat Sheets.

From Stress to Success

Watch From Stress to Success, a brief but insightful YouTube video that offers the tips, tricks, and secrets experts use to score higher on the exam.

Reviews

Leave a review, send us helpful feedback, or sign up for Accepted promotions—including free books!

Access these materials at:

www.acceptedinc.com/ati-teas-online-resources

INTRODUCTION

The Test of Essential Academic Skills (TEAS) VI is a part of the admissions process for nursing and allied health programs around the country. Schools use the test to assess applicants' capabilities in four subject areas: reading, mathematics, science, and English and language usage. This guide will allow you to review your knowledge in these subject areas, apply your knowledge, and answer test questions.

What's on the TEAS VI?

There are 170 multiple-choice questions on the TEAS, 150 of which will be scored. The remaining twenty questions are unscored pre-test questions that will not be indicated on the test. The number of questions for each subject area and sub-area is indicated in the following table.

What's on the TEAS VI?

SUBJECT	SUB-AREAS	TIME LIMIT
Reading 53 questions: paragraph and passage comprehension and informational source comprehension	Key ideas and details (22) Craft and structure (14) Integration of knowledge and ideas (11) Pre-test questions (6, unscored)	64 minutes
Mathematics 36 questions: numbers and operations, measurement, data interpretation, and algebra	Numbers and algebra (23) Measurement and data (9) Pre-test questions (4, unscored)	54 minutes
Science 53 questions: scientific reasoning, human body science, life science, Earth science, and physical science	Human anatomy and physiology (32) Life and physical sciences (8) Scientific reasoning (7) Pre-test questions (6, unscored)	63 minutes

SUBJECT	SUB-AREAS	TIME LIMIT
English and language usage 28 questions: grammar, punctuation, spelling, word meaning, and sentence structure	Conventions of standard English (9) Knowledge of language (9) Vocabulary acquisition (6) Pre-test questions (4, unscored)	28 minutes
Total	170 questions, of which 150 are scored	3 hours and 29 minutes (209 minutes)

Scoring

You cannot pass or fail the TEAS VI exam. Instead, you will receive a score report that details the number of questions you got right in each section and also gives your percentile rank, which shows how you did in comparison to other test takers. Each school has its own entrance requirements, so be sure to check the requirements of the institutions you want to attend so that you can set appropriate goals for yourself.

Each section contains a number of pre-test questions that are unscored, for a total of twenty on the exam. While you must complete these items, they will not be considered as part of your score.

Examinees who take the online version of the TEAS will receive their scores immediately after the test. If you take the paper-and-pencil version, ATI will score your exam within forty-eight hours of receiving it from the testing site. Your scores are automatically sent to the school you chose upon registering for the exam. You must contact the administrators of the exam, the Assessment Technologies Institute (ATI), to send your scores to any other programs.

How is the Exam Administered?

The TEAS is administered by the Assessment Technologies Institute (ATI) at testing centers nationwide. To register for the exam, refer to the ATI website. You may choose to take a pencil-and-paper or computerized test. Both test types contain the same information and number of questions. You are encouraged the take the test in the format that is most comfortable for you.

On the day of your test, arrive early and be sure to bring government-issued, photo identification; two No. 2 pencils; and your ATI login information. You are required to put away all personal belongings before the test begins. Cell phones and other electronic, photographic, recording, or listening devices are not permitted in the testing center. Calculators and scratch paper will be provided by the testing center. You will be permitted a ten-minute break after the mathematics section. For the most up-to-date details on what to expect on test day, refer to the ATI website.

How to Use This Guide

The chapters in this book are divided into a review of the topics covered on the exam. This is not intended to teach you everything you'll see on the test: there is no way to cram all of that material into one book! Instead, we are going to help you recall information that you've already learned, and even more importantly, we'll show you how to apply that knowledge. Each chapter includes an extensive review with practice questions at the end to test your knowledge. With time, practice, and determination, you'll be well-prepared for test day.

This guide will help you master the most important test topics and also develop critical test-taking skills. To support this effort, the guide provides:

- organized concepts with detailed explanations
- practice questions with worked-through solutions
- key test-taking strategies
- simulated one-on-one tutor experience
- tips, tricks, and test secrets

About Accepted, Inc.

Accepted, Inc. uses industry professionals with decades' worth of knowledge in their fields, proven with degrees and honors in law, medicine, business, education, the military, and more, to produce high-quality test prep books for students.

Our study guides are specifically designed to increase any student's score, regardless of his or her current skill level. Our books are also shorter and more concise than typical study guides, so you can increase your score while significantly decreasing your study time.

We Want to Hear from You

Here at Accepted, Inc. our hope is not only that we taught you the relevant information needed to pass the exam, but that we also helped you exceed all previous expectations. Our goal is to keep our guides concise, show you a few test tricks along the way, and ultimately help you succeed in your goals.

On that note, we are always interested in your feedback. To let us know if we've truly prepared you for the exam, please email us at support@acceptedinc.com. Feel free to include your test score!

Your success is our success. Good luck on the exam and in your future ventures.

Sincerely,

– The Accepted, Inc. Team –

PART I: READING

The TEAS VI Reading test includes questions about a wide range of media, including fiction and nonfiction passages, diagrams, graphs, sets of directions, and professional communications like emails and memos. Generally, these questions fall into three categories.

KEY IDEAS AND DETAILS questions test your comprehension of the text on a broad level. You will need to see the text as a whole, identify the main ideas, and explain how they lead to specific inferences and conclusions. You will also need to discern the overall theme of a text and summarize it accurately.

CRAFT AND STRUCTURE questions test your understanding of the craft of writing. You might see questions about the use of language, point of view, and organization. You will need to analyze the details of the passage and relate them to the overall organization and meaning of the passage.

INTEGRATION OF KNOWLEDGE questions ask you to incorporate your skills from the other categories to answer complex questions. Questions might ask you to evaluate a text, compare multiple texts, or examine other kinds of texts, such as visual media. In order to answer questions like this, you will need to synthesize the skills applied to other types of questions and go beyond analyzing texts to evaluating and judging them.

expository
narrative
persuasive
descriptive

INTERPRETING TEXT

The Main Idea

The MAIN IDEA of a text describes the text's main topic and the author's perspective on that topic. On the TEAS, you will be asked to identify the topic and main idea of a text, and you may have to use this information to concisely summarize a passage.

To find the main idea, first identify the TOPIC, which is simply what the passage is about. The TOPIC SENTENCE is generally the first sentence, or very near the first sentence, in the paragraph. It introduces the reader to the topic by making a general statement about that topic so that the reader knows what to expect in the rest of the passage. Once you've identified the topic, use the text to figure out what the author wants to say about that topic.

> To determine the topic, ask yourself what you're reading about. To determine the main idea, ask yourself how the author feels about that topic.

As you read the following passage, think about the topic and what the author wants to communicate about that topic.

> Swimmers and beachgoers may look nervously for the telltale fin skimming the surface of the ocean, but the reality is that shark bites are extremely rare and almost never unprovoked. Sharks attack people at very predictable times and for very predictable reasons: rough surf, poor visibility, or a swimmer sending visual and physical signals that mimic a shark's normal prey are just a few examples. The "shark mania" of recent years can be largely pinned on the sensationalistic media surrounding the animals. The release of *Jaws* in 1975 to the ultra-hyped shark feeding frenzies and "worst shark attacks" countdowns known as *Shark Week* are just some examples. Popular culture both demonizes and fetishizes sharks until the public cannot get enough.

The topic of the passage is the single thing that is discussed throughout the passage: the danger of sharks. To identify the main idea of the passage, ask yourself what the author wants to say about this topic. What does she want the reader to think about the danger of sharks after reading this passage? It's clear from the author's opening sentence that she wants the reader to understand that shark attacks are not nearly as common or dangerous as popular culture makes them seem. The author includes details about the reasons shark bites happen in the real world, then explains how this danger is exaggerated in movies and on TV.

EXAMPLES

Tourists flock to Yellowstone National Park each year to view the geysers that bubble and erupt throughout it. What most of these tourists do not know is that these geysers are formed by a caldera, a hot crater in the earth's crust that was created by a series of three eruptions from an ancient supervolcano. These eruptions, which began 2.1 million years ago, spewed between 1,000 and 2,450 cubic kilometers of volcanic matter at such a rate that the volcano's magma chamber collapsed, creating the craters.

1. Which of the following is the topic of the passage?
    A) tourists
    B) geysers
    C) volcanic eruptions
    D) supervolcanoes

    Answer:
    B) **Correct.** The topic of the passage is geysers. Tourists, volcanic eruptions, and supervolcanoes are all mentioned during the explanation of what geysers are and how they are formed.

The Battle of Little Bighorn (1876), commonly called Custer's Last Stand, was a battle between the Lakota, the Northern Cheyenne, the Arapaho, and the Seventh Calvary Regiment of the US Army. Led by war leaders Crazy Horse and Chief Gall and the religious leader Sitting Bull, the allied tribes of the Plains Indians decisively defeated their US foes. Two hundred sixty-eight US soldiers were killed, including General George Armstrong Custer, two of his brothers, his nephew, his brother-in-law, and six Indian scouts.

2. Which of the following could be considered the main idea of the passage?
    A) Most of General Custer's family died in the Battle of Little Bighorn.
    B) During the nineteenth century, the US Army often fought with Indian tribes.
    C) Sitting Bull and George Custer were fierce enemies.
    D) The Battle of Little Bighorn was a significant victory for the Plains Indians.

    Answer:
    D) **Correct.** The author writes, "the allied tribes decisively defeated their US foes," and the remainder of the passage provides details to support this idea. Choice A is a fact from the passage but is not general enough to be the main idea. Similarly, Choice C can be inferred from the passage but is not what the majority of the passage is about. Choice B is too general and discusses topics outside the content of the passage.

Summarizing Passages

Understanding the main idea can help you summarize a passage. A SUMMARY is a very brief restatement of the most important parts of an argument or text. To build a summary, start by identifying the main idea, then add the most important details that support that main idea. A good summary will address ALL the ideas contained in the passage, not just one or two specific details.

The SUMMARY SENTENCE of a paragraph frequently (but not always!) comes at the end of a paragraph or passage, because it wraps up all of the ideas the passage presents. This sentence gives the reader an understanding of what the author wants to say about the topic and what conclusions can be drawn about it.

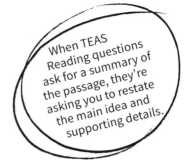

When TEAS Reading questions ask for a summary of the passage, they're asking you to restate the main idea and supporting details.

EXAMPLE

The greatest changes in sensory, motor, and perceptual development happen in the first two years of life. When babies are first born, most of their senses operate in a similar way to those of adults. For example, babies are able to hear before they are born; studies show that babies turn toward the sound of their mother's voice just minutes after being born, indicating they recognize the mother's voice from their time in the womb.

The exception to this rule is vision. A baby's vision changes significantly in the first year of life; initially infants have a range of vision of only 8 – 12 inches and no depth perception. As a result, infants rely primarily on hearing; vision does not become the dominant sense until around the age of 12 months. Babies also prefer faces to other objects. This preference, along with their limited vision range, means that their sight is initially focused on their caregiver.

Which of the following is a concise summary of the passage?

A) Babies have no depth perception until 12 months, which is why they focus only on their caregivers' faces.

B) Babies can recognize their mother's voice when born, so they initially rely primarily on their sense of hearing.

C) Babies have senses similar to those of adults except for their sense of sight, which doesn't fully develop until 12 months.

D) Babies' senses go through many changes in the first year of their lives.

Answers:

A) Incorrect. The passage is about babies' senses in general; therefore this answer choice is too specific.

B) Incorrect. The passage is about babies' senses in general; therefore this answer choice is too specific.

C) Correct. The passage states that babies' senses are much like those of adults with the exception of their vision, which develops later.

D) Incorrect. The passage indicates that a baby's vision "changes significantly in the first year of life" but suggests that other senses are relatively well-developed at birth.

Supporting Details

An author makes her argument using SUPPORTING DETAILS, which make up the majority of a text passage. Supporting details can include FACTS, which can be verified as true, and OPINIONS, which are the author's personal beliefs.

Supporting details are often introduced by SIGNAL WORDS that explain to the reader how one sentence or idea is connected to another and hint at supporting ideas. Signal words can indicate new information, counterarguments, or conclusions.

When reading a text, underline key signal words like *for example* and *because* to help you identify important points.

- adding information: additionally, also, in addition, furthermore, too
- give an example: for example, for instance, in other words, in particular
- show cause and effect: because, so, therefore, consequently
- comparing: in the same way, like, likewise, similarly
- contrasting: alternatively, conversely, instead of, otherwise, unlike
- sequence: first, second, next, after, before, then, finally

EXAMPLES

Increasingly, companies are turning to subcontracting services rather than hiring full-time employees. This provides companies with many advantages. For example, subcontractors offer greater flexibility, reduced legal responsibility to employees, and lower possibility of unionization within the company. However, it has also led to increasing confusion and uncertainty over the legal definition of employment. Recently, the courts have grappled with questions about the hiring company's responsibility in maintaining fair labor practices. Companies argue that they delegate that authority to the subcontractors, while unions and other worker advocate groups argue that companies still have a legal obligation to the workers who contribute to their business.

1. According to the passage, which of the following is NOT an advantage of using subcontracting services?
   A) greater flexibility
   B) uncertainty about the legal definition of employment
   C) reduced legal responsibility to employees
   D) lower possibility of unionization within the company

Answer:
   B) **Correct.** Choices A, C, and D are listed as advantages of using subcontracting services (introduced after the signal words *for example*). Uncertainly about the legal definition of employment is given later as one of the disadvantages of using subcontracting services.

2. Which of the following statements from the passage is an opinion?

   A) Companies are turning to subcontracting services rather than hiring full-time employees.

   B) Subcontractors offer greater flexibility, reduced legal responsibility to employees, and lower possibility of unionization within the company.

   C) The courts have grappled with questions about the hiring company's responsibility in maintaining fair labor practices.

   D) Companies still have a legal obligation to the workers who contribute to their business.

   Answer:

   D) **Correct.** Choices A, B, and C are all facts that can be proven with evidence. For example, employment data could show that companies now choose subcontracting services over full-time employees (Choice A). Choice D is an opinion held by unions and advocate groups.

After looking at five houses, Robert and I have decided to buy the one on Forest Road. The first two homes we visited didn't have the space we need—the first had only one bathroom, and the second did not have a guest bedroom. The third house, on Pine Street, had enough space inside but didn't have a big enough yard for our three dogs. The fourth house we looked at, on Rice Avenue, was stunning but well above our price range. The last home, on Forest Road, wasn't in the neighborhood we wanted to live in. However, it had the right amount of space for the right price.

3. Which of the following lists the author's actions in the correct sequence?

   A) The author looked at the house on Forest Road, then at a house with a yard that was too small, then at two houses that were too small, and then finally at a house that was too expensive.

   B) The author looked at the house on Forest Road, then at two houses that were too small, then at a house with a yard that was too small, and then finally at a house that was too expensive.

   C) The author looked at two homes with yards that were too small, then a house with only one bathroom, then a house that was too expensive, and then finally the house on Forest Road.

   D) The author looked at two homes that were too small, then a house with a yard that was too small, then a house that was too expensive, and then finally the house on Forest Road.

   Answer:

   D) **Correct.** Choice D correctly chronologically lists the houses the author visited in the passage.

Text Structure

The structure of a text describes how the author chooses to organize the supporting details in a passage. To identify the organizing structure of a passage, look at the order in which the author presents information and the transitions used to connect those pieces. Specific text structures are described in the table below.

Table 1.1 Text Structure

Name	Structure	Words to Look For
Cause and effect	The author describes a situation and then its effects.	because, as a result, consequently, therefore, for this reason
Compare and contrast	The author explores the similarities and differences between two or more things.	similarly, like, in addition, however, alternatively, unlike, but
Problem and solution	The author presents a problem and offers a solution.	if...then, problem, solution, answer
Description	The author describes a thing or process.	for example, for instance, such as, to illustrate
Chronological	The author lists events in the order in which they happened.	first, second, next, after, before

Underline signal words like *first*, *after*, *then*, and *consequently* to help identify the sequence of events in a passage.

EXAMPLE

In an effort to increase women's presence in government, several countries in Latin America, including Argentina, Brazil, and Mexico, have implemented legislated candidate quotas. These quotas require that at least 30 percent of a party's candidate list in any election cycle consists of women who have a legitimate chance at election. As a result, Latin America has the greatest number of female heads of government in the world, and the second highest percentage of female members of parliament after Nordic Europe. However, these trends do not carry over outside of politics. While 25 percent of legislators in Latin America are now women, less than 2 percent of CEOs in the region are female.

Which of the following best describes the organization of the passage?

A) compare and contrast

B) chronological

C) cause and effect

D) description

Answer:

C) **Correct.** The passage starts by introducing the topic of candidate quotas, then goes on to explain how these quotas have affected the number of female legislators and CEOs. The transition *as a result* links the cause to the effect.

Drawing Conclusions

Understanding a reading passage begins with understanding the explicit, or clearly stated, information in the text. Using that information, the reader can make conclusions or inferences about what the text suggests or implies but does not explicitly say.

To draw a CONCLUSION, readers must consider the details or facts in a passage, then determine what event or idea would logically follow at the end of the passage. For example, a story describes an old man sitting alone in a café. The young waiter says that the café is closing, but the old man continues to drink. The waiter starts closing up, and the old man tries to order another drink. Based on these details, the reader might conclude that the waiter will not bring the man another drink.

An INFERENCE is slightly different from a conclusion. An inference is an educated guess that readers make based on details in the text as well as their own knowledge and experiences. Returning to the story about the old man, the reader might use her own experiences to infer that the old man is lonely and so is reluctant to leave the café. Note that nothing in the passage explicitly states that the man is lonely—it is simply a possible interpretation of the situation.

EXAMPLE

Alfie closed his eyes and took several deep breaths. He was trying to ignore the sounds of the crowd, but even he had to admit that it was hard not to notice the tension in the stadium. He could feel 50,000 sets of eyes burning through his skin—this crowd expected perfection from him. He took another breath and opened his eyes, setting his sights on the soccer ball resting peacefully in the grass. One shot, just one last shot, between his team and the championship. He didn't look up at the goalie, who was jumping nervously on the goal line just a few yards away. Afterward, he would swear he didn't remember anything between the referee's whistle and the thunderous roar of the crowd.

Which of the following conclusions is BEST supported by the passage?
A) Alfie passed out on the field and was unable to take the shot.
B) The goalie blocked Alfie's shot.
C) Alfie scored the goal and won his team the championship.
D) The referee declared the game a tie.

Answer:
C) **Correct.** The crowd's support for Alfie and the collective roar after the shot implies that Alfie scored the goal and won the championship.

The Author's Purpose

Every author chooses text structure, words, and content with a specific purpose and intention. The TEAS will ask several types of questions that require you to figure out what the author is trying to say and what tools she is using to send that message.

Finding the AUTHOR'S PURPOSE requires identifying the author's main idea and intended audience: What is the author trying to accomplish by writing this text? The purpose of most text passages will fall into one of four MODES: narrative, expository, technical, or persuasive.

In a NARRATIVE, the author tells the reader a story, often to illustrate a theme or idea the reader needs to consider. The author will use the characteristics of storytelling, such as chronological order, characters, and a defined setting.

In an EXPOSITORY passage, the author simply explains an idea or topic to the reader. The main idea will probably be a factual statement or a direct assertion of a broadly held opinion. Expository writing can come in many forms, but one essential feature is a fair and balanced representation of a topic: the author may explore one detailed aspect or a broad range of characteristics, but he or she intends mainly to present the details or ideas to the reader to make a decision.

Similarly, in TECHNICAL writing, the author's purpose is to explain specific processes, techniques, or equipment so the reader can use that process, technique, or equipment to obtain the desired result. In this writing, look for chronological or spatial organization, specialized vocabulary, and imperative or directive structures.

The categories of writing discussed above mostly communicate information to a reader so that he or she can take action or make a decision. In contrast, in PERSUASIVE writing, the author actively sets out to convince the reader to accept an opinion or belief.

EXAMPLE

It could be said that the great battle between the North and South we call the Civil War was a battle for individual identity. The states of the South had their own culture, one based on farming, independence, and the rights of both man and state to determine their own paths. Similarly, the North had forged its own identity as a center of centralized commerce and manufacturing. This clash of lifestyles was bound to create tension, and this tension was bound to lead to war. But people who try to sell you this narrative are wrong. The Civil War was not a battle of cultural identities—it was a battle about slavery. All other explanations for the war are either a direct consequence of the South's desire for wealth at the expense of her fellow man or a fanciful invention to cover up this sad portion of our nation's history. And it cannot be denied that this time in our past was very sad indeed.

Which of the following best describes the mode of the passage?

A) expository

B) narrative

C) persuasive

D) technical

Answer:

C) **Correct.** The author of the passage is trying to persuade the reader that the "Civil War was not a battle of cultural identities—it was a battle about slavery." Phrases like "people…are wrong" and "it cannot be denied" suggest that the author is trying to convince the reader that a particular viewpoint is true.

Words in Context

The TEAS will ask you to determine the definition of words in context, meaning as they appear within the text. This can be slightly more difficult than simply knowing the definition of a word, as you may be required to figure out how the author is using the word in the specific text.

Context Clues

To grasp the meaning of unfamiliar words, readers may use context clues or hints in the text. Using context clues is especially helpful for determining the appropriate meaning of a word with multiple definitions.

One type of context clue is a DEFINITION or DESCRIPTION CLUE. Sometimes, authors may use a difficult word and then say "that is" or "which is" to signal the reader that they are providing a definition. An author may also provide a synonym or restate the idea in familiar words:

> Read the sentence with each answer choice plugged in for the vocabulary word to see which choice best matches the context.

> Teachers often prefer teaching students with intrinsic motivation; these students have an internal desire to learn.

The meaning of *intrinsic* is restated as *internal*.

Similarly, authors may include EXAMPLE CLUES by providing an example of the unfamiliar word close to the word:

> Teachers may view extrinsic rewards as efficacious; however, an individual student may not be interested in what the teacher offers. For example, a student who is diabetic may not feel any incentive to work when offered a sweet treat.

Efficacious is explained with an example demonstrating the effectiveness (and lack thereof) of extrinsic rewards.

Another commonly used context clue is the CONTRAST/ANTONYM CLUE. In this case, authors indicate that the unfamiliar word is the opposite of a familiar word:

> In contrast to intrinsic motivation, extrinsic motivation is contingent on teachers offering rewards that are appealing.

The phrase *in contrast* tells the reader that *extrinsic* is the opposite of *intrinsic*.

EXAMPLES

1. One challenge of teaching is finding ways to incentivize, or to motivate, learning. Which of the following is the meaning of *incentivize* as used in the sentence?

   A) encourage

   B) reward

   C) challenge

   D) improve

Answer:

A) **Correct.** The word *incentivize* is defined immediately with the synonym *motivate*, or *encourage*.

2. If an extrinsic reward is extremely desirable, a student may become so apprehensive he or she cannot focus. That is, the student may experience such intense pressure to perform that the reward undermines its intent.

   Which of the following is the meaning of *apprehensive* as used in the sentence?

   A) uncertain

   B) distracted

   C) anxious

   D) forgetful

Answer:

C) **Correct.** The reader can infer that the pressure to perform is making the student anxious.

Figurative Language

FIGURES OF SPEECH are expressions that are understood to have a nonliteral meaning. Instead of meaning what is actually said, figurative language suggests meaning by speaking of a subject as if it is something else. When Shakespeare says, "All the world's a stage, / And all men and women merely players," he isn't stating that the world is literally a stage. Instead, it functions like a stage, with men and women giving performances as if they were actors on a stage.

A METAPHOR is a figure of speech that works like an analogy. It uses something familiar and obvious to help the reader understand something that is new or hard to describe. For example, the phrase "the elephant in the room" is used to describe the concept of something unspoken but obvious. The unspoken idea is abstract, but the reader can grasp the concrete idea of an elephant as something so large and imposing that everyone is aware of it.

A SIMILE is figurative language that directly points to similarities between two things. Saying that someone runs "as fast as lightning" doesn't mean they're actually running at the speed of light; the simile just emphasizes that the person is very fast.

EXAMPLE

The coach was thrilled his team won its final game. The fact that his son scored the winning goal was just the icing on the cake.

In the sentence, "icing on the cake" refers to which of the following?

A) an unfortunate occurrence

B) an added benefit

C) a surprise event

D) an expected result

Research Skills

RESEARCH is the process of searching for credible information, or sources. SOURCES take various forms, such as written documentation, audio-visual materials, information found over the internet, in-person interviews, and more. Sources may answer specific questions posed in a text, enrich the information the writer provided on a topic, or support a writer's argument. In the twenty-first century, locating sources is easy; however, finding and determining quality sources involves careful evaluation of each one. The TEAS Reading test will include questions that ask you to categorize types of sources and evaluate which sources are appropriate for a specific task.

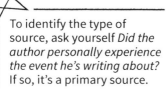

To identify the type of source, ask yourself *Did the author personally experience the event he's writing about?* If so, it's a primary source.

Types of Sources

The sources researchers use depend on their purpose. If the researcher's purpose is to analyze, interpret, or critique a historical event, a creative work, or a natural phenomenon, the researcher will use PRIMARY or original sources. Primary sources were produced by people with firsthand experience of an event. Examples of primary sources include:

- letters and emails
- autobiographies, diaries, and memoirs
- firsthand or eyewitness accounts or descriptions of events
- interviews, questionnaires, and surveys
- speeches and lectures
- photographs, drawings, and paintings
- news stories written at the time of the event

The written analysis or interpretation of a primary source is considered a SECONDARY SOURCE. These sources are written by people who did not have firsthand experience of the topic being described. Instead, authors of secondary sources examine primary sources in order to draw conclusions or make generalizations about people, events, and ideas. Examples of secondary sources include:

- literary criticism and interpretation
- biographies
- historical criticism
- political analyses
- essays on ethics and social policies

A TERTIARY SOURCE is a list or compilation of primary and secondary sources. A tertiary source doesn't provide analysis or new information—it simply lists other sources. Examples of tertiary sources include:

- bibliographies
- encyclopedias
- almanacs
- textbooks

EXAMPLE

Which of the following is an example of a secondary source for an article on local highways?

A) an online opinion column promoting tax incentives for those who carpool

B) photographs of traffic accidents

C) data from the city's transportation department

D) an autobiography of a city official who led efforts to improve local infrastructure

Answer:

A) Correct. It describes a secondary source that analyzes a topic rather than presenting firsthand experience of it.

Evaluating Sources

It is best to begin evaluating sources by evaluating the credibility of the author. Consideration should be given to the motivation of the author: the author's purpose or reason for writing the text may indicate whether the text is biased. Next, researchers must identify the author's background and expertise. Although educational credentials are significant, firsthand experience offers equally reliable information.

Questions to consider include:

- Is the source current?
- If it is a secondary source, is it based on both primary as well as other secondary sources?
- Is the author an expert in the area of study? Does he or she cite relevant information from other authorities on the topic?
- Is the author's purpose clear? That is, is there any apparent bias?
- What does the author assume is true?
- Does the author present multiple viewpoints?
- Does the content align with other reliable sources on the topic?

It can also be helpful to look at where the text was published. Sources like academic journals and established newspapers are more likely to have rigorous standards for publication, which means their articles are fairly reliable. On the other hand, open-source platforms like blogs and websites are more likely to contain biased material.

To evaluate a website, determine who the intended audience is and if there's an agenda in terms of selling something or promoting a belief system. For example, a health website created by a company selling nutritional supplements will not be as authoritative as a site maintained by a government health organization, since the company might omit relevant information that would hinder its sales. Similarly, a website for a particular candidate for public office might not be as good a source of unbiased policy information as a website maintained by a neutral nonprofit organization if elements or consequences of those policies do not align with the candidate's platform.

EXAMPLE

Which of the following sources is most appropriate for researching the health effects of smoking?

A) the personal website of a local doctor

B) a commercial produced by tobacco farming advocates

C) a website run by the Centers for Disease Control and Prevention

D) a book titled *101 Ways to Quit Smoking*

Answer:

C) Correct. The Centers for Disease Control and Prevention, as a government agency, will most likely offer the least biased information out of the four choices.

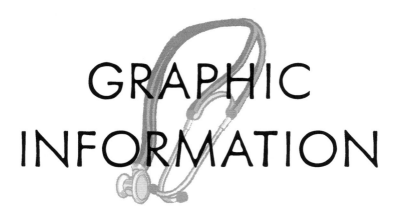

two

GRAPHIC INFORMATION

In addition to locating information in text passages, the TEAS also requires test takers to answer questions about a variety of figures, including maps, graphs and charts, illustrations, and advertisements. The TEAS will test your ability to use these graphic representations of information to answer similar questions to those asked about text passages. You'll be asked to:

- ◆ identify specific facts or patterns from the figure
- ◆ identify how the author uses specific features in the figure
- ◆ make connections between the figure and a related text passage

Maps

A MAP is a visual representation of space. It shows the relative location of a number of features, including roads, buildings, cities, and natural features like bodies of water and mountains. Many of these features will likely be represented by symbols. For example, a forested area might be marked with a drawing of a single tree, and railroad tracks might be indicated using a dotted line. The meanings of these symbols will be shown in the LEGEND. Specific features that do appear in the legend will be labeled on the map itself.

The spatial relationship between the features on a map is indicated both by their position on the page and by the SCALE, which shows the relationship between distance on the map and distance in real life. The scale will be a short line marked with a specific measurement like 100 kilometers or 10 miles. This measurement provides a conversion factor to find the real-life distance between features on the map. For example, if the scale line is 1 inch long and corresponds to 50 miles in real life, then 2 inches on the map equals 100 miles in real life, and so on.

Maps will also include a COMPASS, which shows the four cardinal directions: north, south, east, and west. Traditionally, maps are oriented with the top of the page being north and the right side of the page being east, although this is not an absolute.

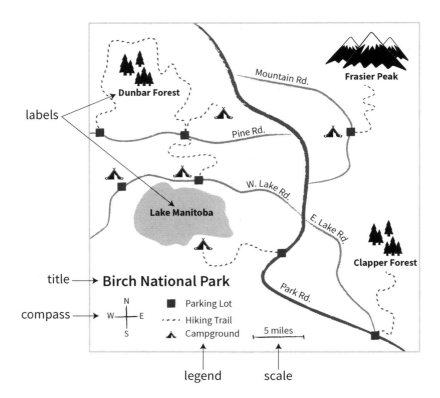

Figure 2.1. Map

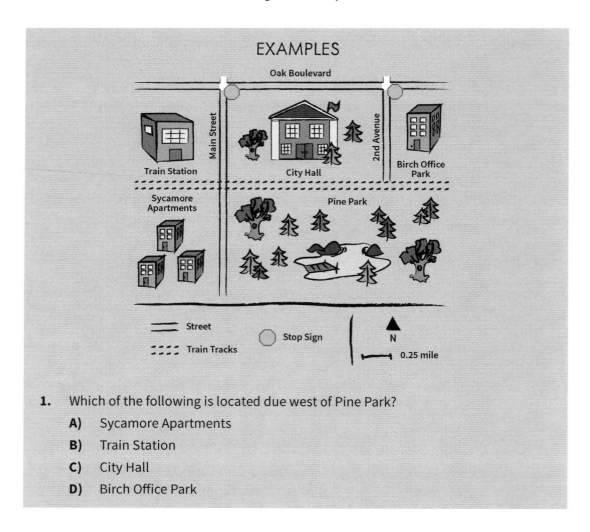

1. Which of the following is located due west of Pine Park?

   A) Sycamore Apartments

   B) Train Station

   C) City Hall

   D) Birch Office Park

Graphs and Charts

GRAPHS and CHARTS are visual representations of data. These figures include line graphs, bar graphs, pie charts, scatter plots, and histograms. These figures have a number of key features that you will need to identify. Graphs and charts will always have a TITLE that provides a brief description of the data being described. The title will often include information that is vital for understanding the graph. For example, the title *Graduating Students in the Class of 2016* tells the reader that the data set to follow includes students who graduated in 2016. The graph may also include a SUBTITLE that provides more detailed information.

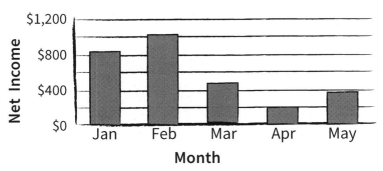

Figure 2.2. Sam's Income

Graphs also include horizontal and vertical AXES with LABELS describing the data being charted on each axis. Both labels should show the units of the data being displayed on that axis. Axes showing countable data, such as money or the number of students, will include a numeric SCALE that allows the reader to determine the value of each point or bar on the graph. Axes that show categorical data, such as time or location, will include text with the name for each category.

Average Student Score by Test

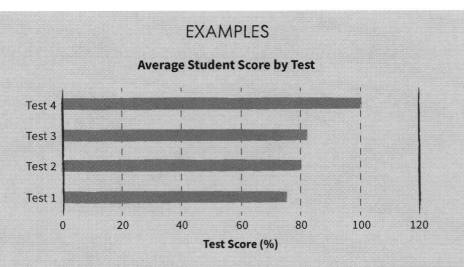

1. Which of the following statements is accurate based on the graph?

   A) The average score for students was lower for Test 4 than for Test 2.

   B) The average score for students was higher for Test 3 than for Test 1.

   C) More students took Test 4 than took Test 2.

   D) Fewer students took Test 3 than took Test 1.

   Answer:

   B) is correct. The title of the graph states that the bars show the average student score, not the number of students who took the test. The bar length shows that the average student score was higher for Test 3 than for Test 1.

2. Which of the following features on a graph will show the units of the data being displayed?

   A) scale

   B) title

   C) axis label

   D) subtitle

   Answer:

   C) is correct. The axis label will show the units for the data shown on that axis.

Other Informational Figures

The TEAS Reading test will include questions about an assortment of other information figures, including flowcharts, diagrams, and print media like brochures and flyers. There's no simple set of rules for handling these questions, but many of the same strategies that are used for other figures and for text passages are applicable.

Always start with the title of a figure—it will provide information that is likely crucial to understanding the figure. An anatomical diagram might have a title such as *Lobes of the Brain* that tells the viewer that the diagram will likely show the names and locations of the brain's lobes. Similarly, a flyer for a local garage sale might have a title like *Biggest Garage Sale in the Neighborhood* that tells the viewer exactly what the flyer is promoting.

Also make sure to examine any labels, legends, or scales provided with the figure. Anatomical diagrams, for example, will likely include labels for specific anatomical features, and a flowchart will have arrows indicating an ordered sequence. These labels can be read just like they would be on a map or graph.

Many of the strategies needed to interpret traditional reading passages can also be used for graphic representations of information, particularly those that may be text heavy. When looking at a flyer or advertisement, it will help to identify:

◆ the purpose of the author

◆ the intended audience

◆ rhetorical strategies designed to influence the viewer

A flyer for a local bake sale, for example, may be designed to appeal to the viewer's emotions by including pictures of local schoolchildren. Similarly, a computer advertisement meant to appeal to corporate buyers would probably use more formal language than one aimed at teenagers.

Most figures on the TEAS Reading will not require any outside knowledge to use. However, some questions may be easier if you have a basic understanding of common tools. For example, you may be asked to interpret the display for a blood pressure monitor or read a scale.

EXAMPLES

1. The device in the illustration above is used to measure which of the following?

   A) bone density

   B) tidal volume

   C) blood sugar

   D) blood pressure

   Answer:

   D) is correct. The illustration shows the display from a blood pressure monitor; the display gives systolic pressure, diastolic pressure, and heart rate.

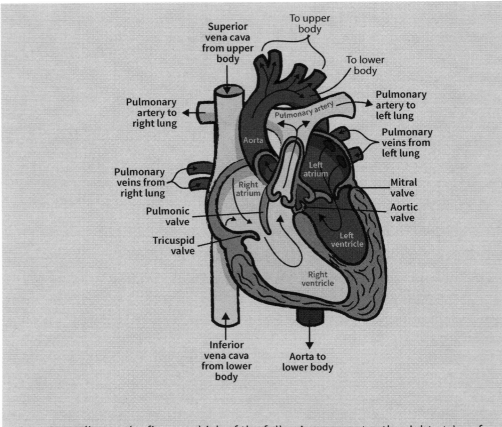

2. According to the figure, which of the following separates the right atrium from the right ventricle?

   A) mitral valve

   B) tricuspid valve

   C) aortic valve

   D) pulmonic valve

   Answer:

   B) is correct. The diagram shows that the tricuspid valve is located between the right atrium and the right ventricle.

Following Directions

DIRECTIONS provide step-by-step instructions for completing a particular task; these appear in all aspects of life, from instructions on microwave dinners to best practices for sterile technique. On the TEAS, directions may appear as simple lists, although they are often accompanied by shapes or figures to be manipulated as part of the directions. For example, a question may present a series of shapes, each of which may be rotated, moved, or deleted as designated by the directions.

Following directions requires the ability to identify the initial conditions, understand sequences, and analyze relationships among steps. First, identify the initial conditions laid out by the problem. This might be a spatial relationship between figures or a certain number of items (e.g., three red marbles and two green marbles).

Next, look for markers that indicate sequence. That may be as simple as identifying numbered steps, or the problem might require a closer reading. Certain words provide clues to the sequence of steps. Transition words like *first*, *next*, *then*, and *finally* indicate the order of tasks to be carried out. Once the order of steps has been identified, they can be carried out in that order.

When working through directions, pay special attention to the relationships between the steps. The action carried out in step 1 will likely affect the action in step 2, so make sure that each step is completed correctly before moving on. These questions are a test of the reader's attention to detail.

> When working through a set of directions, ALWAYS write down the result of each step. This will help you avoid making simple mistakes and will also help you check your work if you find an error.

EXAMPLES

Directions:

1. Imagine three apples, two oranges, and two limes in a fruit bowl.
2. Remove one apple.
3. Add two oranges.
4. Add one lime.
5. Add three apples.
6. Remove one orange.

1. Which of the following is the number of each fruit now in the bowl?
   A) 4 apples, 2 oranges, 3 limes
   B) 4 apples, 4 oranges, 2 limes
   C) 5 apples, 3 oranges, 3 limes
   D) 5 apples, 4 oranges, 2 limes

Answer:

C) is correct. Following the directions step by step gives the following number of fruit:

1. 3 apples, 2 oranges, 2 limes
2. 2 apples, 2 oranges, 2 limes
3. 2 apples, 4 oranges, 2 limes
4. 2 apples, 4 oranges, 3 limes
5. 5 apples, 4 oranges, 3 limes
6. 5 apples, 3 oranges, 3 limes

2. Start with the figure below. Follow the directions.

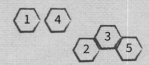

1. Remove block 3.
2. Place block 4 where block 3 used to be.

3. Swap blocks 1 and 2.

4. Move block 5 up one spot.

5. Place block 3 where block 5 used to be.

Which of the following is the resulting arrangement of the blocks?

A)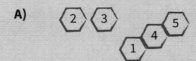

B)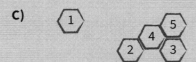

C)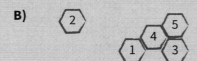

D)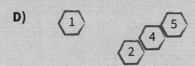

Answer:

B) is correct. Choice B shows the correct order of the blocks after the directions have been followed.

PART II: MATHEMATICS

three

NUMBERS AND OPERATIONS

Types of Numbers

Numbers are placed in categories based on their properties.

- A **NATURAL NUMBER** is greater than zero and has no decimal or fraction attached. These are also sometimes called counting numbers. {1, 2, 3, 4, ...}

- **WHOLE NUMBERS** are natural numbers and the number zero. {0, 1, 2, 3, 4, ...}

- **INTEGERS** include positive and negative natural numbers and zero. {. . ., -4, -3, -2, -1, 0, 1, 2, 3, 4, ...}

- A **RATIONAL NUMBER** can be represented as a fraction. Any decimal part must terminate or resolve into a repeating pattern. Examples include -12, $-\frac{4}{5}$, 0.36, $7.\overline{7}$, $26\frac{1}{2}$, etc.

- An **IRRATIONAL NUMBER** cannot be represented as a fraction. An irrational decimal number never ends and never resolves into a repeating pattern. Examples include $-\sqrt{7}$, π, and 0.34567989135 ...

- A **REAL NUMBER** is a number that can be represented by a point on a number line. Real numbers include all the rational and irrational numbers.

If a real number is a natural number (e.g. 50), then it is also an integer, a whole number, and a rational number.

Every natural number (except 1) is either a prime number or a composite number. A **PRIME NUMBER** is a natural number greater than 1 which can only be divided evenly by 1 and itself. For example, 7 is a prime number because it can only be divided by the numbers 1 and 7.

On the other hand, a **COMPOSITE NUMBER** is a natural number greater than 1 which can be evenly divided by at least one other number besides 1 and itself. For example, 6 is a composite number because it can be divided by 1, 2, 3, and 6.

Composite numbers can be broken down into prime numbers using factor trees. For example, the number 54 is 2 × 27, and 27 is 3 × 9, and 9 is 3 × 3, as shown in Figure 3.1.

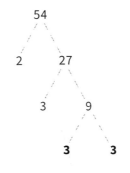

Figure 3.1. Factor Tree

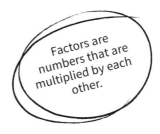
Factors are numbers that are multiplied by each other.

Once the number has been broken down into its simplest form, the composite number can be expressed as a product of prime factors. Repeated factors can be written using exponents. An EXPONENT shows how many times a number should be multiplied by itself. As shown in the factor tree, the number 54 can be written as $2 \times 3 \times 3 \times 3$ or 2×3^3.

EXAMPLES

Classify the following numbers as natural, whole, integer, rational, or irrational. (The numbers may have more than one classification.)

1. 72

   Answer:

   natural, **whole**, **integer**, and **rational** (72 can be written as the fraction $\frac{72}{1}$)

2. $-\frac{2}{3}$

   Answer:

   rational (the number is a fraction)

3. $\sqrt{5}$

   Answer:

   irrational (the number cannot be written as a fraction, and written as a decimal it is approximately 2.2360679... Notice this decimal does not terminate, nor does it have a repeating pattern.)

Scientific Notation

SCIENTIFIC NOTATION is a method of representing very large and small numbers in the form $a \times 10^n$ where a is a value between 1 and 10, and n is an integer. For example, the number 927,000,000 is written in scientific notation as 9.27×10^8. Multiplying 9.27 by 10 eight times gives 927,000,000. When performing operations with scientific notation, the final answer should be in the form $a \times 10^n$.

Table 3.1. Place Value

1,000,000	100,000	10,000	1,000	100	10	1	•	$\frac{1}{10}$	$\frac{1}{100}$
10^6	10^5	10^4	10^3	10^2	10^1	10^0		10^{-1}	10^{-2}
Millions	Hundred Thousands	Ten Thousands	Thousands	Hundreds	Tens	Ones	Decimal	Tenths	Hundreths

When adding and subtracting numbers in scientific notation, the power of 10 must be the same for all numbers. This results in like terms in which the a terms are added or subtracted and the 10^n remains unchanged. When multiplying numbers in scientific notation, multiply the a factors and add the exponents. For division, divide the a factors and subtract the exponents.

EXAMPLES

1. Simplify: $(3.8 \times 10^3) + (4.7 \times 10^2)$

    Answer:

    In order to add, the exponents of 10 must be the same. Change the first number so the power of 10 is 2:

    $3.8 \times 10^3 = 3.8 \times 10 \times 10^2 = 38 \times 10^2$

    Add the terms together and write the number in proper scientific notation:

    $38 \times 10^2 + 4.7 \times 10^2 = 42.7 \times 10^2 = \mathbf{4.27 \times 10^3}$

2. Simplify: $(8.1 \times 10^{-5})(1.4 \times 10^7)$

    Answer:

    Multiply the factors and add the exponents on the base of 10:

    $(8.1 \times 1.4)(10^{-5} \times 10^7) = 11.34 \times 10^2$

    Write the number in proper scientific notation: (Place the decimal so that the first number is between 1 and 10 and adjust the exponent accordingly.)

    $11.34 \times 10^2 = \mathbf{1.134 \times 10^3}$

Positive and Negative Numbers

POSITIVE NUMBERS are greater than zero, and NEGATIVE NUMBERS are less than zero. Both positive and negative numbers can be shown on a NUMBER LINE.

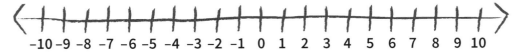

Figure 3.2. Number Line

Positive and negative numbers can be added, subtracted, multiplied, and divided. The sign of the resulting number is governed by a specific set of rules shown in the table below.

Table 3.2. Operations with Positive and Negative Numbers

ADDING REAL NUMBERS	
Positve + Positive = Positive	$7 + 8 = 15$
Negative + Negative = Negative	$-7 + (-8) = -15$
Negative + Positive = Keep the sign of the number with the larger absolute value	$-7 + 8 = 1$ $7 + (-8) = -1$

Table 3.2. Operations with Positive and Negative Numbers (continued)

SUBTRACTING REAL NUMBERS

Change the subtraction to addition, change the sign of the second number, and use addition rules.

Negative – Positive = Negative	$-7 - 8 = -7 + (-8) = -15$
Positive – Negative = Positive	$7 - (-8) = 7 + 8 = 15$
Negative – Negative = Keep the sign of the number with the larger absolute value.	$-7 - (-8) = -7 + 8 = 1$ $-8 - (-7) = -8 + 7 = -1$
Positive – Positive = Positive if the first number is larger Negative if the second number is larger	$8 - 4 = 4$ $4 - 8 = -4$

MULTIPLYING REAL NUMBERS

Positive × Positive = Positive	$8 \times 4 = 32$
Negative × Negative = Positive	$-8 \times (-4) = 32$
Negative × Positive = Negative	$8 \times (-4) = -32$ $-8 \times 4 = -32$

DIVIDING REAL NUMBERS

Positive ÷ Positive = Positive	$8 \div 4 = 2$
Negative ÷ Negative = Positive	$-8 \div (-4) = 2$
Positive ÷ Negative OR Negative ÷ Positive = Negative	$8 \div (-4) = -2$ $-8 \div 4 = -2$

EXAMPLES

Add or subtract the following real numbers:

1. $-18 + 12$

    Answer:

    Since $|-18| > |12|$, the answer is negative. $|-18| - |12| = 6$. So the answer is **−6**.

2. $-3.64 + (-2.18)$

    Answer:

    Adding two negative numbers results in a negative number. Add the values: **−5.82**

3. $9.37 - 4.25$

    Answer:

    5.12

4. $86 - (-20)$

    Answer:

    Change the subtraction to addition, change the sign of the second number, then add: $86 - (-20) = 86 + (+20) = $ **106**

Multiply or divide the following real numbers:

5. $\frac{10}{3}\left(-\frac{9}{5}\right)$

Answer:

Multiply the numerators, multiply the denominators, then simplify: $\frac{-90}{15} = $ **−6**

6. $\frac{-64}{-10}$

Answer:

A negative divided by a negative is a positive number: **6.4**

7. $(2.2)(3.3)$

Answer:

The parentheses indicate multiplication: **7.26**

8. $-52 \div 13$

Answer:

A negative divided by a positive is negative: **−4**

Order of Operations

When solving a multi-step equation, the **ORDER OF OPERATIONS** must be used to get the correct answer. Generally speaking, the problem should be worked in the following order: 1) parentheses and brackets; 2) exponents and square roots; 3) multiplication and division; 4) addition and subtraction. The acronym PEMDAS can be used to remember the order of operations.

Please **E**xcuse (**M**y **D**ear) (**A**unt **S**ally)

1. **P** — Parentheses: Calculate expressions inside parentheses, brackets, braces, etc.
2. **E** — Exponents: Calculate exponents and square roots.
3. **M** — Multiply and **D** — Divide: Calculate any remaining multiplication and division in order from left to right.
4. **A** — Add and **S** — Subtract: Calculate any remaining addition and subtraction in order from left to right.

The steps "Multiply-Divide" and "Addition-Subtraction" go in order from left to right. In other words, divide before multiplying if the division problem is on the left.

For example, the expression $(3^2 - 2)^2 + (4)5^3$ is simplified using the following steps:

1. Parentheses: Because the parentheses in this problem contain two operations (exponents and subtraction), use the order of operations within the parentheses. Exponents come before subtraction.
   $(3^2 - 2)^2 + (4)5^3 = (9 - 2)^2 + (4)5^3 = (7)^2 + (4)5^3$
2. Exponents: $(7)^2 + (4)5^3 = 49 + (4)125$
3. Multiplication and division: $49 + (4)125 = 49 + 500$
4. Addition and subtraction: $49 + 500 = 549$

EXAMPLES

1. Simplify: $2(21 - 14) + 6 \div (-2) \times 3 - 10$

   Answer:

   Calculate the expressions inside the parenthesis:

   $2(21 - 14) + 6 \div (-2) \times 3 - 10 =$

   $2(7) + 6 \div (-2) \times 3 - 10$

   There are no exponents or radicals, so perform multiplication and division from left to right:

   $2(7) + 6 \div (-2) \times 3 - 10 =$

   $14 + 6 \div (-2) \times 3 - 10 =$

   $14 + (-3) \times 3 - 10 =$

   $14 + (-9) - 10$

   Lastly, perform addition and subtraction from left to right:

   $14 + (-9) - 10 =$

   $5 - 10 = \mathbf{-5}$

2. Simplify: $-3^2 + 4(5) + (5 - 6)^2 - 8$

   Answer:

   Calculate the expressions inside the parentheses:

   $-(3)^2 + 4(5) + (5 - 6)^2 - 8 =$

   $-(3)^2 + 4(5) + (-1)^2 - 8$

   Simplify exponents and radicals:

   $-(3)^2 + 4(5) + (-1)^2 - 8 =$

   $-9 + 4(5) + 1 - 8$

   Note that $-(3)^2 = -1(3)^2 = -9$ but $(-1)^2 = (-1)(-1) = 1$

   Perform multiplication and division from left to right:

   $-9 + 4(5) + 1 - 8 =$

   $-9 + 20 + 1 - 8$

   Lastly, perform addition and subtraction from left to right:

   $-9 + 20 + 1 - 8 =$

   $11 + 1 - 8 = 12 - 8 = \mathbf{4}$

3. Simplify: $\dfrac{(7 - 9)^3 + 8(10 - 12)}{4^2 - 5^2}$

   Answer:

   Simplify the top and bottom expressions separately using the same steps described above:

   $\dfrac{(-2)^3 + 8(-2)}{4^2 - 5^2} =$

   $\dfrac{(-2)^3 + (-16)}{4^2 - 5^2} =$

   $\dfrac{-8 + (-16)}{16 - 25} =$

   $\dfrac{-24}{-9} = \dfrac{8}{3}$

Decimals and Fractions

Decimals

A DECIMAL is a number that contains a decimal point. The place value for a decimal includes TENTHS (one place after the decimal point), HUNDREDTHS (two places after the decimal point), THOUSANDTHS (three places after the decimal point), etc.

5	4	•	3	2
5×10^1	4×10^0		3×10^{-1}	2×10^{-2}
5×10	4×1		$3 \times \frac{1}{10}$	$2 \times \frac{1}{100}$
50	4		0.3	0.02
Tens	Ones	Decimal Point	Tenths	Hundredths

$$50 + 4 + 0.3 + 0.02 = 54.32$$

Figure 3.3. Decimals and Place Value

Decimals can be added, subtracted, multiplied, and divided:

To add or subtract decimals, line up the decimal points and perform the operation, keeping the decimal point in the same place in the answer.

$$12.35$$
$$+\ 3.63$$
$$=\ 15.98$$

To multiply decimals, first multiply the numbers without the decimal points. Then, add the number of decimal places to the right of the decimal point in the original numbers and place the decimal point in the answer so that there are that many places to the right of the decimal.

$$12.35 \times 3.63 =$$
$$1235 \times 363 = 448305 \rightarrow 44.8305$$

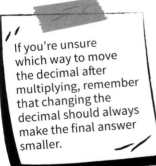

If you're unsure which way to move the decimal after multiplying, remember that changing the decimal should always make the final answer smaller.

When dividing decimals move the decimal point to the right in order to make the divisor a whole number and move the decimal the same number of places in the dividend. Divide the numbers without regard to the decimal. Then, place the decimal point of the quotient directly above the decimal point of the dividend.

$$\frac{12.35}{3.63} = \frac{1235}{363} =$$

$$363 \overline{\big)\ 1235.0}^{\ \ 3.4}$$

EXAMPLES

1. Simplify: 24.38 + 16.51 – 29.87

Answer:

Apply the order of operations left to right:

24.38 + 16.51 = 40.89

40.89 − 29.87 =

11.02

2. Simplify: (10.4)(18.2)

Answer:

Multiply the numbers ignoring the decimals: 104 × 182 = 18,928

The original problem includes two decimal places (10.4 has one place after the decimal point and 18.2 has one place after the decimal point), so place the decimal point in the answer so that there are two places after the decimal point. Estimating is a good way to check the answer (10.4 ≈ 10, 18.2 ≈ 18, 10 × 18 = 180)

18,928 → **189.28**

3. Simplify: 80 ÷ 2.5

Answer:

The divisor is 2.5. Move the decimal one place to the right (multiply 2.5 by 10) so that the divisor is a whole number. Since the decimal point of the divisor was moved one place to the right, the decimal point in the dividend must be moved one place to the right (multiplying it by 10 as well).

80 → 800 and 2.5 → 25

Divide normally: 800 ÷ 25 = **32**

Fractions

A **FRACTION** is a number that can be written in the form $\frac{a}{b}$ where b is not equal to zero. The a part of the fraction is the numerator (top number) and b part of the fraction is the denominator (bottom number).

If the denominator of a fraction is greater than the numerator, the value of the fraction is less than 1 and it is called a **PROPER FRACTION** (e.g., $\frac{3}{5}$ is a proper fraction).

In an **IMPROPER FRACTION**, the denominator is less than the numerator and the value of the fraction is greater than one (e.g., $\frac{8}{3}$ is an improper fraction). An improper fraction can be written as a whole number or a mixed number. A **MIXED NUMBER** has a whole number part and a proper fraction part. Improper fractions can be converted to mixed numbers by dividing the numerator by the denominator, which gives the whole number part, and the remainder becomes the numerator of the proper fraction part (for example: improper fraction $\frac{25}{9}$ is equal to mixed number $2\frac{7}{9}$ because 9 divides into 25 two times, with a remainder of 7).

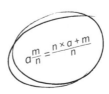

Conversely, mixed numbers can be converted to improper fractions. To do so, determine the numerator of the improper fraction by multiplying the denominator by the whole number, then adding the numerator. The final number is written as the (now larger) numerator over the original denominator.

Fractions with the same denominator can be added or subtracted by simply adding or subtracting the numerators; the denominator will remain unchanged. If the fractions to be added or subtracted do not have a common denominator, the least common multiple of the denominators must be found. The quickest way to find a common denominator of a set of values is simply to multiply all the values together. The result might not be the least common denominator, but it will get the job done.

In the operation $\frac{2}{3} - \frac{1}{2}$, the common denominator will be a multiple of both 3 and 2. Multiples are found by multiplying the denominator by whole numbers until a common multiple is found:

◆ multiples of 3 are **3** (3 × 1), **6** (3 × 2), **9** (3 × 3) …
◆ multiples of 2 are **2** (2 × 1), **4** (2 × 2), **6** (2 × 3) …

Since 6 is the smallest multiple of both 3 and 2, it is the least common multiple and can be used as the common denominator. Both the numerator and denominator of each fraction should be multiplied by the appropriate whole number:

$$\frac{2}{3}\left(\frac{2}{2}\right) - \frac{1}{2}\left(\frac{3}{3}\right) = \frac{4}{6} - \frac{3}{6} = \frac{1}{6}.$$

When multiplying fractions, simply multiply each numerator together and each denominator together, reducing the result if possible. To divide two fractions, invert the second fraction (swap the numerator and denominator) then multiply normally. If there are any mixed numbers when multiplying or dividing, they should first be changed to improper fractions. Note that multiplying proper fractions creates a value smaller than either original value.

$$\frac{5}{6} \times \frac{2}{3} = \frac{10}{18} = \frac{5}{9}$$

$$\frac{5}{6} \div \frac{2}{3} = \frac{5}{6} \times \frac{3}{2} = \frac{15}{12} = \frac{5}{4}$$

EXAMPLES

1. Simplify: $2\frac{3}{5} + 3\frac{1}{4} - 1\frac{1}{2}$

   Answer:

   The first step is to change each fraction so it has a denominator of 20, which is the LCD of 5, 4, and 2:

   $2\frac{3}{5} + 3\frac{1}{4} - 1\frac{1}{2} = 2\frac{12}{20} + 3\frac{5}{20} - 1\frac{10}{20}$

   Next, add and subtract the whole numbers together and the fractions together:

   $2 + 3 - 1 = 4$

   $\frac{12}{20} + \frac{5}{20} - \frac{10}{20} = \frac{7}{20}$

   Lastly, combine to get the final answer (a mixed number): **$4\frac{7}{20}$**

2. Simplify: $\frac{7}{8}\left(3\frac{1}{3}\right)$

   Answer:

   Change the mixed number to an improper fraction:

   $3\frac{1}{3} = \frac{10}{3}$

   Multiply the numerators together and the denominators together, and then reduce the fraction:

   $\frac{7}{8}\left(\frac{10}{3}\right) = \frac{7 \times 10}{8 \times 3} = \frac{70}{24} = \frac{35}{12} = \mathbf{2\frac{11}{12}}$

3. Simplify: $4\frac{1}{2} \div \frac{2}{3}$

Answer:

Change the mixed number to an improper fraction. Then, multiply the first fraction by the reciprocal of the second fraction and simplify:

$$\frac{9}{2} \div \frac{2}{3} = \frac{9}{2} \times \frac{3}{2} = \frac{27}{4} = 6\frac{3}{4}$$

Converting Between Fractions and Decimals

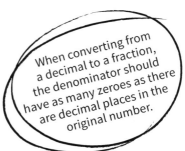

When converting from a decimal to a fraction, the denominator should have as many zeroes as there are decimal places in the original number.

A fraction is converted to a decimal by using long division until there is no remainder or a pattern of repeating numbers occurs.

$$\frac{1}{2} = 1 \div 2 = 0.5$$

To convert a decimal to a fraction, place the numbers to the right of the decimal over the appropriate base-10 power and simplify the fraction.

$$0.375 = \frac{375}{1000} = \frac{3}{8}$$

EXAMPLES

1. Write the fraction $\frac{7}{8}$ as a decimal.

Answer:

Divide the denominator into the numerator using long division:

```
        0.875
   8 | 7.0000
      -64
        60
       -56
        60
       -56
        40
       -40
         0
```

2. Write the fraction $\frac{5}{11}$ as a decimal.

Answer:

Dividing using long division yields a repeating decimal:

```
         0.4545
   11 | 5.0000
       -44
         60
        -55
         50
        -44
         60
        -55
          5
```

3. Write the decimal 0.125 as a fraction.

Place the numbers to the right of the decimal (125) in the numerator. There are three numbers, so put the number 1000 in the denominator, and then reduce:

$$\frac{125}{1000} = \frac{1}{8}$$

Rounding and Estimation

ROUNDING is a way of simplifying a complicated number. The result of rounding will be a less precise value that is easier to write or perform operations on. Rounding is performed to a specific place value, such as the thousands or tenths place.

The rules for rounding are as follows:

1. Underline the place value being rounded to.
2. Locate the digit one place value to the right of the underlined value. If this value is less than 5, keep the underlined value and replace all digits to the right of the underlined value with zero. If the value to the right of the underlined digit is more than 5, increase the underlined digit by one and replace all digits to the right of it with zero.

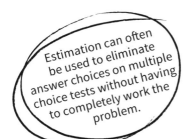

Estimation can often be used to eliminate answer choices on multiple choice tests without having to completely work the problem.

ESTIMATION is when numbers are rounded and then an operation is performed. This process can be used when working with large numbers to find a close, but not exact, answer.

EXAMPLES

1. Round the number 138,472 to the nearest thousand.

Answer:

The 8 is in the thousands place, and the number to its right is a 4. Because 4 is less than 5, the 8 remains and all numbers to the right become zero:

138,472 ≈ **138,000**

2. The populations of five local towns are 12,341, 8,975, 9,431, 10,521, and 11,427. Estimate the population to the nearest 1,000 people.

Answer:

Round each value to the thousands place and add:

12,341 ≈ 12,000

8,975 ≈ 9,000

9,431 ≈ 9,000

10,521 ≈ 11,000

11,427 ≈ 11,000

12,000 + 9,000 + 9,000 + 11,000 + 11,000 = **52,000**

Ratios

A **RATIO** is a comparison of two numbers and can be represented as $\frac{a}{b}$ ($b \neq 0$), $a{:}b$, or a to b. The two numbers represent a constant relationship, not a specific value: for every a number of items in the first group, there will be b number of items in the second. For example, if the ratio of blue to red candies in a bag is 3:5, the bag will contain 3 blue candies for every 5 red candies. So the bag might contain 3 blue candies and 5 red candies, or it might contain 30 blue candies and 50 red candies, or 36 blue candies and 60 red candies. All of these values are representative of the ratio 3:5 (which is the ratio in its lowest, or simplest, terms).

To find the "whole" when working with ratios, simply add the values in the ratio. For example, if the ratio of boys to girls in a class is 2:3, the "whole" is five: 2 out of every 5 students are boys, and 3 out of every 5 students are girls.

EXAMPLES

1. There are 10 boys and 12 girls in a first grade class. What is the ratio of boys to the total number of students? What is the ratio of girls to boys?

   Answer:

   There are 22 total students in the class. The ratio can be written as $\frac{10}{22}$, and reduced to $\frac{5}{11}$. The ratio of girls to boys is **12:10 or 6:5**.

2. A family spends \$600 a month on rent, \$400 on utilities, \$750 on groceries, and \$550 on miscellaneous expenses. What is the ratio of the family's rent to their total expenses?

   Answer:

   The family's total expenses for the month add up to \$2,300. The ratio of the rent to total amount of expenses can be written as $\frac{600}{2300}$ and reduced to $\frac{6}{23}$.

Proportions

A **PROPORTION** is an equation which states that two ratios are equal. Proportions are given in the form $\frac{a}{b} = \frac{c}{d}$, where the a and d terms are the extremes and the b and c terms are the means. A proportion is solved using **CROSS-MULTIPLICATION** to create an equation with no fractional components: $\frac{a}{b} = \frac{c}{d} \rightarrow ad = bc$

EXAMPLES

1. Solve the proportion for: $\frac{3-5}{2} = \frac{-8}{3}$.

   Answer:

   Start by cross multiplying:

   $\frac{3-5}{2} = \frac{-8}{3} \rightarrow 3(3-5) = 2(-8)$

   Then, solve the equation:

   $9 - 15 = 2 - 16$

   $7 - 15 = -16$

$$7 = -1$$

$$x = -\frac{1}{7}$$

2. A map is drawn such that 2.5 inches on the map equates to an actual distance of 40 miles. If the distance between two cities measured on the map is 17.25 inches, what is the actual distance between them in miles?

Answer:

Write a proportion where x equals the actual distance and each ratio is written as inches:miles.

$$\frac{2.5}{40} = \frac{17.25}{x}$$

Then, cross-multiply and divide to solve:

$$2.5x = 690$$

$$x = 276$$

The two cities are 276 miles apart.

3. At a certain factory, every 4 out of 1,000 parts made will be defective. If in a month there are 125,000 parts made, how many of these parts will be defective?

Answer:

Write a proportion in which x is the number of defective parts made and both ratios are written as defective parts:total parts.

$$\frac{4}{1000} = \frac{x}{125,000}$$

Then, cross-multiply and divide to solve for x:

$$1000x = 500,000$$

$$x = 500$$

There are 500 defective parts for the month.

Percentages

A PERCENT (or percentage) means per hundred and is expressed with a percent symbol (%). For example, 54% means 54 out of every 100. A percent can be converted to a decimal by removing the % symbol and moving the decimal point two places to the left, while a decimal can be converted to a percent by moving the decimal point two places to the right and attaching the % sign.

A percent can be converted to a fraction by writing the percent as a fraction with 100 as the denominator and reducing. A fraction can be converted to a percent by performing the indicated division, multiplying the result by 100 and attaching the % sign.

The percent equation has three variables: the part, the whole, and the percent (which is expressed in the equation as a decimal). The equation, as shown below, can be rearranged to solve for any of these variables.

$$part = whole \times percent$$

$$percent = \frac{part}{whole}$$

$$whole = \frac{part}{percent}$$

This set of equations can be used to solve percent word problems. All that is needed is to identify the part, whole, and/or percent, then to plug those values into the appropriate equation and solve.

EXAMPLES

1. Write 18% as a fraction.

   Answer:

   The percent is written as a fraction over 100 and reduced: $\frac{18}{100} = \frac{9}{50}$.

2. Write $\frac{3}{5}$ as a percent.

   Answer:

   Dividing 5 by 3 gives the value 0.6, which is then multiplied by 100: **60%**.

3. Write 1.125 as a percent.

   Answer:

   The decimal point is moved two places to the right: **112.5%**.

4. Write 84% as a decimal.

   Answer:

   The decimal point is moved two places to the left:
   84% = **0.84**.

5. In a school of 650 students, 54% of the students are boys. How many students are girls?

   Answer:

   The first step is to find the percent of students who are girls by subtracting from 100%: 100% − 54% = 46%

   Next, identify the variables and plug into the appropriate equation:

   percent = 46% = 0.46

   whole = 650 students

   part = ?

   part = *whole* × *percent* = 0.46 × 650 = 299

   There are 299 girls.

Percent Change

Key terms associated with percent change problems include discount, sales tax, growth, and markup.

Percent change problems involve a change from an original amount. Often percent change problems appear as word problems that include discounts, growth, or markups. In order to solve percent change problems, it is necessary to identify the percent change (as a decimal), the amount of change, and the original amount. (Keep in mind that one of these will be the value being solved for.) These values can then be plugged into the equations below:

$$\text{amount of change} = \text{original amount} \times \text{percent change}$$

$$\text{percent change} = \frac{\text{amount of change}}{\text{original amount}}$$

$$\text{original amount} = \frac{\text{amount of change}}{\text{percent change}}$$

EXAMPLES

1. A Smart HDTV that originally cost $1,500 is on sale for 45% off. What is the sale price for the item?

   Answer:

   The first step is to identify the necessary values. These can then be plugged into the appropriate equation:

   original amount = 1,500

   percent change = 45% = 0.45

   amount of change = ?

   amount of change = *original amount* × *percent change* = 1,500 × 0.45 = 675

   To find the new price, subtract the amount of change from the original price:

   1,500 − 675 = 825

   The final price is **$825**.

2. A house was purchased in 2000 for $100,000 and sold in 2015 for $120,000. What was the percent growth in the value of the house from 2000 to 2015?

   Answer:

   Identify the necessary values and plug into the appropriate equation:

   original amount = 100,000

   amount of change = 120,000 − 100,000 = 20,000

   percent change = ?

   $$\textit{percent change} = \frac{\text{amount of change}}{\text{original amount}} = \frac{20,000}{100,000} = 0.20$$

   To find the percent growth, multiply by 100: 0.20 × 100 = **20%**

Comparison of Rational Numbers

Rational numbers can be ordered from least to greatest (or greatest to least) by placing them in the order in which they fall on a number line. When comparing a set of fractions, it is often easiest to convert each value to a common denominator. Then, it is only necessary to compare the numerators of each fraction.

When working with numbers in multiple forms (for example, a group of fractions and decimals), convert the values so that the set contains only fractions or only decimals. When ordering negative numbers, remember that the negative number with the largest absolute value is furthest from 0 and is therefore the smallest number. (For example, –75 is smaller than –25.)

Drawing a number line can help when comparing numbers: the final list should go in order from left to right (least to greatest) or right to left (greatest to least) on the line.

EXAMPLES

1. Order the following numbers from greatest to least:
   $-\frac{2}{3}, 1.2, 0, -2.1, \frac{5}{4}, -1, \frac{1}{8}$.

   Answer:

   Change each fraction to a decimal:

   $-\frac{2}{3} = -0.\overline{66}$

   $\frac{5}{4} = 1.25$

   $\frac{1}{8} = 0.125$

   Now place the decimals in order from greatest to least:

   $1.25, 1.2, 0.125, 0, -0.\overline{66}, -1, -2.1$

   Lastly, convert back to fractions if the problem requires it:

   $\mathbf{\frac{5}{4}, 1.2, \frac{1}{8}, 0, -\frac{2}{3}, -1, -2.1}$

2. Order the following numbers from least to greatest:
   $\frac{1}{3}, -\frac{5}{6}, 1\frac{1}{8}, \frac{7}{12}, -\frac{3}{4}, -\frac{3}{2}$

   Answer:

   Convert each value using the least common denominator value of 24:

   $\frac{1}{3} = \frac{8}{24}$

   $-\frac{5}{6} = -\frac{20}{24}$

   $1\frac{1}{8} = \frac{9}{8} = \frac{27}{24}$

   $\frac{7}{12} = \frac{14}{24}$

   $-\frac{3}{4} = -\frac{18}{24}$

   $-\frac{3}{2} = -\frac{36}{24}$

   Next, put the fractions in order from least to greatest by comparing the numerators:

   $-\frac{36}{24}, -\frac{20}{24}, -\frac{18}{24}, \frac{8}{24}, \frac{14}{24}, \frac{27}{24}$

   Finally, put the fractions back in their original form if the problem requires it:

   $\mathbf{-\frac{3}{2}, -\frac{5}{6}, -\frac{3}{4}, \frac{1}{3}, \frac{7}{12}, 1\frac{1}{8}}$

four

ALGEBRA

Algebraic Expressions

The foundation of algebra is the VARIABLE, an unknown number represented by a symbol (usually a letter such as x or a). Variables can be preceded by a COEFFICIENT, which is a constant (i.e., a real number) in front of the variable, such as $4x$ or $-2a$. An ALGEBRAIC EXPRESSION is any sum, difference, product, or quotient of variables and numbers (for example $3x^2$, $2x + 7y - 1$, and $\frac{5}{x}$ are algebraic expressions). TERMS are any quantities that are added or subtracted (for example, the terms of the expression $x^2 - 3x + 5$ are x^2, $3x$, and 5). A POLYNOMIAL EXPRESSION is an algebraic expression where all the exponents on the variables are whole numbers. A polynomial with two terms is known as a BINOMIAL, and one with three terms is a TRINOMIAL.

EXAMPLE

If $m = 4$, find the value of the following expression: $5(m - 2)^3 + 3m^2 - \frac{m}{4} - 1$

Answer:

First, plug the value 4 in for m in the expression:

$5(m - 2)^3 + 3m^2 - \frac{m}{4} - 1$

$= 5(4 - 2)^3 + 3(4)^2 - \frac{4}{4} - 1$

Then, simplify using PEMDAS:

P: $5(2)^3 + 3(4)^2 - \frac{4}{4} - 1$

E: $5(8) + 3(16) - \frac{4}{4} - 1$

M and D, working left to right: $40 + 48 - 1 - 1$

A and S, working left to right: 86

The answer is 86.

Operations with Expressions

Adding and Subtracting

Expressions can be added or subtracted by simply adding and subtracting LIKE TERMS, which are terms with the same variable part (the variables must be the same, with the same exponents on each variable). For example, in the expressions $2x + 3xy - 2z$ and $6y + 2xy$, the like terms are $3xy$ and $2xy$. Adding the two expressions yields the new expression $2x + 5xy - 2z + 6y$. Note that the other terms did not change; they cannot combine because they have different variables.

EXAMPLE

If $a = 12x + 7xy - 9y$ and $b = 8x - 9xz + 7z$, what is $a + b$?

Answer:

The only like terms in both expressions are $12x$ and $8x$, so these two terms will be added, and all other terms will remain the same:

$a + b = (12x + 8x) + 7xy - 9y - 9xz + 7z$

$= 20x + 7xy - 9y - 9xz + 7z$

Distributing and Factoring

Often, simplifying expressions requires distributing and factoring, which can be seen as two sides of the same coin. **DISTRIBUTION** multiplies each term in the first factor by each term in the second factor to clear off parentheses, while **FACTORING** reverses this process, taking a polynomial in standard form and writing it as a product of two or more factors.

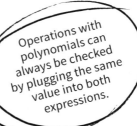
Operations with polynomials can always be checked by plugging the same value into both expressions.

When distributing a monomial through a polynomial, the expression outside the parentheses is multiplied by each term inside the parentheses. Remember, coefficients are multiplied and exponents are added, following the rules of exponents.

The first step in factoring a polynomial is always to "undistribute," or factor out, the greatest common factor (GCF) among the terms. The GCF is multiplied by, in parentheses, the expression that remains of each term when the GCF is divided out of each term. Factoring can be checked by multiplying the GCF factor through the parentheses again.

EXAMPLES

1. Expand the following expression: $5x(x^2 - 2c + 10)$

    Answer:

    The term outside the parentheses must be distributed and multiplied by all three terms inside the parentheses:

    $(5x)(x^2) = 5x^3$

$(5x)(-2c) = -10xc$

$(5x)(10) = 50x$

$5x(x^2 - 2c + 10) \rightarrow$

$5x^3 - 10xc + 50x$

2. Expand the following expression: $x(5 + z) - z(4x - z^2)$

Answer:

Start by distributing for each set of parentheses:

$x(5 + z) - z(4x - z^2)$

Notice that $-z$ is distributed and that $(-z)(-z^2) = +z^3$. **Failing to distribute the negative is a very common error.**

$5x + xz - 4zx + z^3$

Note that xz is a like term with zx (commutative property), and they can therefore be combined.

Now combine like terms and place terms in the appropriate order (highest exponents first):

$z^3 - 3xz + 5x$

Linear Equations

An **EQUATION** states that two expressions are equal to each other. Polynomial equations are categorized by the highest power of the variables they contain. For instance, the highest power of any exponent of a linear equation is 1, a quadratic equation has a variable raised to the second power, a cubic equation has a variable raised to the third power, and so on.

Solving Linear Equations

Solving an equation means finding the value(s) of the variable that make the equation true. To solve a linear equation, it is necessary to manipulate the terms so that the variable being solved for appears alone on exactly one side of the equal sign while everything else in the equation is on the other side.

The way to solve linear equations is to "undo" all the operations that connect numbers to the variable of interest. Follow these steps:

1. Eliminate fractions by multiplying each side by the least common multiple of any denominators.
2. Distribute to eliminate parentheses, braces, and brackets.
3. Combine like terms.
4. Use addition or subtraction to collect all terms containing the variable of interest to one side, and all terms not containing the variable to the other side.
5. Use multiplication or division to remove coefficients from the variable being solved for.

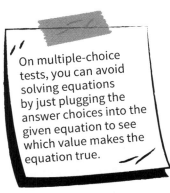

On multiple-choice tests, you can avoid solving equations by just plugging the answer choices into the given equation to see which value makes the equation true.

Sometimes there are no numeric values in the equation, or there will be a mix of numerous variables and constants. The goal will be to solve the equation for one of the variables in terms of the other variables. In this case, the answer will be an expression involving numbers and letters instead of a numeric value.

EXAMPLES

1. Solve for x: $\left(\dfrac{100(x+5)}{20} \right) = 1$

   Answer:

   To cancel out the denominator, multiply both sides by 20:

   $20 \dfrac{100(x+5)}{20} = 1 \times 20$

   $100(x + 5) = 20$

   Next, distribute 100 through the parentheses:

   $100(x + 5) = 20$

   $100x + 500 = 20$

   "Undo" the +500 by subtracting 500 from both sides of the equation to isolate the variable term: $100x = -480$

   Finally, "undo" the multiplication by 100: divide by 100 on both sides to solve for x:

   $x = \dfrac{-480}{100} = -4.8$

2. Solve for x: $2(x + 2)^2 - 2x^2 + 10 = 20$

   Answer:

   First, simplify the left-hand side of the equation using order of operations and combining like terms.

   $2(x + 2)^2 - 2x^2 + 10 = 20$

   Do the exponent first: $2(x + 2)(x + 2) - 2x^2 + 10 = 20$

   FOIL: $2(x^2 + 4x + 4) - 2x^2 + 10 = 20$

   Distribute the 2: $2x^2 + 8x + 8 - 2x^2 + 10 = 20$

   Combine like terms on the left-hand side: $8x + 18 = 20$

   Now, isolate the variable.

   "Undo" +18 by subtracting 18 from both sides: $8x + 18 = 20$

   $8x = 2$

   "Undo" multiplication by 8 by dividing both sides by 8:

   $x = \dfrac{2}{8}$ or $\dfrac{1}{4}$

Graphs of Linear Equations

The most common way to write a linear equation is SLOPE-INTERCEPT FORM:

$$y = mx + b$$

In this equation, m is the SLOPE, and b is the Y-INTERCEPT. Slope is often described as "rise over run" because it is calculated as the difference in y-values (rise) over the difference in x-values (run). The slope of the line is also the RATE OF CHANGE of the dependent variable y with respect to the independent variable x. The y-intercept is the point where the line crosses the y-axis, or where x equals zero.

To graph a linear equation, identify the y-intercept and place that point on the y-axis. Then, starting at the y-intercept, use the slope to count up (or down if negative) the "rise" part of the slope and to the right the "run" part of the slope to find a second point. These points can then be connected to draw the line. To find the equation of a line, identify the y-intercept, if possible, on the graph and use two easily identifiable points to find the slope.

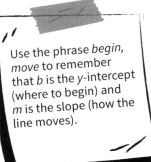
Use the phrase *begin, move* to remember that b is the y-intercept (where to begin) and m is the slope (how the line moves).

EXAMPLES

1. What is the slope of the line whose equation is $6x - 2y - 8 = 0$?

   Answer:

   Rearrange the equation into slope-intercept form by solving the equation for y. Isolate $-2y$ by subtracting $6x$ and adding 8 to both sides of the equation.

   $-2y = -6x + 8$

   Divide both sides by -2:

   $y = \frac{-6x + 8}{-2}$

   Simplify the fraction.

   $y = 3x - 4$

   The slope is 3, since it is the coefficient of x.

2. What is the equation of the following line?

   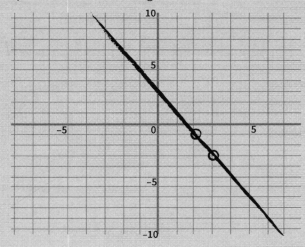

   Answer:

   The y-intercept can be identified on the graph as $(0, 3)$. Thus, $b = 3$.

   To find the slope, choose any two points and plug the values into the slope equation. The two points chosen here are $(2, -1)$ and $(3, -3)$.

   $m = \frac{(-3) - (-1)}{3 - 2} = \frac{-2}{1} = -2$

   Replace m with -2 and b with 3 in $y = mx + b$.

   The equation of the line is **$y = -2x + 3$.**

Building Equations

In word problems, it is often necessary to translate a verbal description of a relationship into a mathematical equation. No matter the problem, this process can be done using the same steps:

1. Read the problem carefully and identify what value needs to be solved for.
2. Identify the known and unknown quantities in the problem, and assign the unknown quantities a variable.
3. Create equations using the variables and known quantities.
4. Solve the equations.
5. Check the solution: Does it answer the question asked in the problem? Does it make sense?

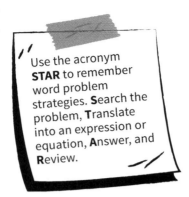

Use the acronym **STAR** to remember word problem strategies. **S**earch the problem, **T**ranslate into an expression or equation, **A**nswer, and **R**eview.

EXAMPLES

1. A school is holding a raffle to raise money. There is a $3.00 entry fee, and each ticket costs $5.00. If a student paid $28.00, how many tickets did he or she buy?

   Answer:

   The problem is asking for the number of tickets. First, identify the quantities:

   number of tickets = x

   cost per ticket = 5

   cost for x tickets = $5x$

   total cost = 28

   entry fee = 3

   Now, set up an equation. The total cost for x tickets will be equal to the cost for x tickets plus the $3 entry fee: $5x + 3 = 28$

   Now solve the equation:

   $5x + 3 = 28$

   $5x = 25$

   $x = 5$

   The student bought 5 tickets.

2. Abby needs $395 to buy a new bicycle. She has borrowed $150 from her parents, and plans to earn the rest of the money working as a waitress. If she makes $10 per hour, how many hours will she need to work to pay for her new bicycle?

   Answer:

   The problem asks for the number of hours Abby will have to work. First, identify the quantities:

   number of hours = x

   amount earned per hour = 10

   amount of money earned = $10x$

   price of bicycle = 395

money borrowed = 150

Now, set up an equation. The amount of money she has borrowed plus the money she earned as a waitress needs to equal the cost of the bicycle:

$10x + 150 = 395$

Now solve the equation:

$10x + 150 = 395$

$10x = 245$

$x = 24.5$ hours

She will need to work 24.5 hours.

Inequalities

INEQUALITIES are similar to equations, but both sides of the problem are not equal ($\neq$). Inequalities may be represented as follows: greater than ($>$), greater than or equal to ($\geq$), less than ($<$), or less than or equal to ($\leq$). For example, the statement "12 is less than 4 times x" would be written as $12 < 4x$.

Inequalities can be solved by manipulating them much like equations. However, the solution to an inequality is a set of numbers, not a single value. For example, simplifying $4x + 2 \leq 14$ gives the inequality $x \leq 3$, meaning every number less than 3 would also be included in the set of correct answers.

EXAMPLES

1) Solve the inequality: $4x + 10 > 58$

Answer:

Inequalities can be solved using the same steps used to solve equations. Start by subtracting 10 from both sides:

$4x + 10 > 58$

$4x > 48$

Now divide by 4 to isolate x:

$x > 12$

2) The students on the track team are buying new uniforms. T-shirts cost $12, pants cost $15, and a pair of shoes costs $45. If they have a budget of $2,500, write a mathematical sentence that represents how many of each item they can buy.

Answer:

They have to spend less than $2,500 on uniforms, so this problem is an inequality. First, identify the quantities:

number of t-shirts = t

total cost of t-shirts = $12t$

number of pants = p

total cost of pants = $15p$

number of pairs of shoes = s

total cost of shoes = 45s

The cost of all the items must be less than $2,500: **$12t + 15p + 45s < 2{,}500$**

five

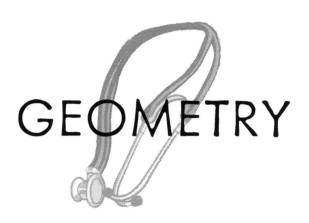

GEOMETRY

Units of Measurement

The standard units for the metric and American systems are shown below along with the prefixes used to express metric units.

Table 5.1. American and SI Units

Dimension	American	SI
length	inch/foot/yard/mile	meter
mass	ounce/pound/ton	gram
volume	cup/pint/quart/gallon	liter
force	pound-force	newton
pressure	pound-force per square inch	pascal
work and energy	cal/British thermal unit	joule
temperature	Fahrenheit	kelvin
charge	faraday	coulomb

Table 5.2. Metric Prefixes

Prefix	Symbol	Multiplication Factor
tera	T	1,000,000,000,000
giga	G	1,000,000,000
mega	M	1,000,000
kilo	k	1,000
hecto	h	100
deca	da	10
base unit	--	--
deci	d	0.1
centi	c	0.01
milli	m	0.001
micro	μ	0.000001
nano	n	0.000000001
pico	p	0.000000000001

Table 5.3. Conversion Factors

1 in. = 2.54 cm	1 lb. = 0.454 kg
1 yd. = 0.914 m	1 cal = 4.19 J
1 mi. = 1.61 km	$1°F = \frac{9}{5}°C + 32°C$
1 gal. = 3.785 L	$1 cm^3 = 1 mL$
1 oz. = 28.35 g	1 hr = 3600 s

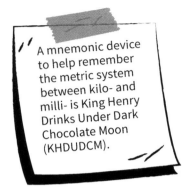

A mnemonic device to help remember the metric system between kilo- and milli- is King Henry Drinks Under Dark Chocolate Moon (KHDUDCM).

Units can be converted within a single system or between systems. When converting from one unit to another unit, a **CONVERSION FACTOR** (a fraction used to convert a value with a unit into another unit) is used. For example, there are 2.54 centimeters in 1 inch, so the conversion factor from inches to centimeters is $\frac{2.54 \text{ centimeters}}{1 \text{ inch}}$.

To convert between units, multiply the original value by a conversion factor (or several if needed) so that the original units cancel, leaving the desired unit. Remember that the original value can be made into a fraction by placing it over 1.

$$\frac{3 \text{ inches}}{1} \times \frac{2.54 \text{ centimeters}}{1 \text{ inch}} = 7.62 \text{ centimeters}$$

Units can be canceled (meaning they disappear from the expression) when they appear on the top and the bottom of a fraction. If the same unit appears in the top (or bottom) of both fractions, you probably need to flip the conversion factor.

EXAMPLES

1. Convert 4.25 kilometers to meters.

   Answer:

   $4.25 \text{ km} \left(\frac{1000 \text{ m}}{1 \text{ km}}\right) = \textbf{4250 m}$

2. Convert 12 feet to inches.

   Answer:

   $12 \text{ ft} \left(\frac{12 \text{ in}}{1 \text{ ft}}\right) = \textbf{144 in}$

Geometric Figures

Classifying Geometric Figures

GEOMETRIC FIGURES are shapes comprised of points, lines, or planes. A **POINT** is simply a location in space; it does not have any dimensional properties like length, area, or volume. A collection of points that extend infinitely in both directions is a **LINE**, and one that extends infinitely in only one direction is a **RAY**. A section of a line with a beginning and end point is a **LINE SEGMENT**. Lines, rays, and line segments are examples of **ONE-DIMENSIONAL** objects because they can only be measured in one dimension (length).

Figure 5.1. One-Dimensional Object

Lines, rays, and line segments can intersect to create ANGLES, which are measured in degrees or radians. Angles between zero and 90 degrees are ACUTE, and angles between 90 and 180 degrees are OBTUSE. An angle of exactly 90 degrees is a RIGHT ANGLE, and two lines that form right angles are PERPENDICULAR. Lines that do not intersect are described as PARALLEL.

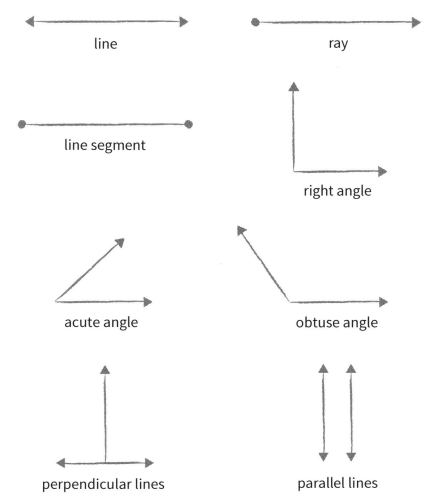

Figure 5.2. Lines and Angles

TWO-DIMENSIONAL objects can be measured in two dimensions—length and width. A PLANE is a two-dimensional object that extends infinitely in both directions. POLYGONS are two-dimensional shapes, such as triangles and squares, which have three or more straight sides. Regular polygons are polygons whose sides are all the same length.

Figure 5.3. Two-Dimensional Object

THREE-DIMENSIONAL objects, such as cubes, can be measured in three dimensions—length, width, and height.

Figure 5.4. Three-Dimensional Object

Calculating Geometric Quantities

The LENGTH, or distance from one point to another on an object, can be determined using a tape measure or a ruler. The size of the surface of a two-dimensional object is its AREA. Generally, finding area involves multiplying one dimension of an object by another, such as length by width. For example, if a window is 3 feet long and 2 feet wide, its area would be 6 ft².

The distance around a two dimensional figure is its PERIMETER, which can be found by adding the lengths of all the sides. The distance around a circle is referred to as its CIRCUMFERENCE.

Table 5.4. Area and Perimeter of Basic Shapes

SHAPE	EXAMPLE	AREA	PERIMETER
Triangle		$A = \frac{1}{2}bh$	$P = s_1 + s_2 + s_3$
Square		$A = s^2$	$P = 4s$
Rectangle		$A = l \times w$	$P = 2l + 2w$
Trapezoid		$A = \frac{1}{2}h(b_1 + b_2)$	$P = b_1 + b_2 + l_1 + l_2$
Circle		$A = \pi r^2$	$C = 2\pi r$
Sector		$A = \frac{x°}{360°}(\pi r^2)$	$arc\ length = \frac{x°}{360°}(2\pi r)$

For the rectangle below, the area would be 8 m² because 2 m × 4 m = 8 m². The perimeter of the rectangle would be $P = 2l + 2w = 2(4\ m) + 2(2\ m) = 12$ m.

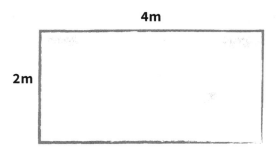

4m

2m

Figure 5.5. Perimeter

The SURFACE AREA of a three-dimensional object can be figured by adding the areas of all the sides. For example, the box below is 4 feet long, 3 feet wide, and 1 foot deep. The surface area is found by adding the areas of each face:

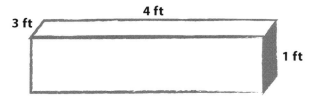

4 ft

3 ft

1 ft

Figure 5.6. Surface Area

- top: 4 ft × 3 ft = 12 ft²
- bottom: 4 ft × 3 ft = 12 ft²
- front: 4 ft × 1 ft = 4 ft²
- back: 4 ft × 1 ft = 4 ft²
- right: 1 ft × 3 ft = 3 ft²
- left: 1 ft × 3 ft = 3 ft²

The TEAS will also ask test takers to find the perimeter and area of compound shapes, which will include parts of circles, squares, triangles, or other polygons joined together to create an irregular shape. For these types of problems, the first step is to divide the figure into shapes whose area (or perimeter) can easily be solved for. Then, solve each part separately and add (or subtract) the parts together for the final answer.

> The test won't provide formulas for the area and perimeter of basic shapes, so you need to memorize them. Don't worry if you see questions on the test about more complicated shapes like cylinders or spheres—the formulas you need will be given in the question.

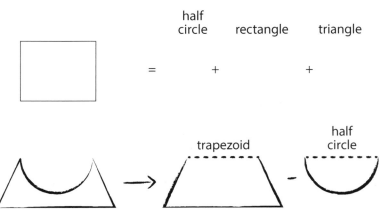

half circle   rectangle   triangle

trapezoid   half circle

Figure 5.7. Compound Shapes

EXAMPLES

1. What is the area of the figure shown below?

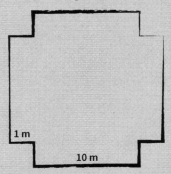

Answer:

The figure can be broken apart into three rectangles:

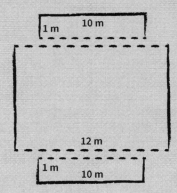

The area of each smaller rectangle is 1 m × 10 m = 10 m². The area of the larger rectangle is 10 m × 12 m = 120 m². Together, the area of the three shapes is 10 m² + 10 m² + 120 m² = **140 m²**

2. What is the area of the shaded region in the figure below?

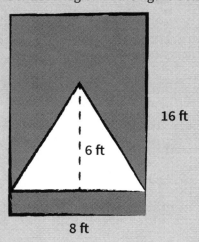

Answer:

The area of the shaded region is the area of the rectangle minus the area of the triangle:

rectangle – triangle = (8 ft × 16 ft) – (0.5 × 8 ft × 6 ft) = 128 ft² – 24 ft² = **104 ft²**

six

STATISTICS

Statistics

STATISTICS is the study of data. Analyzing data requires using MEASURES OF CENTRAL TENDENCY (mean, median, and mode) to identify trends or patterns.

The MEAN is the average; it is determined by adding all outcomes and then dividing by the total number of outcomes. For example, the average of the data set {16, 19, 19, 25, 27, 29, 75} is equal to $\frac{16 + 19 + 19 + 25 + 27 + 29 + 75}{7} = \frac{210}{7} = 30$.

The MEDIAN is the number in the middle when the data set is arranged in order from least to greatest. For example, in the data set {16, 19, 19, **25**, 27, 29, 75}, the median is 25. When a data set contains an even number of values, finding the median requires averaging the two middle values. In the data set {75, 80, 82, 100}, the two numbers in the middle are 80 and 82. Consequently, the median will be the average of these two values: $\frac{80 + 82}{2} = 81$.

Finally, the MODE is the most frequent outcome in a data set. In the set {16, 19, 19, 25, 27, 29, 75}, the mode is 19 because it occurs twice, which is more than any of the other numbers. If several values appear an equal, and most frequent, number of times, both values are considered the mode. If every value in a data set appears only once, the data set has no mode.

Other useful indicators include range and outliers. The RANGE is the difference between the highest and the lowest values in a data set. For example, the range of the set {16, 19, 19, 25, 27, 29, 75} is 75 − 16 = 59.

OUTLIERS, or data points that are much different from other data points, should be noted as they can skew the central tendency. In the data set {16, 19, 19, 25, 27, 29, 75}, the value 75 is far outside the other values and raises the value of the mean. Without the outlier, the mean is much closer to the other data points.

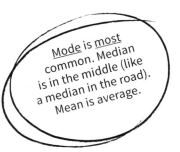

Mode is <u>most</u> common. Median is in the middle (like a median in the road). Mean is average.

- $\frac{16 + 19 + 19 + 25 + 27 + 29 + 75}{7} = \frac{210}{7} = 30$
- $\frac{16 + 19 + 19 + 25 + 27 + 29}{6} = \frac{135}{6} = 22.5$

Generally, the median is a better indicator of a central tendency if outliers are present to skew the mean.

Trends in a data set can also be seen by graphing the data as a dot plot. The distribution of the data can then be described based on the shape of the graph. A SYMMETRIC distribution looks like two mirrored halves, while a SKEWED distribution is weighted more heavily toward the right or the left. Note the direction of the skew describes the side of the graph with fewer data points. In a UNIFORM data set, the points are distributed evenly along the graph.

A symmetric or skewed distribution may have peaks, or sets of data points that appear more frequently. A UNIMODAL distribution has one peak while a BIMODAL distribution has two peaks. A normal (or bell-shaped) distribution is a special symmetric, unimodal graph with a specific distribution of data points.

EXAMPLES

1. Which of the following is the mean of the data set?

   14, 18, 11, 28, 23, 14

   A) 11

   B) 14

   C) 18

   D) 28

   Answer:

   C) is correct. The mean is the average:

   $$\frac{14 + 18 + 11 + 28 + 23 + 14}{6} = \frac{108}{6} = 18$$

2. Which of the following best describes the distribution of the graph?

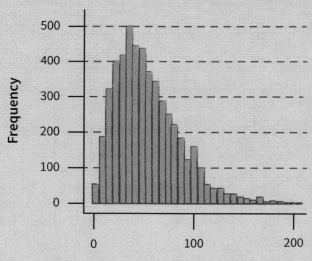

   A) Skewed left

   B) Skewed right

   C) Bimodal

   D) Uniform

Data Presentation

Data can be presented in a variety of ways. In addition to a simple table, there are a number of different graphs and charts that can be used to visually represent data. The most appropriate type of graph or chart depends on the data being displayed.

BOX PLOTS (also called box and whisker plots) show data using the median, range, and outliers of a data set. They provide a helpful visual guide, showing how data is distributed around the median. In the example below, 70 is the median and the range is 0 – 100, or 100.

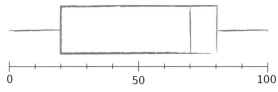

Figure 6.1. Box Plot

BAR GRAPHS use bars of different lengths to compare data. The independent variable on a bar graph is grouped into categories such as months, flavors, or locations, and the dependent variable is a quantity. Thus, comparing the length of bars provides a visual guide to the relative amounts in each category. **DOUBLE BAR GRAPHS** show more than one data set on the same set of axes.

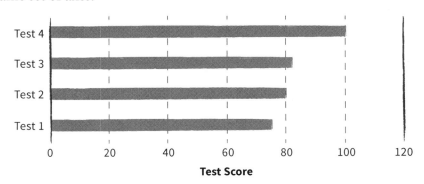

Figure 6.2. Bar Graph

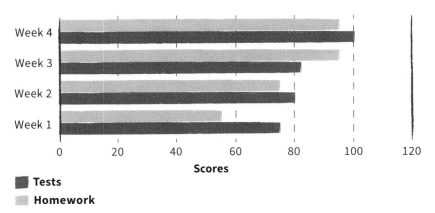

Figure 6.3. Double Bar Graph

HISTOGRAMS similarly use bars to compare data, but the independent variable is a continuous variable that has been "binned" or divided into categories. For example, the time of day can be broken down into 8:00 a.m. to 12:00 p.m., 12:00 p.m. to 4:00 p.m., and so on. Usually (but not always), a gap is included between the bars of a bar graph but not a histogram. The bars of a bar graph show actual data, but the bars (or bins) of a histogram show the frequency of the data in various ranges.

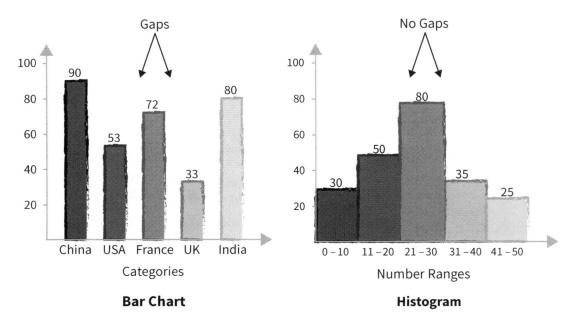

Figure 6.4. Bar Chart vs. Histogram

DOT PLOTS display the frequency of a value or event data graphically using dots, and thus can be used to observe the distribution of a data set. Typically, a value or category is listed on the x-axis, and the number of times that value appears in the data set is represented by a line of vertical dots. Dot plots make it easy to see which values occur most often.

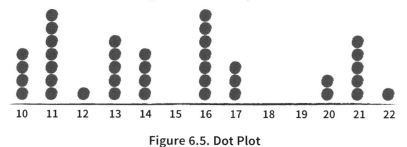

Figure 6.5. Dot Plot

SCATTER PLOTS use points to show relationships between two variables which can be plotted as coordinate points. One variable describes a position on the x-axis, and the other a point on the y-axis. Scatter plots can suggest relationships between variables. For example, both variables might increase together, or one may increase when the other decreases.

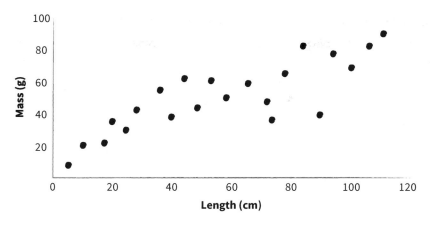

Figure 6.6. Scatter Plot

LINE GRAPHS show changes in data by connecting points on a scatter graph using a line. These graphs will often measure time on the *x*-axis and are used to show trends in the data, such as temperature changes over a day or school attendance throughout the year.

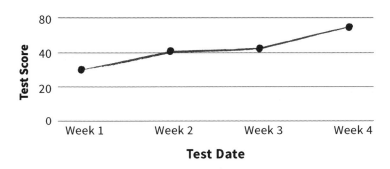

Figure 6.7. Line Graph

DOUBLE LINE GRAPHS present two sets of data on the same set of axes.

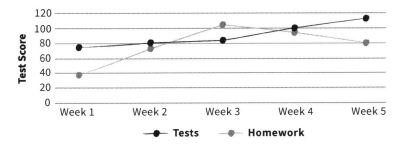

Figure 6.8. Double Line Graph

CIRCLE GRAPHS (also called pie charts) are used to show parts of a whole: the "pie" is the whole, and each "slice" represents a percentage or part of the whole.

Test Scores

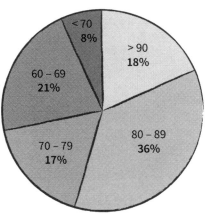

Figure 6.9. Circle Graph

EXAMPLE

Students are asked if they prefer vanilla, chocolate, or strawberry ice cream. The results are tallied on the following table.

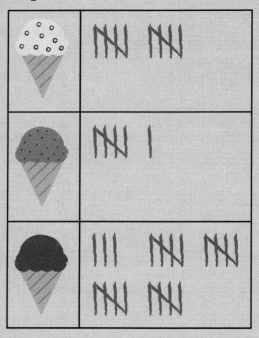

Four students display the information from the table in a bar graph. Which student completes the bar graph correctly?

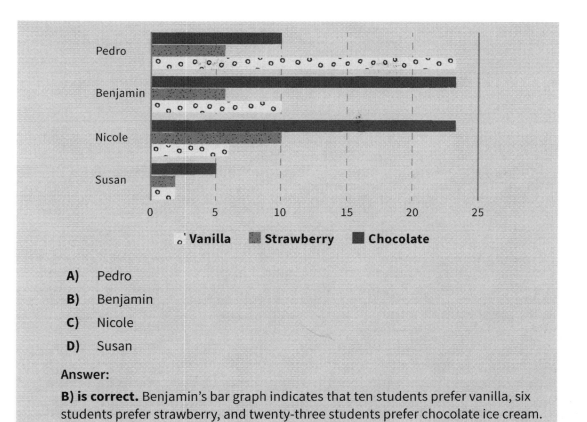

A) Pedro

B) Benjamin

C) Nicole

D) Susan

Answer:

B) is correct. Benjamin's bar graph indicates that ten students prefer vanilla, six students prefer strawberry, and twenty-three students prefer chocolate ice cream.

PART III: SCIENCE

seven

ANATOMY AND PHYSIOLOGY

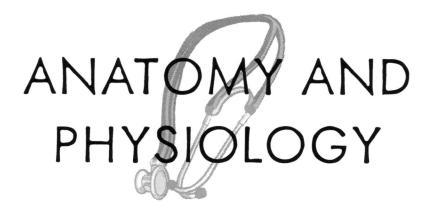

Anatomical Terminology

The Biological Hierarchy

Organisms are living things consisting of at least one cell, which is the smallest unit of life that can reproduce on its own. Unicellular organisms, such as the amoeba, are made up of only one cell, while multicellular organisms are comprised of many cells. In a multicellular organism, the cells are grouped together into TISSUES, and these tissues are grouped into ORGANS, which perform a specific function. The heart, for example, is the organ that pumps blood throughout the body. Organs are further grouped into ORGAN SYSTEMS, such as the digestive or respiratory systems.

A system is a collection of interconnected parts that make up a complex whole with defined boundaries. Systems may be closed, meaning nothing passes in or out of them, or open, meaning they have inputs and outputs. Organ systems are open and will have a number of inputs and outputs.

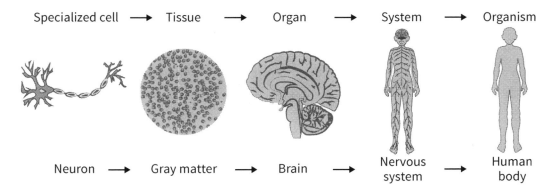

Specialized cell → Tissue → Organ → System → Organism

Neuron → Gray matter → Brain → Nervous system → Human body

Figure 7.1. The Biological Hierarchy

Directional Terms

Learning anatomy requires an understanding of the terminology used to describe the location of a particular structure. Anatomical science uses common terms to describe spatial relationships, often in pairs of opposites. These terms usually refer to the position of a structure in an organism that is upright with respect to its environment (e.g., in its typical orientation while moving forward).

Table 7.1. Directional Terms

Term	Meaning	Example
inferior	away from the head	The pelvis is inferior to the head.
superior	closer to the head	The head is superior to the pelvis.
anterior	toward the front	The eyes are anterior to the ears.
posterior	toward the back	The ears are posterior to the eyes.
ventral	toward the front	The stomach is ventral to the spine.
dorsal	toward the back	The spine is dorsal to the stomach.
medial	toward the midline of the body	The heart is medial to the arm.
lateral	further from the midline of the body	The arm is lateral to the chest.
proximal	closer to the trunk	The knee is proximal to the ankle.
distal	away from the trunk	The ankle is distal to the knee.

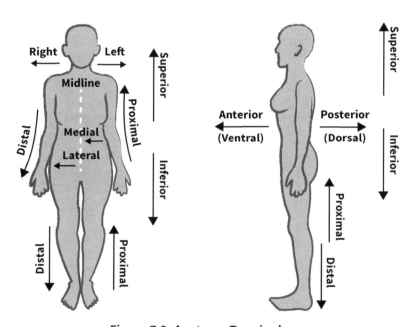

Figure 7.2. Anatomy Terminology

Body Cavities

The internal structure of the human body is organized into compartments called CAVITIES, which are separated by membranes. There are two main cavities in the human body: the dorsal cavity and the ventral cavity (both named for their relative positions).

The DORSAL CAVITY is further divided into the CRANIAL CAVITY, which holds the brain, and the SPINAL CAVITY, which surrounds the spine. The two sections of the dorsal cavity are continuous with each other. Both sections are lined by the MENINGES, a three-layered membrane that protects the brain and spinal cord.

The VENTRAL CAVITY houses the majority of the body's organs. It also can be further divided into smaller cavities. The THORACIC CAVITY holds the heart and lungs, the ABDOMINAL CAVITY holds the digestive organs and kidneys, and the PELVIC CAVITY holds the bladder and reproductive organs. Both the abdominal and pelvic cavities are enclosed by a membrane called the PERITONEUM.

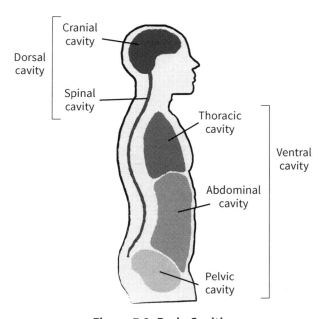

Figure 7.3. Body Cavities

The Respiratory System

Structure and Function of the Respiratory System

Mammalian cells require oxygen for glucose metabolism and release carbon dioxide as a byproduct. This process requires constant gas exchange between the human body and the environment to replenish the oxygen supply and remove carbon dioxide. This exchange is accomplished through the efforts of the **RESPIRATORY SYSTEM**, in which powerful muscles force oxygen-rich air into the lungs and carbon dioxide-rich air out of the body.

Gas exchange takes place in the **LUNGS**. Humans have two lungs, a right and a left, with the right being slightly larger than the left due to the heart's placement in the left side of the chest cavity. The right lung has three **LOBES**, and the left has two. The lungs are surrounded by a thick membrane called the **PLEURA**.

In anatomy, the terms *right* and *left* are used with respect to the subject, not the observer.

Air enters the body through the mouth or nasal cavity and passes through the **TRACHEA** (sometimes called the windpipe) and into the two bronchi, each of which leads to one lung. Within the lung, the bronchi branch into smaller passageways called **BRONCHIOLES** and then terminate in sac-like structures called **ALVEOLI**, which is where gas exchange between the air and the capillaries occurs. The large surface area of the alveoli allows for efficient exchange of gases through diffusion (movement of particles from areas of high to low concentration). Alveoli are covered in a layer of **SURFACTANT**, which lubricates the sacs and prevents the lungs from collapsing.

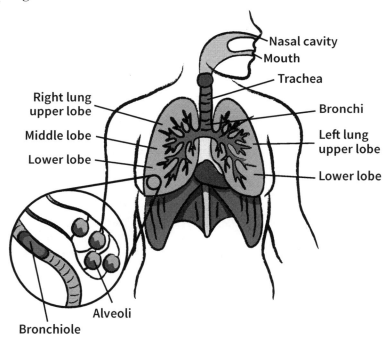

Figure 7.4. The Respiratory System

The heart pumps deoxygenated blood into the lungs via the **PULMONARY ARTERY**. This blood is oxygenated in the alveoli and then delivered back into the heart by the **PULMONARY VEINS** for distribution to the body.

The DIAPHRAGM contributes to the activity of ventilation—the process of inhalation and exhalation. The contraction of the diaphragm creates a vacuum, forcing air into the lungs. Relaxation of the diaphragm compresses the lungs, forcing carbon dioxide-enriched gas out in exhalation. The amount of air breathed in and out is the TIDAL VOLUME, and the RESIDUAL CAPACITY is the small volume of air left in the lungs after exhalation.

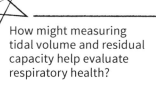

How might measuring tidal volume and residual capacity help evaluate respiratory health?

Pathologies of the Respiratory System

The body's critical and constant need for the exchange of carbon dioxide for oxygen makes the pulmonary system a locus of many serious diseases. Lung diseases that result in the continual restriction of airflow are known as CHRONIC OBSTRUCTIVE PULMONARY DISEASE (COPD). These include EMPHYSEMA, which is the destruction of lung tissues, and ASTHMA, in which the airways are compromised due to a dysfunctional immune response. The main causes of COPD are smoking and air pollution, but genetic factors can also influence the severity of the disease.

The system is also prone to RESPIRATORY TRACT INFECTIONS, with upper respiratory tract infections affecting air inputs in the nose and throat and lower respiratory tract infections affecting the lungs and their immediate pulmonary inputs. Viral infections of the respiratory system include influenza and the common cold; bacterial infections include tuberculosis and pertussis (whooping cough). PNEUMONIA, which affects alveoli, is a bacterial or viral infection that is often seen in people whose respiratory system has been weakened by other conditions.

EXAMPLES

1. Which of the following structures are small air sacs that function as the site of gas exchange in the lungs?
   A) capillaries
   B) bronchi
   C) alveoli
   D) cilia

   Answer:

   C) is correct. The alveoli are sacs found at the terminal end of each bronchiole in the lungs and are the site of gas exchange with the blood.

2. Which of the following conditions is caused by an immune response?
   A) COPD
   B) influenza
   C) asthma
   D) emphysema

   Answer:

   C) is correct. Asthma is a negative reaction of the body to otherwise harmless particles.

The Cardiovascular System

Structure and Function of the Cardiovascular System

The cardiovascular system circulates blood throughout the body. Blood carries a wide range of molecules necessary for the body to function, including nutrients, wastes, hormones, and gases. Blood is broken into a number of different parts. Red blood cells, which contain the protein HEMOGLOBIN, transport oxygen, and white blood cells circulate as part of the immune system. Both red and white blood cells are suspended in a fluid called PLASMA, which the other molecules transported by the blood are dissolved in.

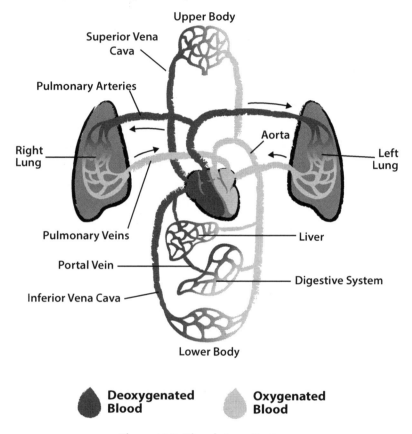

Figure 7.5. Circulatory System

Blood is circulated by a muscular organ called the HEART. The circulatory system includes two closed loops. In the pulmonary loop, deoxygenated blood leaves the heart and travels to the lungs, where it loses carbon dioxide and becomes rich in oxygen. The oxygenated blood then returns to the heart, which pumps it through the systemic loop. The systemic loop delivers oxygen to the rest of the body and returns deoxygenated blood to the heart. The pumping action of the heart is regulated primarily by two neurological nodes, the SINOATRIAL and ATRIOVENTRICULAR NODES, whose electrical activity sets the rhythm of the heart.

Deoxygenated blood from the body enters the heart via the RIGHT ATRIUM. It then passes through the TRICUSPID valve into the RIGHT VENTRICLE and is pumped out to the lungs. Oxygenated blood returns from the lungs into the LEFT ATRIUM. It then passes through the MITRAL VALVE into the LEFT VENTRICLE and is pumped out to the body through the AORTA. The contraction of the heart during this process is called SYSTOLE, and the relaxation of the heart is DIASTOLE.

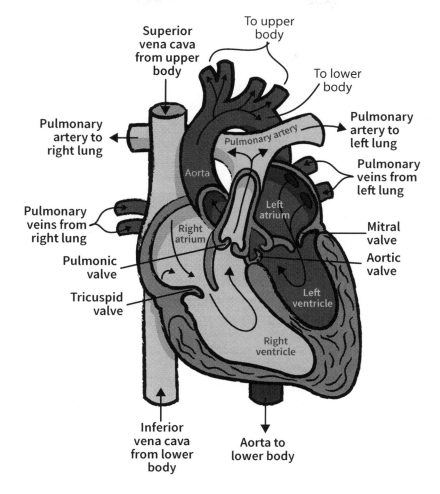

Figure 7.6. The Heart

Blood is carried through the body in a system of blood vessels. Oxygenated blood leaves the heart in large vessels called ARTERIES, which branch into smaller and smaller vessels. The smallest vessels, CAPILLARIES, are where the exchange of molecules between blood and cells takes place. Deoxygenated blood returns to the heart in VEINS.

Blood leaves the heart to travel to the body through the AORTA; in the lower body, the aorta branches into the ILIAC ARTERIES. Deoxygenated blood returns to the heart from the body via the SUPERIOR VENA CAVA (upper body) and INFERIOR VENA CAVA (lower body). Blood then leaves the heart again to travel to the lungs through the PULMONARY ARTERIES, and returns from the lungs via the PULMONARY VEINS.

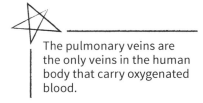

The pulmonary veins are the only veins in the human body that carry oxygenated blood.

The Lymphatic System

The LYMPHATIC SYSTEM is an open circulatory system that functions alongside the cardiovascular system. It facilitates the movement of substances between cells and the blood by removing interstitial fluid (the fluid between cells). It also plays an important role

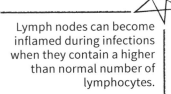

Lymph nodes can become inflamed during infections when they contain a higher than normal number of lymphocytes.

in the immune system by circulating white blood cells. The system is composed of LYMPHATIC VESSELS that carry LYMPH, a clear fluid containing lymphocytes and waste products. Lymph passes through LYMPH NODES, which are collections of tissue rich in white blood cells that filter out harmful substances such as pathogens and cell waste. The lymph is then returned to the circulatory system through the veins near the heart.

Pathologies of the Cardiovascular System

The cardiovascular system is subject to a number of pathologies. In a HEART ATTACK, blood flow to part of the heart is stopped, causing damage to the heart muscle. An irregular heartbeat, called an ARRHYTHMIA, is caused by disruptions with the electrical signals in the heart. Many arrhythmias can be treated—with a pacemaker, for example—or do not cause any symptoms.

Problems with blood vessels include ATHEROSCLEROSIS, in which white blood cells and plaque build up in arteries, and HYPERTENSION, or high blood pressure. In a stroke, blood flow is blocked in the brain, resulting in damage to brain cells.

EXAMPLES

1. The mitral valve transports blood between which of the following two regions of the heart?
   A) aorta and left atrium
   B) aorta and right atrium
   C) right atrium and right ventricle
   D) left atrium and left ventricle

   Answer:

   D) is correct. These two structures form a junction at the mitral valve.

2. Which of the following supplies blood to the lower body?
   A) superior vena cava
   B) inferior vena cava
   C) iliac artery
   D) aortic arch

   Answer:

   C) is correct. The iliac artery receives blood from the aorta to supply blood to the lower body.

3. Which of the following electrically signals the heart to pump?
   A) sinoatrial node
   B) aorta
   C) mitral valve
   D) left ventricle

The Nervous System

The nervous system is made up of two distinct parts: the central nervous system (brain and spinal cord) and the peripheral nervous system. However, the fundamental physiological principles underlying both systems are similar. In both systems, NEURONS communicate electrically and chemically with one another along pathways. These pathways allow the nervous system as a whole to conduct its incredibly broad array of functions, from motor control and sensory perception to complex thinking and emotions.

Nerve Cells

Neurons, a.k.a. nerve cells, have several key anatomical features that contribute to their specialized functions. These cells typically contain an AXON, a long projection from the cell that sends information over a distance. These cells also have DENDRITES, which are long, branching extensions of the cell that receive information from neighboring cells. The number of dendrites and the extent of their branching varies widely, distinguishing the various types of these cells.

Neurons and nerve cells do not touch; instead, communication occurs across a specialized gap called a SYNAPSE. The chemicals that facilitate communication across synapses are known as NEUROTRANSMITTERS, and include serotonin and dopamine. Communication occurs when electrical signals cause the AXON TERMINAL to release neurotransmitters.

Nerve cell signaling is controlled by moving ions across the cell membrane to maintain an action potential. Depolarizing the cell, or lowering the action potential, triggers the release of neurotransmitters.

Nerve cells are accompanied by glia, or supporting cells, that surround the cell and provide support, protection, and nutrients. In the peripheral nervous system, the primary glial cell is a SCHWANN CELL. Schwann cells secrete a fatty substance called MYELIN that wraps around the neuron and allows much faster transmission of the electrical signal the neuron is sending. Gaps in the myelin sheath are called nodes of Ranvier.

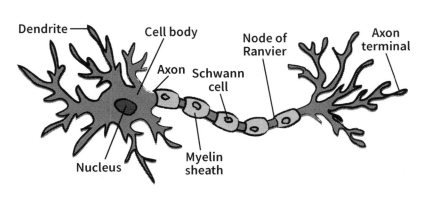

Figure 7.7. Nerve Cell

The Central Nervous System

The central nervous system, which includes the brain and spinal cord, is responsible for arguably the body's most complex and abstract functions, including cognition, emotion, and behavioral regulation. The brain is divided into six general regions:

- **CEREBRUM**: the largest part of the brain; responsible for voluntary movement, language, learning, and memory
- **DIENCEPHALON**: includes the thalamus, hypothalamus, and pineal body; relays sensory information and controls some automatic functions of the peripheral nervous system
- **MESENCEPHALON** (midbrain): processes hearing and visual information; maintains sleep/wake cycles and temperature
- **PONS**: controls many involuntary processes, including respiration, bladder control, and sleep; also responsible for facial movements and eye movement
- **CEREBELLUM**: responsible for motor control and motor learning
- **MEDULLA OBLONGATA**: controls involuntary processes of the cardiac and respiratory systems; responsible for reflexes such as sneezing and vomiting

Alzheimer's disease, which causes dementia, is the result of damaged neurons in the cerebral cortex, the area of the brain responsible for higher order functions like information processing and language.

The cerebrum and cerebellum are further broken down into **LOBES** that each carry out a broad common function. For example, in the cerebrum, the processing of visual information occurs in the **OCCIPITAL LOBE,** and the **TEMPORAL LOBE** is involved in language comprehension and emotional associations.

In addition to its organization by lobes and structures, regions of the brain are also designated by myelination status: **WHITE MATTER** regions are myelinated and **GRAY MATTER** regions are unmyelinated. Brain structures in the cerebral cortex (the outermost brain layer) form a convoluted pattern of **GYRI** (ridges) and **SULCI** (valleys) that maximize the ratio of surface area to volume.

The Peripheral Nervous System

The peripheral nervous system, which includes all the nerve cells outside the brain and spinal cord, has one main function and that is to communicate between the CNS and the rest of the body.

The peripheral nervous system is further divided into two systems. The **AUTOMATIC NERVOUS SYSTEM** (ANS) is the part of the peripheral nervous system that controls involuntary bodily functions such as digestion, respiration, and heart rate. The autonomic nervous system is further broken down into the sympathetic nervous system and parasympathetic nervous system.

The "fight or flight" reaction includes accelerated breathing and heart rate, dilation of blood vessels in muscles, release of energy molecules for use by muscles, relaxation of the bladder, and slowing or stopping movement in the upper digestive tract.

The **SYMPATHETIC NERVOUS SYSTEM** is responsible for the body's reaction to stress and induces a "fight or flight" response to stimuli. For instance, if an individual is frightened, the sympathetic nervous system increases the person's heart rate and blood pressure to prepare that person to either fight or flee.

In contrast, the PARASYMPATHETIC NERVOUS SYSTEM is stimulated by the body's need for rest or recovery. The parasympathetic nervous system responds by decreasing heart rate, blood pressure, and muscular activation when a person is getting ready for activities such as sleeping or digesting food. For example, the body activates the parasympathetic nervous system after a person eats a large meal, which is why that individual may then feel sluggish.

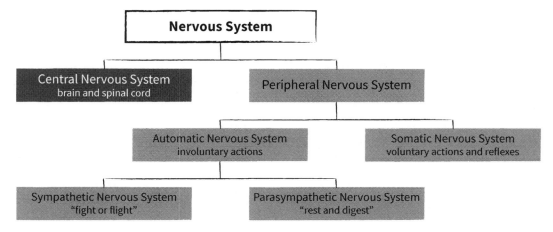

Figure 7.8. Divisions of the Nervous System

The second part of the peripheral nervous system, called the SOMATIC NERVOUS SYSTEM, controls sensory information and motor control. Generally, nerve cells can be divided into two types. AFFERENT (sensory) cells relay messages to the central nervous system, and EFFERENT (motor) cells carry messages to the muscles. In the motor nervous system, signals from the brain travel down the spinal cord before exiting and communicating with motor nerve cells, which synapse on muscle fibers at NEUROMUSCULAR JUNCTIONS. Because individuals can control the movement of skeletal muscle, this part of the nervous system is considered voluntary.

Some REFLEXES, or automatic response to stimuli, are able to occur rapidly by bypassing the brain altogether. In a REFLEX ARC, a signal is sent from the peripheral nervous system to the spinal cord, which then sends a signal directly to a motor cells, causing movement.

Pathologies of the Nervous System

The nervous system can be affected by a number of degenerative diseases that result from the gradual breakdown of nervous tissue. These include:

- PARKINSON'S DISEASE: caused by cell death in the basal ganglia; characterized by gradual loss of motor function
- MULTIPLE SCLEROSIS (MS): caused by damage to the myelin sheath; characterized by muscle spasms and weakness, numbness, loss of coordination, and blindness
- AMYOTROPHIC LATERAL SCLEROSIS (ALS): caused by the death of neurons that control voluntary muscle movement; characterized by muscle stiffness, twitches, and weakness
- ALZHEIMER'S DISEASE: caused by damaged neurons in the cerebral cortex; characterized by memory loss, confusion, mood swings, and problems with language

The nervous system is also susceptible to infections, some of which can be life threatening. MENINGITIS is inflammation of the meninges, the protective membrane that surrounds the brain and spinal cord, and ENCEPHALITIS is inflammation of the brain. Both conditions can be caused by viral or bacterial pathogens.

EPILEPTIC SEIZURES are brief episodes caused by disturbed or overactive nerve cell activity in the brain. Seizures range widely in severity and may include confusion, convulsions, and loss of consciousness. They have many causes, including tumors, infections, head injuries, and medications.

EXAMPLES

1. Which part of the nervous system controls only voluntary action?
    A) the peripheral nervous system
    B) the somatic nervous system
    C) the sympathetic nervous system
    D) the parasympathetic nervous system

    automatic nervous system

    Answer:
    B) is correct. The somatic nervous system controls voluntary actions.

2. Which of the following is the part of a nerve cell that receives information?
    A) axon
    B) dendrite
    C) Schwann cell
    D) myelin

    Answer:
    B) is correct. Dendrites receive information in nerve cells.

The Gastrointestinal System

Structure and Function of the Gastrointestinal System

Fueling the biological systems mentioned previously is the digestive system. The digestive system is essentially a continuous tube in which food is processed. During digestion, the body extracts necessary nutrients and biological fuels and isolates waste to be discarded.

The breakdown of food into its constituent parts begins as soon as it is put into the mouth. Enzymes in SALIVA such as salivary amylase begin breaking down food, particularly starch, as mastication helps prepare food for swallowing and subsequent digestion. Food from this point is formed into a BOLUS that travels down the esophagus, aided by a process called PERISTALSIS, rhythmic contractions that move the partially digested food towards the stomach. Upon reaching the STOMACH, food

The burning sensation called heartburn occurs when gastric acid from the stomach travels up the esophagus, often as a result of relaxation of the lower esophageal sphincter. This acid can damage the lining of the esophagus.

encounters a powerful acid (composed mainly of hydrochloric acid), which aids the breakdown of food into its absorbable components.

The human body derives fuel primarily from three sources: proteins, sugars, and fats (lipids). Enzymes break proteins down into their constituent amino acids to produce new proteins for the body. Carbohydrates are broken down enzymatically if necessary and used for metabolism. Fats are broken down into constituent fatty acids and glycerol for a number of uses, including dense nutritional energy storage. Digestion of fat requires BILE acids produced by the LIVER; bile is stored in the GALL BLADDER.

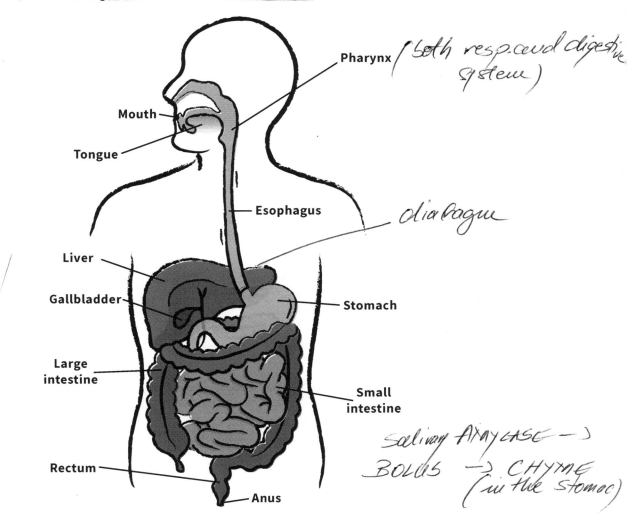

Pharynx (both resp. and digestive system)

Mouth

Tongue

Esophagus

diaphragm

Liver

Gallbladder

Stomach

Large intestine

Small intestine

Rectum

Anus

salivary AMYLASE →
BOLUS → CHYME
(in the stomac)

Figure 7.9. The Digestive System

The stomach produces a semifluid mass of partially digested food called CHYME that passes into the SMALL INTESTINE, where nutrients are absorbed into the bloodstream. This absorption occurs through millions of finger-like projections known as VILLI that increase the surface area available for the absorption of nutrients.

The small intestine itself has three major segments. Proximal to the stomach is the DUODENUM, which combines digestive substances from the liver and pancreas; next is the JEJUNUM, the primary site of nutrient absorption; finally, the ILEUM absorbs remaining nutrients and moves the remaining matter into the large intestine. The LARGE INTESTINE

small intestine: DUODENUM → Jejunum → ILEUM

(also called the colon) absorbs water from the waste, which then passes into the RECTUM and out of the body through the ANUS.

Pathologies of the Digestive System

The digestive system is prone to several illnesses of varying severity. Commonly, gastrointestinal distress is caused by an acute infection (bacterial or viral) affecting the lining of the digestive system. A resulting immune response triggers the body, as an adaptive measure, to void the contents of the digestive system in order to purge the infection. Chronic gastrointestinal disorders include IRRITABLE BOWEL SYNDROME (the causes of which are largely unknown) and CROHN'S DISEASE, an inflammatory bowel disorder with an immune-related etiology.

EXAMPLES

1. Where in the digestive tract are most of the nutrients absorbed?
    A) the small intestine
    B) the rectum
    C) the stomach
    D) the large intestine

    Answer:

    A) is correct. Most nutrients are absorbed by the small intestine.

2. Which of the following initiates the breakdown of carbohydrates?
    A) salivary amylase
    B) stomach acid
    C) bile salts
    D) peristalsis

    Answer:

    A) is correct. Salivary amylase in the mouth begins the breakdown of carbohydrates.

The Skeletal System

Structure and Function of the Skeletal System

The skeletal system is composed of tissue called BONE that helps with movement, provides support for organs, and synthesizes blood cells. The outer layer of bone is composed of a matrix made of collagen and minerals that gives bones their strength and rigidity. The matrix is formed from functional units called OSTEONS that include layers of compact bone called LAMELLAE. The lamellae surround a cavity called the HAVERSIAN CANAL, which houses the bone's blood supply. These canals are in turn connected to the PERIOSTEUM, the bone's outermost membrane, by another series of channels called VOLKMANN'S CANALS.

Within osteons are blood cells called OSTEOBLASTS, mononucleate cells that produce bone tissue. When the bone tissue hardens around these cells, the cells are known as OSTEOCYTES, and the space they occupy within the bone tissue is known as LACUNAE. The lacunae are connected by a series of channels called CANALICULI. OSTEOCLASTS, a third type of bone cell, are responsible for breaking down bone tissue. They are located on the surface of bones and help balance the body's calcium levels by degrading bone to release stored calcium. The fourth type of bone cell, LINING CELLS are flatted osteoblasts that protect the bone and also help balance calcium levels.

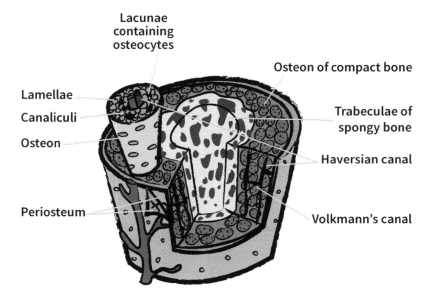

Figure 7.10. Bone Structure

Within the hard outer layer of bone is the spongy layer called CANCELLOUS BONE, which is made up of support structures called TRABECULAE. Within this layer is the bone marrow, which houses cells that produce red blood cells in a process called HEMATOPOIESIS. Bone marrow also produces many of the lymphocytes that play an important role in the immune system.

Bones are divided into four main categories. LONG BONES, such as the femur and humerus, are longer than they are wide. SHORT BONES, in contrast, are wider than they are long. These include the clavicle and carpals. FLAT BONES are wide and flat, and usually provide protection. Examples of flat bones include the bones of the skull, pelvis, and rib cage. IRREGULAR BONES, as the name suggests, have an irregular shape that doesn't fit into the other categories. These bones include the vertebrae and bones of the jaw.

How might diet affect the body's ability to rebuild bone after a fracture?

Bones are held together (articulated) at JOINTS by connective tissue called LIGAMENTS. Joints can be classified based on the tissue that connects the bone. FIBROUS JOINTS are connected by dense, collagen-rich fibers, while CARTILAGINOUS JOINTS are joined by special tissue called HYALINE CARTILAGE. Cartilage is more flexible than bone but denser than muscles. In addition to joining together bone, it also helps hold open passageways and provides support in structures like the nose and ears. The third type of joint, SYNOVIAL JOINTS, are joined by synovial fluid, which lubricates the joint and allows for movement. Bones are also joined to muscles by connective tissue called TENDONS.

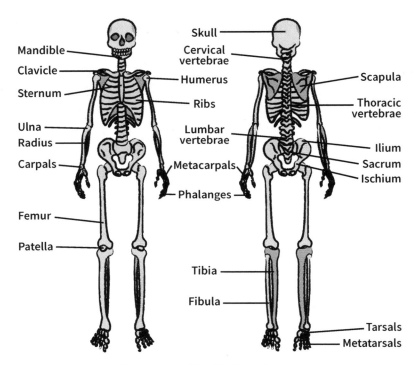

Figure 7.11. The Skeletal System

Table 7.2. Types of Synovial Joints

Name	Movement	Found In
Hinge joint	movement through one plane of motion as flexion/extension	elbows, knees, fingers
Ball-and-socket joint	range of motion through multiple planes and rotation about an axis	hips, shoulders
Saddle joint	movement through multiple planes, but cannot rotate about an axis	thumbs
Gliding joint	sliding movement in the plane of the bones' surfaces	vertebrae, small bones in the wrists and ankles
Condyloid joint	movement through two planes as flexion/extension and abduction/adduction, but cannot rotate about an axis	wrists
Pivot joint	only movement is rotation about an axis	elbows, neck

Pathologies of the Skeletal System

Important pathologies of the skeletal system include OSTEOPOROSIS, which occurs when minerals are leached from the bone, making bones more likely to break. Broken bones can also be caused by BRITTLE BONE DISEASE, which results from a genetic defect that affects collagen production. Joint pain can be caused by OSTEOARTHRITIS, which is the breakdown of cartilage in joints, and RHEUMATOID ARTHRITIS, which is an autoimmune disease that affects synovial membranes.

The Muscular System

Types of Muscle

The muscular system is composed of **MUSCLES** that move the body, support bodily functions, and circulate blood. The human body contains three types of muscles. **SKELETAL MUSCLES** are voluntarily controlled and attach to the skeleton to allow movement in the body. **SMOOTH MUSCLES** are involuntary, meaning they cannot be consciously controlled. Smooth muscles are found in many organs and structures, including the esophagus, stomach, intestines, blood vessels, bladder, and bronchi. Finally, **CARDIAC MUSCLES**, found only in the heart, are the involuntary muscles that contract the heart in order to pump blood through the body.

Some skeletal muscles, such as the diaphragm and those that control blinking, can be voluntarily controlled but usually operate involuntarily.

Muscle Cell Structure

The main structural unit of a muscle is the **SARCOMERE**. Sarcomeres are composed of a series of **MUSCLE FIBERS**, which are elongated individual cells that stretch from one end of the muscle to the other. Within each fiber are hundreds of **MYOFIBRILS**, long strands within the cells that contain alternating layers of thin filaments made of the protein **ACTIN** and thick filaments made of the protein **MYOSIN**. Each of these proteins plays a role in muscle contraction and relaxation.

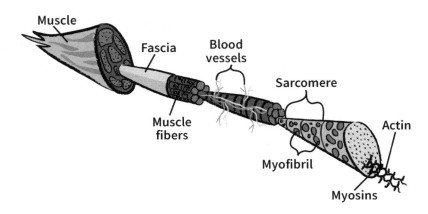

Figure 7.12. Structure of Skeletal Muscle

Muscle contraction is explained by the SLIDING FILAMENT THEORY. When the sarcomere is at rest, the thin filaments containing actin are found at both ends of the muscle, while the thick filaments containing myosin are found at the center. Myosin filaments contain "heads," which can attach and detach from actin filaments. The myosin attaches to actin and pulls the thin filaments to the center of the sarcomere, forcing the thin filaments to slide inward and causing the entire sarcomere to shorten, or contract, creating movement. The sarcomere can be broken down into zones that contain certain filaments.

◆ The Z-LINE separates the sarcomeres: a single sarcomere is the distance between two Z-lines.

◆ The A-BAND is the area of the sarcomere in which thick myosin filaments are found and does not shorten during muscular contraction.

◆ The I-BAND is the area in the sarcomere between the thick myosin filaments in which only thin actin filament is found.

◆ The H-ZONE is found between the actin filaments and contains only thick myosin filament.

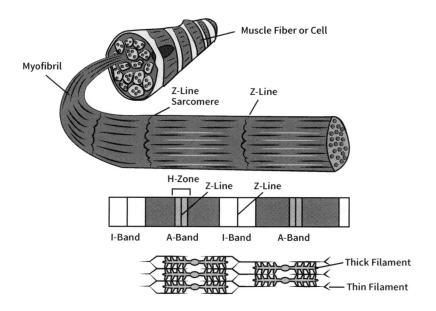

Figure 7.13. Sliding Filament Theory

Pathologies of the Muscular System

Injuries to muscle can impede movement and cause pain. When muscle fibers are over-stretched, the resulting MUSCLE STRAIN can cause pain, stiffness, and bruising. Muscle fibers can also be weakened by diseases, as with MUSCULAR DYSTROPHY (MD). MD is a genetically inherited condition that results in progressive muscle wasting, which limits movement and can cause respiratory and cardiovascular difficulties.

Overstretching a ligament is called a sprain.

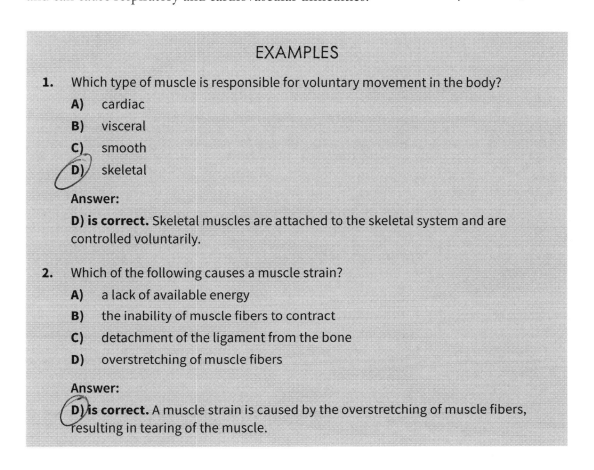

EXAMPLES

1. Which type of muscle is responsible for voluntary movement in the body?
   A) cardiac
   B) visceral
   C) smooth
   D) skeletal

   Answer:

   D) is correct. Skeletal muscles are attached to the skeletal system and are controlled voluntarily.

2. Which of the following causes a muscle strain?
   A) a lack of available energy
   B) the inability of muscle fibers to contract
   C) detachment of the ligament from the bone
   D) overstretching of muscle fibers

   Answer:

   D) is correct. A muscle strain is caused by the overstretching of muscle fibers, resulting in tearing of the muscle.

The Immune System

The human immune system protects the body against bacteria and viruses that cause disease. The system is composed of two parts. The INNATE system includes nonspecific defenses that work against a wide range of infectious agents. This system includes both physical barriers that keep out foreign particles and organisms along with specific cells that attack invaders that move past barriers. The second part of the immune system is the ADAPTIVE immune system, which "learns" to respond only to specific invaders.

Table 7.3. Lines of Defense in the Immune System

1. external barriers	skin, enzymes, mucus, earwax, native bacteria
2. the innate response	inflammation, neutrophils (a white blood cell), antimicrobial peptides, natural killer lymphocytes, interferon
3. the adaptive response	helper T-cells, cytotoxic T-cells, B-cells, memory B-cells

The Innate Immune System

The first line of defense in the immune system are barriers to entry. The most prominent is the SKIN, which leaves few openings for an infection-causing agent to enter. Bodily orifices exhibit other methods for preventing infection. The mouth is saturated with native bacteria that dominate the resources in the microenvironment, making it inhospitable to invading bacteria. In addition, enzymes in the mouth create a hostile environment for foreign organisms. The urethra flushes away potentially invasive microorganisms mechanically through the outflow of urine, while the vagina maintains a consistently low pH, deterring potential infections. The eyes and nose constantly produce and flush away tears and MUCUS, which trap pathogens before they can replicate and infect. Similarly, EARWAX serves as an additional barrier to entry.

Pathogens do occasionally breach these barriers and arrive within the body, where they attempt to replicate and cause an infection. When this occurs, the body mounts a number of nonspecific responses. The body's initial response is INFLAMMATION: infected cells release signaling molecules indicating that an infection has occurred, which causes increased blood flow to the area. This increase in blood flow includes the increased presence of WHITE BLOOD CELLS, also called LEUKOCYTES. The most common type of leukocyte found at sites of inflammation are NEUTROPHILS, which engulf and destroy invaders.

Phagocytosis occurs when a cell completely surrounds a particle to form an enclosed vesicle. The particle can then be broken down either for nutrients or to neutralize a threat. Cells in the immune system that use phagocytosis are called macrophages.

Other innate responses include ANTIMICROBIAL PEPTIDES, which destroy bacteria by interfering with the functions of their membranes or DNA, and NATURAL KILLER LYMPHOCYTES, which respond to virus-infected cells. Because they can recognize damaged cells with the presence of antibodies, they are important in early defense against bacterial infection. In addition, infected cells may release INTERFERON, which causes nearby cells to increase their defenses.

Table 7.4. Types of White Blood Cells

TYPE OF CELL	NAME OF CELL	ROLE	INNATE OR ADAPTIVE	PREVALENCE
Granulocytes	Neutrophil	First responders that quickly migrate to the site of infections to destroy bacterial invaders	Innate	Very common
	Eosinophil	Attack multicellular parasites	Innate	Rare
	Basophil	Large cell responsible for inflammatory reactions, including allergies	Innate	Very rare
Lymphocyte	B-cells	Respond to antigens by releasing antibodies	Adaptive	Common
	T-cells	Respond to antigens by destroying invaders and infected cells	Adaptive	
	Natural killer cells	Destroy virus-infected cells and tumor cells	Innate and adaptive	
Monocyte	Macrophage	Engulf and destroy microbes, foreign substances, and cancer cells	Innate and adaptive	Rare

auca Whitacre / Nursing /

The Adaptive Immune System

The adaptive immune system is able to recognize molecules called ANTIGENS on the surface of pathogens to which the system has previously been exposed. Antigens are displayed on the surface of cells by the MAJOR HISTOCOMPATIBILITY COMPLEX (MHC), which can display either "self" proteins from their own cells or proteins from pathogens. In an ANTIGEN-PRESENTING CELL, the MHC on the cell's surface displays a particular antigen, which is recognized by HELPER T-CELLS. These cells produce a signal (cytokines) that activates CYTOTOXIC T-CELLS, which then destroy any cell that displays the antigen.

The presence of antigens also activates B-CELLS, which rapidly multiply to create PLASMA CELLS, which in turn release ANTIBODIES. Antibodies will bind only to specific antigens, and in turn result in the destruction of the infected cell. Some interfere directly with the function of the cell, while others draw the attention of macrophages. MEMORY B-CELLS are created during infection. These cells "remember" the antigen that their parent cells responded to, allowing them to respond more quickly if the infection appears again.

Memory B-cells are the underlying mechanisms behind vaccines, which introduce a harmless version of a pathogen into the body to active the body's adaptive immune response.

Together, T- and B-cells are known as LYMPHOCYTES. T-cells are produced in the thymus, while B-cells mature in bone marrow. These cells circulate through the lymphatic system.

Pathologies of the Immune System

The immune system itself can be pathological. The immune system of individuals with an AUTOIMMUNE DISEASE will attack healthy tissues, as is the case in lupus, psoriasis, and multiple sclerosis. The immune system may also overreact to harmless particles, a condition known as an ALLERGY. Some infections will attack the immune system itself. HUMAN IMMUNODEFICIENCY VIRUS (HIV) attacks helper T-cells, eventually causing ACQUIRED IMMUNODEFICIENCY SYNDROME (AIDS), which allows opportunistic infections to overrun the body.

EXAMPLES

1. Which of the following is NOT part of the innate immune system?
   A) interferon
   B) neutrophils
   C) antibodies
   D) natural killer lymphocytes

   Answer:

   C) is correct. Antibodies are part of the body's adaptive immune system and only respond to specific pathogens.

ANATOMY AND PHYSIOLOGY 87

The Reproductive System

The Male Reproductive System

The male reproductive system produces SPERM, or male gametes, and passes them to the female reproductive system. Sperm are produced in the TESTES (also called testicles), which are housed externally in a sac-like structure called the SCROTUM. The scrotum contracts and relaxes to move the testes closer or farther from the body. This process keeps the testes at the appropriate temperature for sperm production, which is slightly lower than regular body temperature.

Mature sperm are stored in the EPIDIDYMIS. During sexual stimulation, sperm travel from the epididymis through a long, thin tube called the VAS DEFERENS. Along the way, the sperm is joined by fluids from three glands to form SEMEN. The SEMINAL VESICLES secrete the bulk of the fluid which makes up semen, which is composed of various proteins, sugars, and enzymes. The PROSTATE contributes an alkaline fluid that counteracts the

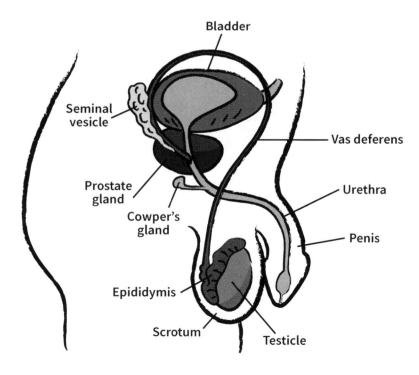

Figure 7.14. The Male Reproductive System

acidity of the vaginal tract. Finally, the COWPER GLAND secretes a protein-rich fluid that acts as a lubricant. Semen travels through the URETHRA and exits the body through the PENIS, which becomes rigid during sexual arousal.

The main hormone associated with the male reproductive system is TESTOSTERONE, which is released by the testes (and in the adrenal glands in much smaller amounts). Testosterone is responsible for the development of the male reproductive system and male secondary sexual characteristics, including muscle development and facial hair growth.

The Female Reproductive System

The female reproductive system produces EGGS, or female gametes, and gestates the fetus during pregnancy. Eggs are produced in the OVARIES and travel through the FALLOPIAN TUBES to the UTERUS, which is a muscular organ that houses the fetus during pregnancy. The uterine cavity is lined with a layer of blood-rich tissue called the ENDOMETRIUM. If no pregnancy occurs, the endometrium is shed monthly during MENSTRUATION.

FERTILIZATION occurs when the egg absorbs the sperm; it usually takes place in the fallopian tubes but may happen in the uterus itself. After fertilization the new zygote implants itself in the endometrium, where it will grow and develop over thirty-eight weeks (roughly nine months). During gestation, the developing fetus acquires nutrients and passes waste through the PLACENTA. This temporary organ is attached to the wall of the uterus and is connected to the baby by the UMBILICAL CORD.

What type of muscle is most likely found in the myometrium of the uterus? smooth

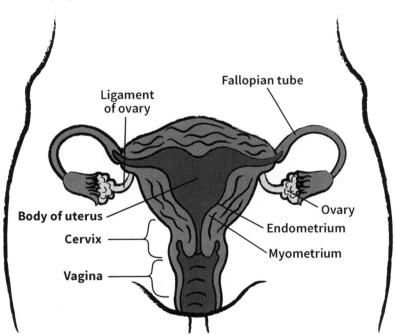

Figure 7.15. The Female Reproductive System

When the fetus is mature, powerful muscle contractions occur in the myometrium, the muscular layer next to the endometrium. These contractions push the fetus through an opening called the CERVIX into the vagina, from which it exits the body. The placenta and umbilical cords are also expelled through the vagina shortly after birth.

The female reproductive cycle is controlled by a number of different hormones. Estrogen, produced by the ovaries, stimulates Graafian follicles, which contain immature eggs cells. The pituitary gland then releases luteinizing hormone, which causes the egg to be released into the fallopian tubes during OVULATION. During pregnancy, estrogen and progesterone are released in high levels to help with fetal growth and to prevent further ovulation.

EXAMPLES

1. Which of the following organs transports semen through the penis?
   A) urethra
   B) vas deferens
   C) prostate
   D) seminal vesicles

   Answer:

   A) is correct. The urethra carries semen through the penis.

2. Which of the following organs provides nutrients to a fetus during gestation?
   A) ovary
   B) placenta
   C) uterus
   D) cervix

   Answer:

   B) is correct. The placenta provides nutrients to the growing fetus and also removes waste products.

The Endocrine System

Structure and Function of the Endocrine System

The endocrine system is composed of a network of organs called GLANDS that produce signaling chemicals called HORMONES. These hormones are released by glands into the bloodstream and then travel to the other tissues and organs whose functions they regulate. When they reach their target, hormones bond to a specific receptor on cell membranes, which affects the machinery of the cell. Hormones play an important role in regulating almost all bodily functions, including digestion, respiration, sleep, stress, growth, development, reproduction, and immune response.

Much of the action of the endocrine system runs through the HYPOTHALAMUS, which is highly integrated into the nervous system. The hypothalamus receives signals from the brain and in turn will release hormones that regulate both other endocrine organs and important metabolic processes. Other endocrine glands include the pineal, pituitary, thyroid, parathyroid, thymus, and adrenal glands.

Organs from other systems, including the reproductive and digestive systems, can also secrete hormones, and thus are considered part of the endocrine system. The reproductive organs in both males (testes) and females (ovaries and placenta) release important hormones, as do the pancreas, liver, and stomach.

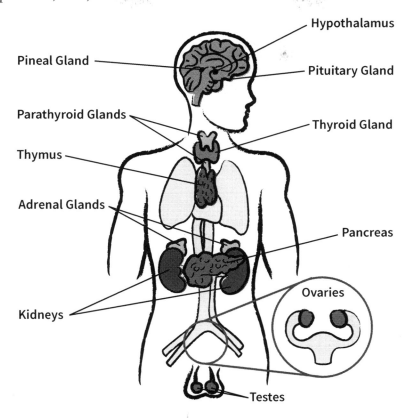

Figure 7.16. The Endocrine System

Table 7.5. Endocrine Glands

GLAND	REGULATES	HORMONES PRODUCED
pineal gland	circadian rhythms (the sleep/wake cycle)	melatonin
pituitary gland	growth, blood pressure, reabsorption of water by the kidneys, temperature, pain relief, and some reproductive functions related to pregnancy and childbirth	human growth hormone (HGH), thyroid-stimulating hormone (TSH), prolactin (PRL), luteinizing hormone (LH), follicle-stimulating hormone (FSH), oxytocin, antidiuretic hormone (ADH)
hypothalamus	pituitary function and metabolic processes including body temperature, hunger, thirst, and circadian rhythms	thyrotropin-releasing hormone (TRH), dopamine, growth-hormone-releasing hormone (GHRH), gonadotropin-releasing hormone (GnRH), oxytocin, vasopressin
thyroid gland	energy use and protein synthesis	thyroxine (T4), triiodothyronine (T3), calcitonin
parathyroid	calcium and phosphate levels	parathyroid hormone (PTH)
adrenal glands	"fight or flight" response, regulation of salt and blood volume	epinephrine, norepinephrine, cortisol, androgens
pancreas	blood sugar levels and metabolism	insulin, glucagon, somatostatin

Table 7.5. Endocrine Glands

GLAND	REGULATES	HORMONES PRODUCED
testes	maturation of sex organs, secondary sex characteristics	androgens (e.g., testosterone)
ovaries	maturation of sex organs, secondary sex characteristics, pregnancy, childbirth, and lactation	progesterone, estrogens
placenta	gestation and childbirth	progesterone, estrogens, human chorionic gonadotropin, human placental lactogen

Pathologies of the Endocrine System

Disruption of hormone production in specific endocrine glands can lead to disease. An inability to produce insulin results in uncontrolled blood glucose levels, a condition called DIABETES. Over- or underactive glands can lead to conditions like HYPOTHYROIDISM, which is characterized by slow metabolism, and hyperparathyroidism, which can lead to osteoporosis. Tumors on endocrine glands can also damage the functioning of a wide variety of bodily systems.

EXAMPLES

1. Which gland in the endocrine system is responsible for regulating blood glucose levels?

   A) adrenal

   B) testes

   C) pineal

   D) pancreas

   Answer:

   D) is correct. The pancreas releases insulin and glucagon, which regulate glucose levels in the blood.

2. Damage to the parathyroid would most likely affect which of the following?

   A) stress levels

   B) bone density

   C) secondary sex characteristics

   D) circadian rhythms

   Answer:

   B) is correct. The parathyroid controls calcium and phosphate levels, which are maintained by producing and reabsorbing bone tissue.

The Integumentary System

The **INTEGUMENTARY SYSTEM** refers to the skin (the largest organ in the body) and related structures, including the hair and nails. Skin is composed of three layers. The **EPIDERMIS** is the outermost layer of the skin. This waterproof layer contains no blood vessels and acts mainly to protect the body. Under the epidermis lies the **DERMIS**, which consists of dense connective tissue that allows skin to stretch and flex. The dermis is home to blood vessels, glands, and **HAIR FOLLICLES**. The **HYPODERMIS** is a layer of fat below the dermis that stores energy (in the form of fat) and acts as a cushion for the body. The hypodermis is sometimes called the **SUBCUTANEOUS LAYER**.

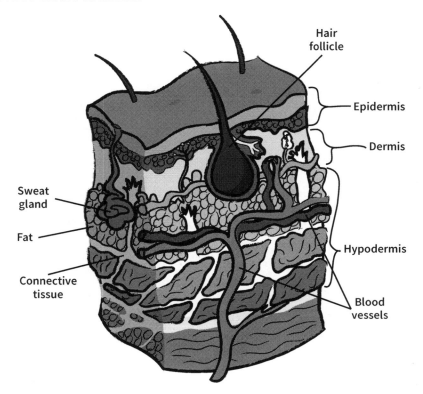

Figure 7.17. The Skin

The skin has several important roles. It acts as a barrier to protect the body from injury, the intrusion of foreign particles, and the loss of water and nutrients. It is also important for **THERMOREGULATION**. Blood vessels near the surface of the skin can dilate, allowing for higher blood flow and the release of heat. They can also constrict to reduce the amount of blood that travels near the surface of the skin, which helps conserve heat. The skin also produces vitamin D when exposed to sunlight.

Because the skin covers the whole body, it plays a vital role in allowing organisms to interact with the environment. It is home to nerve endings that sense temperature, pressure, and pain, and it also houses glands that help maintain homeostasis. **ECCRINE glands**, which are located primarily in the palms of the hands and soles of the feet (and to a lesser degree in other areas of the body), release the water and salt (NaCl) mixture called **SWEAT**. These glands help the body maintain the appropriate salt/water balance. Sweat can also contain small amounts of other substances the body needs to expel, including alcohol, lactic acid, and urea.

Why would flushing—the reddening of the skin caused by dilating blood vessels—be associated with fevers?

APOCRINE glands, which are located primarily in the armpit and groin, release an oily substance that contains pheromones. They are also sensitive to adrenaline, and are responsible for most of the sweating that occurs due to stress, fear, anxiety, or pain. Apocrine glands are largely inactive until puberty.

EXAMPLES

1. Which of the following is NOT a function of the skin?
    A) regulating body temperature
    B) protecting against injury
    C) producing adrenaline
    D) maintaining water/salt balance

    Answer:

    C) is correct. The skin does not produce adrenaline. (Adrenaline is produced and released by the adrenal glands.)

2. Which of the following is the outermost layer of the skin?
    A) hypodermis
    B) dermis
    C) epidermis
    D) apocrine

    Answer:

    C) is correct. The epidermis is the outermost layer of the skin. It is waterproof and does not contain any blood vessels.

The Genitourinary System

The URINARY SYSTEM excretes water and waste from the body and is crucial for maintaining the body's electrolyte balance (the balance of water and salt in the blood). Because many organs function as part of both the reproductive and urinary systems, the two are sometimes referred to collectively as the GENITOURINARY SYSTEM.

The main organs of the urinary system are the KIDNEYS, which filter waste from the blood; maintain the electrolyte balance in the blood; and regulate blood volume, pressure, and pH. The kidneys also function as an endocrine organ and release several important hormones. These include RENIN, which regulates blood pressure, and CALCITRIOL, the active form of vitamin D. The kidney is divided into two regions: the RENAL CORTEX, which is the outermost layer, and the RENAL MEDULLA, which is the inner layer.

A normal human kidney contains around one million nephrons.

The functional unit of the kidney is the NEPHRON, which is a series of looping tubes that filter electrolytes, metabolic waste, and other water-soluble waste molecules from the blood. These wastes include UREA, which is a nitrogenous byproduct of protein catabolism, and URIC ACID, a byproduct of nucleic acid metabolism. Together, these waste products are excreted from the body in URINE.

Filtration begins in a network of capillaries called a GLOMERULUS which is located in the renal cortex of each kidney. This waste is then funneled into COLLECTING DUCTS in the renal medulla. From the collecting ducts, urine passes through the RENAL PELVIS and then through two long tubes called URETERS.

The two ureters drain into the urinary bladder, which holds up to 1000 milliliters of liquid. The bladder exit is controlled by two sphincters, both of which must open for urine to pass. The internal sphincter is made of smooth involuntary muscle, while the external sphincter can be voluntarily controlled. In males, the external sphincter also closes to prevent movement of seminal fluid into the bladder during sexual activity. (A sphincter is a circular muscle that controls movement of substances through passageways. Sphincters are found throughout the human body, including the bladder, esophagus, and capillaries.)

Urine exits the bladder through the URETHRA. In males, the urethra goes through the penis and also carries semen. In females, the much-shorter urethra ends just above the vaginal opening.

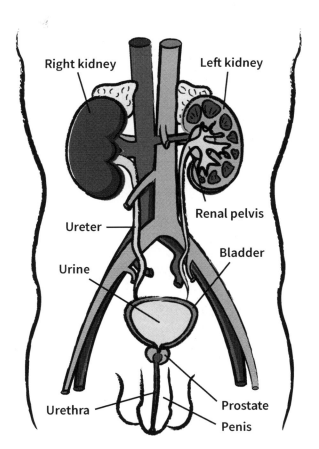

Figure 7.18. Male Genitourinary System

EXAMPLES

1. Which of the following is the outermost layer of the kidney?
   (A) renal cortex
   B) renal medulla
   C) renal pelvis
   D) nephron

   Answer:
   A) is correct. The outermost layer of the kidney is the renal cortex.

2. Which of the following organs holds urine before it passes into the urethra?
   A) prostate
   B) kidney
   C) ureter
   (D) urinary bladder

Answer:

D) is correct. The urinary bladder holds urine before it passes to the urethra to be excreted.

eight

LIFE SCIENCE

Biological Macromolecules

There are four basic biological macromolecules that are common between all organisms: carbohydrates, lipids, nucleic acids, and proteins. These molecules make life possible by performing basic cellular functions.

Macromolecules are **POLYMERS**, which are large molecules comprised of smaller molecules called **MONOMERS**. The monomers are joined together in an endothermic (energy requiring) dehydration reaction, so-called because it releases a molecule of water. Conversely, the bonds in polymers can be broken by an exothermic (energy-releasing) reaction that requires water.

Carbohydrates

CARBOHYDRATES, commonly known as sugars, are made up of carbon, hydrogen, and oxygen. The monomers of carbohydrates, called **MONOSACCHARIDES**, have these elements in the ratio $C_nH_{2n}O_n$. Common monosaccharides include glucose and fructose.

Monosaccharides bond together to build larger carbohydrate molecules. Two monosaccharides bond together to form **DISACCHARIDES** such as sucrose and lactose. **OLIGOSACCHARIDES** are formed when small numbers of monosaccharies (usually between two and ten) bond together, and **POLYSACCHARIDES** can include hundreds or even thousands of monosaccharides.

Carbohydrates are often taken into the body through ingestion of food and serve a number of purposes, acting as:

- fuel sources (glycogen, amylose)
- means of communication between cells (glycoproteins)
- cell structure support (cellulose, chitin)

Carbohydrates are broken down to their constituent parts for fuel and other biological functions. Inability to

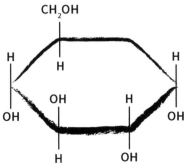

Figure 8.1. Glucose

process sugars can lead to health issues; for example, inability to break down lactose (often due to problems with the enzyme LACTASE, which serves this function) leads to lactose intolerance, and problems with insulin not working properly in the breakdown of sugars can lead to diabetes.

Lipids

LIPIDS, commonly known as fats, are composed mainly of hydrogen and carbon. They serve a number of functions depending on their particular structure: they make up the outer structure of cells, and can act as fuel, as steroids, and as hormones. Lipids are hydrophobic, meaning they repel water.

Cholesterol is one example of a lipid, and is essential for normal functioning, although excessive accumulation can cause inflammation issues and high blood pressure. There are two types of cholesterol: HIGH-DENSITY LIPOPROTEIN (**HDL**) and LOW-DENSITY LIPOPROTEIN (**LDL**), with HDL commonly referred to as "good" cholesterol and LDL as "bad" cholesterol, as high levels of LDL in particular can cause health problems.

Proteins

PROTEINS serve an incredibly wide variety of purposes within the body. As enzymes, they play key roles in important processes like DNA replication, cellular division, and cellular metabolism. Structural proteins provide rigidity to cartilage, hair, nails, and the cytoskeletons (the network of molecules that holds the parts of a cell in place). They are also involved in communication between cells and in the transportation of molecules.

Proteins are composed of individual AMINO ACIDS, each of which has an amino group and carboxylic acid group, along with other side groups. Amino acids are joined together by PEPTIDE BONDS to form polypeptides. There are twenty amino acids, and the order of the amino acids in the polypeptide determines the shape and function of the molecule.

Nucleic Acids

NUCLEIC ACIDS store hereditary information and are composed of monomers called NUCLEOTIDES. Each nucleotide includes a sugar, a phosphate group, and a nitrogenous base.

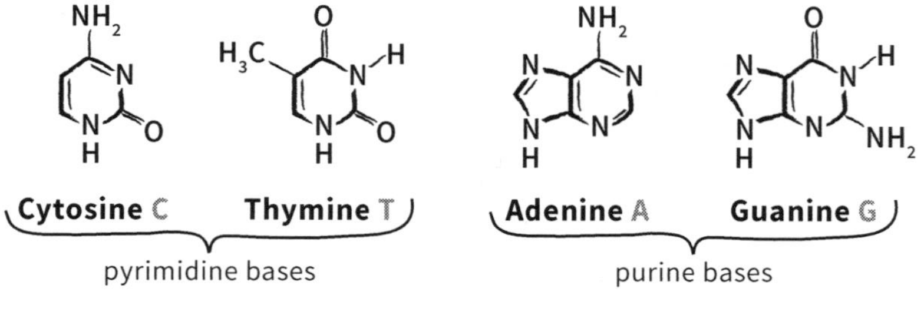

| Cytosine C | Thymine T | Adenine A | Guanine G |
| pyrimidine bases | | purine bases | |

Figure 8.2. DNA Nucleotides

There are two types of nucleic acids. DEOXYRIBONUCLEIC ACID (**DNA**) contains the genetic instructions to produce proteins. It is composed of two strings of nucleotides wound into a double helix shape. The backbone of the helix is made from the nucleotide's sugar (deoxyribose) and phosphate groups. The "rungs" of the ladder are made from one of four nitrogenous bases: adenine, thymine, cytosine, and guanine. These bases bond together in specific pairs: adenine with thymine and cytosine with guanine.

RIBONUCLEIC ACID (RNA) transcribes information from DNA and plays several vital roles in the replication of DNA and the manufacturing of proteins. RNA nucleotides contain a sugar (ribose), a phosphate group, and one of four nitrogenous bases: adenine, uracil, cytosine, and guanine. It is usually found as a single stranded molecule.

There are three main differences between DNA and RNA:

1. DNA contains the nucleotide thymine; RNA contains the nucleotide uracil.
2. DNA is double stranded; RNA is single stranded.
3. DNA is made from the sugar deoxyribose; RNA is made from the sugar ribose.

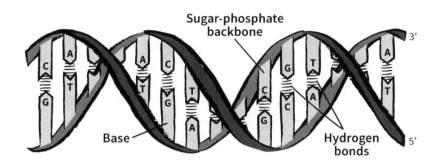

Figure 8.3. DNA

The Structure and Role of DNA

DNA stores information by coding for proteins using blocks of three nucleotides called CODONS. Each codon codes for a specific amino acid; together, all the codons needed to make a specific protein are called a GENE. In addition to codons for specific amino acids, there are also codons that signal "start" and "stop."

The production of a protein starts with TRANSCRIPTION. During transcription, the two sides of the DNA helix unwind and a complementary strand of messenger RNA (mRNA) is manufactured using the DNA as a template.

This mRNA then travels outside the nucleus where it is "read" by a ribosome during TRANSLATION. Each codon on the mRNA is matched to an ANTI-CODON on a strand of tRNA, which carries a specific amino acid. The amino acids bond as they are lined up next to each other, forming a polypeptide.

A MUTATION causes a change in the sequence of nucleotides within DNA. For example, the codon GAC codes for the amino acid aspartic acid. However, if the cytosine is swapped for an adenine, the codon now reads GAA, which corresponds to the amino acid glutamic acid.

When it is not being transcribed, DNA is tightly wound around proteins called HISTONES to create NUCLEOSOMES, which are in turn packaged into CHROMATIN. The structure of chromatin allows large amounts of DNA to be stored in a very small space and helps regulate transcription by controlling access to specific sections of DNA. Tightly

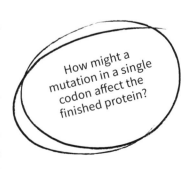

How might a mutation in a single codon affect the finished protein?

folding the DNA also helps prevent damage to the genetic code. Chromatin is further bundled into packages of DNA called CHROMOSOMES. During cell division, DNA is replicated to create two identical copies of each chromosome called CHROMATIDS.

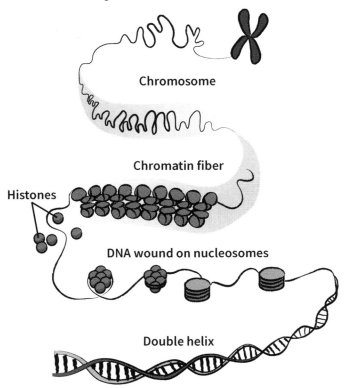

Figure 8.4. DNA, Chromatin, and Chromosomes

EXAMPLES

1. Which of the following is NOT an amino acid found in DNA?
    A) adenine
    B) guanine
    C) uracil
    D) thymine

    Answer:

    C) is correct. Uracil is found only in RNA.

2. Which of the following processes uses the information stored in RNA to produce a protein?
    A) replication
    B) translation
    C) transcription
    D) mutation

    Answer:

    B) is correct. Translation is the process of matching codons in RNA to the correct anti-codon to manufacture a protein.

The Cell

A **CELL** is the smallest unit of life that can reproduce on its own. Unicellular organisms, such as amoebae, are made up of only one cell, while multicellular organisms are comprised of many cells. Cells consist of many different parts that work together to maintain the life of the cell.

Cell Membranes

The outer surface of human cells is made up of a **PLASMA MEMBRANE**, which gives the cell its shape. This membrane is primarily composed of a **PHOSPHOLIPID BILAYER**, which itself is made up of two layers of lipids facing in opposing directions. This functions to separate the inner cellular environment from the **EXTRACELLULAR SPACE**, the space between cells.

Molecules travel through the cell membrane using a number of different methods. During **DIFFUSION**, molecules pass through the membrane from areas of high to low concentration. (When that molecule is water, the process is called **OSMOSIS**.) **FACILITATED DIFFUSION** occurs with the assistance of proteins embedded in the membrane. Diffusion is known as **PASSIVE TRANSPORT** because it does not require energy.

During **ACTIVE TRANSPORT**, proteins in the membrane use energy (in the form of ATP) to move molecules across the membrane. Usually these molecules are large or are being moved against their concentration gradient (from areas of low to high concentration).

Cell Organelles

Within the cell, specialized parts known as **ORGANELLES** serve individual functions to support the cell. The inside of the cell (excluding the nucleus) is the **CYTOPLASM**, which includes both organelles and **CYTOSOL**, a fluid that aids in molecular transport and reactions.

The function of individual organelles can be compared to the functions of components in a city. The "power plant" for the cell is its mitochondria, which produce energy for the cell in the form of **ADENOSINE TRIPHOSPHATE** (**ATP**). This process is known as **CELLULAR RESPIRATION**, as it requires oxygen that is taken in from the lungs and supplied in blood. Byproducts of cellular respiration are water and carbon dioxide, the latter of which is transported into blood and then to the lungs, where it is exhaled.

The "city hall" of the cell is the cell NUCLEUS, which is where the cell's "instructions" governing its functions originate. The nucleus contains the cell's DNA and is surrounded by a NUCLEAR MEMBRANE. Only eukaryotic cells have nuclei; prokaryotic nucleic acids are not contained with a membrane-bound organelle.

The transporting "railway" function is largely served by ENDOPLASMIC RETICULUM. Proteins and lipids travel along endoplasmic reticulum as they are constructed and transported within the cell. There are two types of endoplasmic reticulum, SMOOTH and ROUGH, which are distinguished by the fact that the latter is embedded with RIBOSOMES. Also, smooth endoplasmic reticulum are associated with the production and transport of lipids, whereas rough endoplasmic reticulum are associated with the production and transport of proteins. Ribosomes themselves are sites of protein production; here, molecules produced from the nucleus-encoding proteins guide the assembly of proteins from amino acids.

The GOLGI APPARATUS is another organelle involved in protein synthesis and transport. After a new protein is synthesized at the ribosome and travels along the endoplasmic reticulum, the Golgi apparatus packages it into a VESICLE (essentially a plasma membrane "bubble"), which can then be transported within the cell or secreted outside of the cell, as needed.

Plant cells include a number of structures not found in animal cells. These include the CELL WALL, which provides the cell with a hard outer structure, and CHLOROPLASTS, where photosynthesis occurs. During PHOTOSYNTHESIS, plants store energy from sunlight as sugars, which serve as the main source of energy for cell functions.

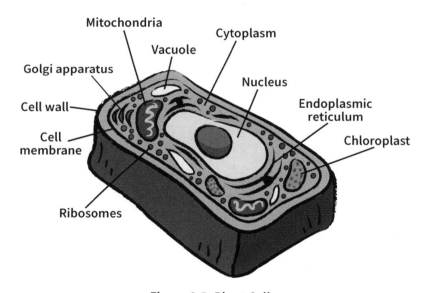

Figure 8.5. Plant Cell

The Cell Cycle

From the very earliest moments of life throughout adulthood, cell division is a critical function of cell biology. The rate of division differs between cell types; hair and skin cells divide relatively rapidly (which is why chemotherapy drugs, which target rapidly-dividing cells in an effort to destroy cancerous cells, often cause hair loss), whereas liver cells rarely divide, except in response to injury. Regardless of cell type (with the exception of reproductive cells), the process of cell division follows consistent stages, which make up the CELL CYCLE.

The cell cycle is made up of five stages. Cells at rest, which are not dividing, are considered to be at the G_0 (GROWTH PHASE 0) stage of the cell cycle. Once cell division is triggered (for example, by extracellular signals in response to nearby damage, requiring new cells to replace the damaged cells), cells enter stage G_1. In this stage, the organelles of the soon-to-be-dividing cell are duplicated, in order to support both daughter cells upon division. Similarly, in the next stage, S (DNA SYNTHESIS) PHASE, the genetic material of the cell (DNA) is duplicated, to ensure that each cell has the full complement of genetic instructions. Additional growth and protein production occurs in the subsequent stage, G_2 PHASE.

G_1, S, and G_2 are collectively known as INTERPHASE, in which the cell is growing and preparing to divide; the subsequent stages in which the cell is actively dividing are stages of MITOSIS. The first mitotic stage is PROPHASE, in which the newly replicated DNA condenses into chromosomes. These chromosomes are in pairs (humans have twenty-three pairs of chromosomes), with each pair joined together at the CENTROMERE.

Next, in PROMETAPHASE, the nuclear membrane breaks down. KINETOCHORES form on chromosomes, which are proteins that attach to kinetochore MICROTUBULES (cellular filaments) anchored at opposite ends of the cell. In METAPHASE, the chromosomes align along the center of the cell, perpendicular to the poles anchoring the microtubules. The alignment is such that one of each chromosome duplicates is attached to each pole by these microtubules.

In ANAPHASE, the microtubules pull the duplicates apart from each other toward each of the poles. In the final stage of mitosis, TELOPHASE, nuclei reform in each pole of the cell, and cellular filaments contract. The process of CYTOKINESIS divides the cell into two daughter cells, both with a full complement of genetic material and organelles.

Following mitosis, both daughter cells return to the G_1 phase, either to begin the process of division once again or to rest without dividing (G_0).

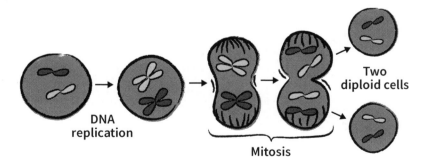

DNA replication

Mitosis

Two diploid cells

Figure 8.6. Mitosis

The process of producing sex cells (GAMETES: OVUM for women and SPERMATOZOA for men) is similar to mitosis, except that it produces cells with only half the normal number of chromosomes. Thus, when two sex cells fuse, the resulting ZYGOTE has the proper amount of chromosomes (and genetic information from both parents). This process is known as MEIOSIS.

In the prophase of meiosis, chromosome pairs align next to each other. At this stage, transfer of genetic material can occur between members of each pair, in a process known as HOMOLOGOUS RECOMBINATION, which can increase the genetic diversity of offspring.

In meiotic metaphase, these chromosomes align as pairs in the center of the cell, and the chromosomes are separated during anaphase. As a result, each gamete cell ends up with one copy of each chromosome pair, and thus one half of the genetic complement necessary for the zygote.

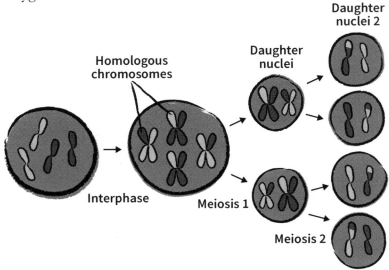

Figure 8.7. Meiosis

EXAMPLES

1. Cellular respiration produces which of the following molecules?
   A) oxygen
   B) DNA
   C) ATP
   D) glucose

   Answer:

   C) is correct. Cellular respiration uses glucose and oxygen to produce ATP.

2. Which of the following houses the cell's DNA?
   A) rough endoplasmic reticulum
   B) smooth endoplasmic reticulum
   C) mitochondrion
   D) nucleus

   Answer:

   D) is correct. Smooth and rough endoplasmic reticula process and transport lipids and proteins, and mitochondria produce the cell's chemical energy.

3. Which of the following processes creates daughter cells with half the number of chromosomes contained in somatic (body) cells?

A) mitosis
B) meiosis
C) recombination
D) the cell cycle

Answer:

B) is correct. Meiosis produces sex cells, which have half the number of chromosomes that somatic cells contain.

Genetics

Heredity

When organisms reproduce, GENETIC information is passed to the next generation through DNA. Within DNA are blocks of nucleotides called genes, each of which contains the code needed to produce a specific protein. Genes are responsible for TRAITS, or characteristics, in organisms such as eye color, height, and flower color. The sequence of nucleotides in DNA is called an organism's GENOTYPE, while the resulting physical traits are the organism's PHENOTYPE.

Many of the rules of genetics were discovered by Gregor Mendel, a nineteenth century abbot who used pea plants to show how traits are passed down through generations.

Different versions of the same gene (e.g., one that codes for blue eyes and one for green eyes) are called ALLELES. During sexual reproduction, the child receives two alleles of each gene—one each on the mother's chromosomes and the father's chromosomes. These alleles can be HOMOZYGOUS (identical) or HETEROZYGOUS (different). If the organism is heterozygous for a particular gene, which allele is expressed is determined by which alleles are dominant and/or recessive. According to the rules of Mendelian heredity, DOMINANT alleles will always be expressed, while RECESSIVE alleles are only expressed if the organism has no dominant alleles for that gene.

The genotype, and resulting phenotype, of sexually reproducing organisms can be tracked using Punnett squares, which show the alleles of the PARENT GENERATION on each of two axes. (Note that dominant alleles are always depicted using capital letters while recessive alleles are written in lower case.) The possible phenotype of the resulting offspring, called the **F1 GENERATION**, are then shown in the body of the square. The squares do not show the phenotypes of any one offspring; instead, they show the ratio of phenotypes found across the generation. In Figure 8.8, two heterozygous parents for trait *R* are mated, resulting in a ratio of 1:2:1 for homozygous dominant, heterozygous, and homozygous recessive. Note that this creates a 3:1 ratio of dominant to recessive phenotypes.

When the F1 generation is mated together, the resulting offspring are called the F2 generation.

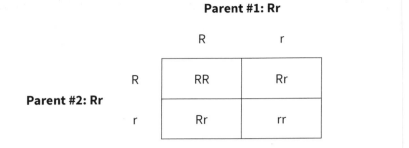

Parent #1: Rr

	R	r
R	RR	Rr
r	Rr	rr

Parent #2: Rr

Figure 8.8. Punnett Square

Similarly, crossing two parents that are heterozygous for two traits (dihybrids) results in a phenotypic ratio of 9:3:3:1, as shown below. This ratio is known as the DIHYBRID RATIO.

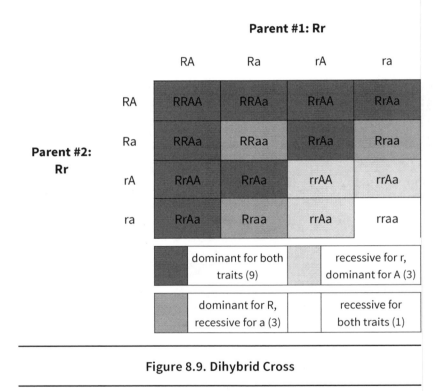

Figure 8.9. Dihybrid Cross

Non-Mendelian inheritance describes patterns in inheritance that do not follow the ratios described above. The patterns can occur for a number of reasons. Alleles might show INCOMPLETE DOMINANCE, where one allele is not fully expressed over the other, resulting in a third phenotype (for example, a red flower and white flower cross to create a pink flower). Alleles can also be CODOMINANT, meaning both are fully expresed (such as the AB blood type).

The expression of genes can also be regulated by mechanisms other than the dominant/recessive relationship. For example, some genes may inhibit the expression of other genes, a process called EPISTASIS. The environment can also impact gene expression. For example, organisms with the same genotype may grow to different sizes depending on the nutrients available to them.

When a person's genetic code is damaged, that organism may have a GENETIC DISORDER. For example, cystic fibrosis, which causes difficulty with basic bodily functions such as breathing and eating, results from damage to the gene which codes for a protein called CFTR. Down syndrome, which causes developmental delays, occurs when a person has three copies of chromosome 21 (meaning they received two copies from a parent as a result of an error in meiosis).

Natural Selection and Evolution

Genes are not static. Over time, MUTATIONS, or changes in the genetic code, occur that can affect an organism's ability to survive. Harmful mutations will appear less often in a population or be removed entirely because those organisms will be less likely to reproduce (and thus will not pass on that trait). Beneficial mutations may help an organism reproduce, and thus that trait will appear more often. Over time, this process, called NATURAL SELECTION, results in the evolution of new species. The theory of evolution was developed by naturalist Charles Darwin based in part on his observations of finches on the Galapagos Islands. These finches had a variety of beak shapes and sizes that allowed them to coexist by using different food sources.

Why might a harmful mutation continue to exist in a population?

As a result of these processes, all organisms share a distant evolutionary predecessor. As evolution progressed, species subsequently split off as different branches of the phylogenetic (evolutionary) tree of species diversity, leading to the complexity of life seen today. For example, humans share a recent evolutionary ancestor with other primates (but did not evolve directly from any of these species).

EXAMPLES

1. If a plant that is homozygous dominant (**T**) for a trait is crossed with a plant that is homozygous recessive (**t**) for the same trait, what will be the phenotype of the offspring if the trait follows Mendelian patterns of inheritance?

    A) All offspring will show the dominant phenotype.

    B) All offspring will show the recessive phenotype.

    C) Half the offspring will show the dominant trait, and the other half will show the recessive phenotype.

    D) All the offspring will show a mix of the dominant and recessive phenotypes.

    Answer:

    A) is correct. Because each offspring will inherit the dominant allele, all the offspring will show the dominant phenotype. The offspring would only show a mix of the two phenotypes if they did not follow Mendelian inheritance patterns.

2. Which of the following mutations would most likely be passed on to an organism's offspring?

    A) a mutation that prevents the production of functioning sperm cells

    B) a mutation that causes the deterioration of nerve cells in mature adults

    C) a mutation that does not cause any changes to the organism's phenotype

    D) a mutation that limits the growth of bone cells in children

Answer:

B) is correct. Because this mutation presents in older adults who have likely already reproduced, it is likely to have been passed on to the next generation. Mutations that affect reproduction and children are much less likely to be passed on. A mutation that causes no changes in phenotype may either disappear or spread as a result of random fluctuations in the gene pool.

nine

PHYSICAL SCIENCE

Properties of Atoms

An ATOM is defined as the smallest constituent unit of an element that still retains all of the original properties of the element, and all matter is composed of atoms. Atoms are not irreducible, however, and may be broken into further components: protons, neutrons, and electrons. All atomic nuclei are comprised of positively charged PROTONS and neutrally charged NEUTRONS, meaning nuclei have an overall positive charge.

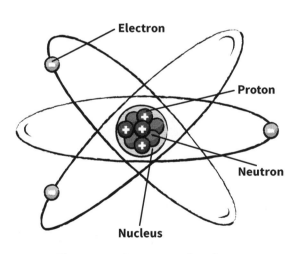

Figure 9.1. Structure of an Atom

Negatively charged ELECTRONS orbit the nucleus in orbitals, with the orbitals closer to the nucleus having less energy than those farther away. Thus, overall atomic charge is determined by the number of positively charged protons and negatively charged electrons in an atom.

Every atom of an element has the same number of protons, which is that element's ATOMIC NUMBER. Elements are arranged on the Periodic Table of the Elements by their atomic number which increases from top to bottom and left to right on the table. Hydrogen, the first element on the periodic table, has one proton while helium, the second element, has two, and so on.

Along with atomic charge, atoms have measurable mass. Protons and neutrons are significantly more massive than electrons (about 1,800 times), so the mass of electrons is not considered when calculating the mass of an atom. Thus, an element's MASS NUMBER is the number of protons and neutrons present in its atoms. The number of neutrons in an atom can be found by subtracting the atomic number from the mass number.

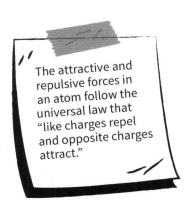

The attractive and repulsive forces in an atom follow the universal law that "like charges repel and opposite charges attract."

While atoms of the same element have the same number of protons, their number of neutrons may vary. Atoms which differ in their number of neutrons but have equal numbers of protons are ISOTOPES of the same element.

When writing the atomic symbol of an element, isotopes are differentiated by writing the mass number in the upper left-hand corner of the symbol. The atomic symbol for ordinary hydrogen is written as ^1H, to signify that it has no neutrons and 1 proton, while deuterium, which is a hydrogen isotope with 1 neutron, is written as ^2H.

The ATOMIC MASS of an atom, which is different from the mass number, is the average mass of all known isotopes of an element. For each element on the Periodic Table, the atomic number is listed above the symbol of the element and the atomic mass (measured in atomic mass units, or AMU) is listed underneath the symbol.

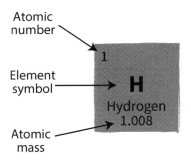

Figure 9.2. Reading the Periodic Table

atomic number = number of protons
mass number = number of protons + number of neutrons
atomic mass = average mass of all isotopes

Atoms may lose or gain electrons, creating charged particles called IONS. Ions are called CATIONS if they are positively charged (due to the loss of electrons) or ANIONS if they are negatively charged (due to the gaining of electrons). Ionic charges are denoted by adding a plus or minus sign onto the elemental symbol; for example, a sodium ion with a charge of +1 would be written as Na^+.

Ions may be composed of two or more atoms known as molecular ions or POLYATOMIC IONS. The overall charge of a polyatomic ion is equal to the sum of the charges of all constituent atoms.

Table 9.1. Common Polyatomic Ions

NH_4^+	ammonium
H_3O^+	hydronium
PO_4^{3-}	phosphate
SO_4^{2-}	sulfate
MnO_4^{2-}	manganate
OH^-	hydroxide
CN^-	cyanide
CO_3^{2-}	carbonate
HCO_3^{1-}	hydrogen carbonate
ClO^{2-}	chlorite

The Periodic Table of the Elements

There are many useful physical and chemical patterns represented in the Periodic Table of the Elements. The periodic table is organized into rows called PERIODS and columns called GROUPS. The position of an element's symbol on the periodic table indicates its electron configuration. The elements in each group on the table all contain the same amount of electrons in their valence shell, which results in all elements in a group having similar chemical properties.

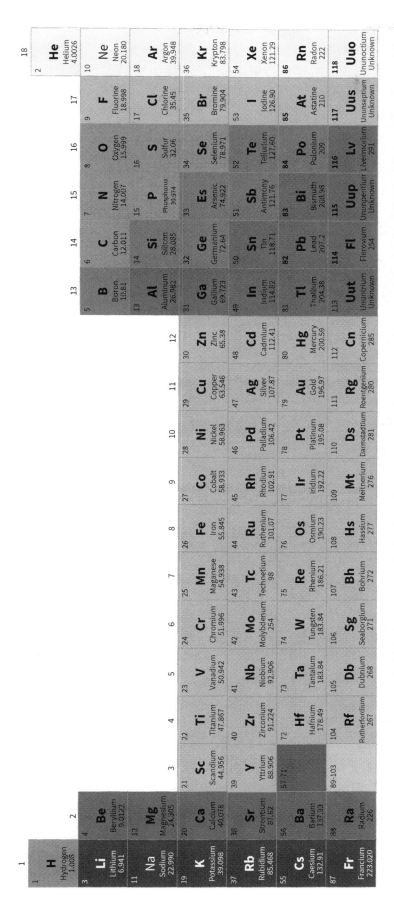

Figure 9.3. Periodic Table of the Elements

The majority of the elements in the periodic table are metals. METALS have the following properties:

- They are ductile and malleable.
- They conduct electricity.
- They can form alloys.
- They are thermally conductive.
- They are hard, opaque, and shiny.
- With the exception of mercury, they are solids.

Solid metals usually consist of tightly packed atoms, resulting in fairly high densities. Metals begin on the left side of the periodic table and span across the middle of the table, almost all the way to the right side. Examples of metals include gold (Au), tin (Sn), and lead (Pb).

NONMETALS are elements that do not conduct electricity and tend to be more volatile than metals. They can be solids, liquids, or gases. The nonmetals are located on the right side of the periodic table. Examples of nonmetals include sulfur (S), hydrogen (H), and oxygen (O).

METALLOIDS, or semimetals, are elements that possess both metal and nonmetal characteristics. For example, some metalloids are shiny but do not conduct electricity well. Many metalloids are semiconductors. Metalloids are located between the metals and nonmetals on the periodic table. Some examples of metalloids are boron (B), silicon (Si), and arsenic (As).

Specific names are given to certain groups on the periodic table. Group 1 elements (belonging to the leftmost column) are known as the ALKALI METALS and are characterized by the fact that they are very unstable and react violently with water. Other notably reactive elements are in Group 17, the HALOGENS. In contrast to both of these groups, Group 18 contains the NOBLE GASES, which are inert and very non-reactive because they have a full outer shell of electrons.

There are two periods below and separated from the main periodic table. These are called LANTHANIDES and ACTINIDES. They are set apart from the other elements for two reasons: first, to consolidate the periodic table, and second, because they are more complicated chemically than the rest of the elements—which means that they do not follow any of the trends outlined below.

The Periodic Table is organized so that element show trends across periods and groups. Some of these trends are summarized below.

ATOMIC NUMBER: The atomic number (equal to the number of protons) of an element increases from left to right and top to bottom on the Periodic Table of the Elements. This means that hydrogen, with the lowest atomic number, is located at the upper left corner of the table.

ATOMIC RADIUS: Atomic radius (the distance from the center of the atom to its outermost electron shell) increases from right to left and top to bottom on the periodic table, with the largest elements residing in the lower left corner.

ELECTRON AFFINITY: An atom's electron affinity describes the amount of energy released or gained when an electron is added to the atom. On the periodic table, electron affinity increases from left to right and bottom to top, with the highest electron affinities belonging to elements residing in the upper right corner.

ELECTRONEGATIVITY: Electronegativity measures how easily an atom can attract electrons and form chemical bonds. In general, electronegativity increases from left to right and bottom to top on the Periodic Table of the Elements, with fluorine being the most electronegative element. Electronegativity decreases from top to bottom of a group on the periodic table because of the increasing atomic radius, which corresponds with a greater distance between the electron orbital shells. One notable exception to these electronegativity trends is Group 18, the noble gases, since they possess a complete valence shell in their ground state and generally do not attract electrons.

IONIZATION ENERGY: The ionization energy of an element is defined as the energy necessary to remove an electron from a neutral atom in its gaseous phase. In other words, the lower this energy is, the more likely an atom is to lose an electron and become a cation. Ionization energies increase from left to right and bottom to top on the periodic table, meaning that the lowest ionization energies are in the lower left corner and the highest are in the upper right corner. This is because elements to the right on the periodic table are unlikely to lose electrons and become cations since their outer valence shells are nearly full.

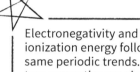

Electronegativity and ionization energy follow the same periodic trends. These two properties are simply different ways of describing the same basic property: the strength with which an atom holds electrons.

Electron Configuration

An atom's ELECTRON CONFIGURATION—the location of its electrons—influences its physical and chemical properties, including boiling point, conductivity, and its tendency to engage in chemical reactions (also called the atom's stability). The chemical reactivity of an atom is determined by the electrons in the outermost shell, as they are first to interact with neighboring atoms.

Conventionally, electrons are depicted as orbiting a nucleus in defined pathways, much like a planet orbits the sun. In reality, electrons move in clouds surrounding the nucleus known as ORBITALS. Each orbital in an atom holds two electrons.

Orbitals are grouped into four types of SUBSHELLS labeled with the letters s, p, d, and f. Each subshell has a specific number of orbitals:

- s has 1 orbital and holds 1 × 2 = 2 electrons
- p has 3 orbitals and holds 3 × 2 = 6 electrons
- d has 5 orbitals and holds 5 × 2 = 10 electrons
- f has 7 orbitals and holds 7 × 2 = 14 electrons

The orbitals in each type of subshell have a particular shape. For example, the *s* subshell is spherical, while the *p* subshell is shaped like a bow tie.

Subshells are further grouped into SHELLS, which are labeled with integers (1, 2, 3, ...). The shell numbered 1 is closest to the nucleus, and the energy of the electrons in shells increases the further the shell is from the nucleus.

The location of a electron is described by its shell number and subshell letter, with the number of electrons in that orbital given as a superscript. The one electron in hydrogen, for example, is written as $1s^1$.

The orbtials for the first four shells are described in the table below.

Table 9.2. Electron Configuration Notation

SHELL	SUBSHELL	No. OF ORBITALS	No. OF ELECTRONS IN SUBSHELL	NOTATION FOR FULL SUBSHELL
1	s	1	2	$1s^2$
2	s	1	2	$2s^2$
	p	3	6	$2p^6$
3	s	1	2	$3s^2$
	p	3	6	$3p^6$
	d	5	10	$3d^{10}$
4	s	1	2	$4s^2$
	p	3	6	$4p^6$
	d	5	10	$4d^{10}$
	f	7	14	$4f^{14}$

Electrons fill orbitals in order of increasing energy, meaning they fill orbitals close to the nucleus before filling in outer orbitals. The order in which orbitals are filled is shown in Figure 9.4.

The electrons in an atom's outermost shell are its **VALENCE ELECTRONS**. Most elements require eight electrons to fill their outermost shell (2 in *s* and 6 in *p*). So, elements with six or seven valence electrons are likely to gain electrons (and become cations). Conversely, elements with one or two electrons are very likely to lose electrons (and become anions). Elements with exactly eight electrons (the noble gases), are almost completely unreactive.

The electron configuration of each element correlates to its position on the periodic table: Group 1 and Group 2 (defined as the **S-BLOCK**) have valence electrons in s-orbitals. Elements in Groups 13 to 18 (defined as the **P-BLOCK**) have

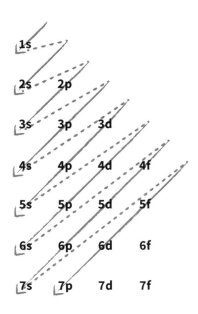

$1s^2 2s^2 2p^6 3s^2 3p^6 4s^2 3d^{10} 4p^6 5s^2...$

Figure 9.4. Electron Configuration

valence electrons in their p-orbitals. These groups (with the exception of the noble gases) are very reactive.

Group 3 through Group 12 elements (defined as the D-BLOCK) have valence electrons in *d*-orbitals. The lanthanides and actinides have valence electrons in their *f*-orbitals (and are called the F-BLOCK). The properties of these elements are less predictable because atoms' *d* and *f* orbitals do not fill in a straightforward order.

You can use the periodic table to remember the order in which orbitals are filled: start at the upper left corner and move from left to right, then move down to the next row.

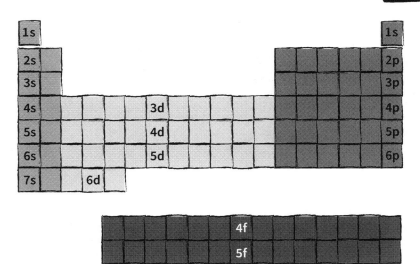

Figure 9.5. Electron Orbitals on the Periodic Table

EXAMPLES

1. Rank the following in order of increasing atomic radius: xenon (Xe), barium (Ba), cesium (Cs).

   A) Xe < Cs < Ba

   B) Cs < Xe < Ba

   C) Ba < Cs < Xe

   D) Xe < Ba < Cs

   Answer:

   D) is correct. Atomic radius increases from the top of the periodic table to the bottom and also from right to left. This means that the largest atoms are found in the lower left-hand corner of the periodic table while the smallest are found in the upper right-hand corner. Of the three elements listed, xenon has the smallest radius, barium is larger as it is further down and to the left, and cesium is the largest as it is furthest to the left of the three: Xe < Ba < Cs.

2. What is the electron configuration of ground-state neutral magnesium (Mg)?

   A) $1s^2 2s^2 2p^6 3s^2$

   B) $1s^2 2s^2 2p^3 3s^2$

   C) $1s^2 2s^6 2p^3 3s^2$

   D) $1s^2 2s^2 2p^3 3s^3$

3.   List the following in order of decreasing electronegativity: fluorine (F), bromine (Br), magnesium (Mg), strontium (Sr).

   A)   F > Mg > Br < Sr

   B)   F > Br > Mg > Sr

   C)   Br > Mg > Sr > F

   D)   Sr > Mg > Br > F

Intramolecular Bonds

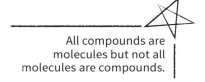

All compounds are molecules but not all molecules are compounds.

Chemical bonds, also called intramolecular bonds, are attractions between atoms that allow for the creation of substances consisting of more than one atom. When all the chemically bonded atoms are the same element, the substance is known as a **MOLECULE**. When two or more different elements bond together, the result is called a **COMPOUND**. (However, the word *molecule* is often used colloquially to refer to both types of substances.)

Table 9.3. Common Molecules and Compounds

H_2O	water
NaCl	table salt
CO_2	carbon dioxide
HCl	hydrochloric acid
O_3	ozone
$C_6H_{12}O_6$	glucose (sugar)
H_2	hydrogen gas

Types of Bonds

Not all chemical bonds are alike. Their causes vary, and thus the strength of those bonds also varies widely. There are two major types of bonds, distinguished from one another based on whether electrons are shared or transferred between the atoms. A **COVALENT BOND** involves a pair of atoms sharing electrons from their outer orbitals to fill their valence shells. These bonds form between non-metals with similar electronegativities.

In an IONIC BOND, one atom "gives" its electrons to the other, resulting in one positively and one negatively charged atom. The bond is a result of the attraction between ions. Ionic bonds form between atoms with very different electronegativities.

Metals can form tightly packed arrays in which each atom is in close contact with many neighbors. So many atomic orbitals overlap with each atom that they form very large molecular orbitals that in turn overlap with each other creating a continuous band in which electrons can move. Any excitation, such as an electrical current, can cause the electrons to move throughout the array. The high electrical and thermal conductivity of metals is due to this ability of electrons to move throughout the lattice. This type of delocalized bonding is called METALLIC BONDING. Metals are ductile or can be bent without breaking because the atoms can slide past each other without breaking the delocalized bonds.

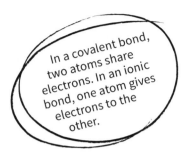

In a covalent bond, two atoms share electrons. In an ionic bond, one atom gives electrons to the other.

Polarity

Polarity is the difference in charge across a compound caused by the uneven partial charge distribution between the atoms. Ionic bonds have higher polarity than covalent bonds because they consist of ions of full opposite charges, meaning one side of the compound is very positive and one very negative. The charge distribution in covalent bonds is more variable, resulting in either polar covalent bonds or non-polar covalent bonds.

NON-POLAR COVALENT BONDS have no uneven distribution of charge. This is because electrons are completely shared between the two atoms, meaning neither has a strong hold on the shared electrons. Non-polar covalent bonds generally arise between two non-metal atoms with equal electronegativity, for example, two hydrogen atoms.

POLAR COVALENT BONDS arise between two non-metal atoms with different electro-negativities. In these bonds, electrons are shared unequally. Neither atom is a completely charged ion; instead, the more electronegative atom will hold onto the electron more often,

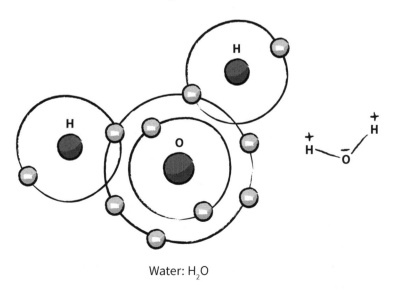

Water: H_2O

Figure 9.6. Polar Covalent Bond

Why would molecules with large dipole moments be more likely to interact than non-polar molecules?

creating a slightly negative charge. The other atom will thus have a slightly positive charge. These slight charges are called DIPOLES.

A DIPOLE MOMENT is a measure of the unequal charge distribution in a polar bond. It is possible for a polar molecule to have no net dipole moment if the dipole moments of each bond are equal in magnitude and opposing in direction. These covalent compounds have a symmetrical molecular geometry, meaning that the dipoles created by the polar bond cancel each other out.

EXAMPLES

1. Which of the following bonds would have the largest dipole moment?
    A) C—H
    B) C—F
    C) C—O
    D) C—N

    Answer:

    B) is correct. The difference in electronegativity is the greatest between carbon and fluorine, so the C—F bond will have the largest dipole moment.

2. Which group on the periodic table will typically adopt a charge of +1 when forming ionic compounds?
    A) alkaline earth metals
    B) lanthanides
    C) halogens
    D) alkali metals

    Answer:

    A) is correct. The alkaline earth metals have a full valence shell when they lose one electron, so they easily form ions of +1.

Intermolecular Bonds

While intramolecular bonds occur within compounds to hold atoms together, it is also possible for bonds to exist between compounds. These intermolecular bonds do not result from the transfer or sharing of electrons. Rather, they are caused by the attraction between the positive and negative parts of separate compounds.

The force of attraction between hydrogen and an extremely electronegative atom, such as oxygen or nitrogen, is known as a HYDROGEN BOND. For example, in water (H_2O), oxygen atoms are attracted to the hydrogen atoms in nearby molecules, creating hydrogen bonds. These bonds are significantly weaker than the chemical bonds that involve sharing or transfer of electrons, and have only 5 to 10 percent of the strength of a covalent bond. Despite its relative weakness, hydrogen bonding is quite important in the natural world;

it has major effects on the properties of water and ice and is important biologically with regard to proteins and nucleic acids as well as the DNA double helix structure.

VAN DER WAALS FORCES are electrical interactions between two or more molecules or atoms. They are the weakest type of intermolecular attraction, but if substantial amounts of these forces are present, their net effect can be quite strong.

There are two major types of van der Waals forces. The LONDON DISPERSION FORCE is a temporary force that occurs when electrons in two adjacent atoms form spontaneous, temporary dipoles due to the positions the atoms are occupying. This is the weakest intermolecular force and it does not exert a force over long distances. Interestingly, London dispersion forces are the only forces that exist between noble gas atoms; without these forces, noble gases would not be able to liquefy.

The second type of van der Waals force is DIPOLE-DIPOLE INTERACTIONS, which are the result of two dipolar molecules interacting with each other. This interaction occurs when the partial positive dipole in one molecule is attracted to the partial negative dipole in the other molecule.

EXAMPLE

Which intermolecular forces would need to be considered in predicting the relative physical properties of CH_3F, CH_3Cl, CH_3Br, and CH_3I?

A) London force only
B) dipole-dipole and London force only
C) dipole-dipole and hydrogen bonding only
D) dipole-dipole, hydrogen bonding, and London force

Answer:

B) is correct. These molecules are polar and so are subject to both dipole-dipole and London forces. There are no hydrogen atoms bound to high electronegative atoms, so there will be no hydrogen bonding.

Properties of Substances
Chemical and Physical Properties

Properties of substances are divided into two categories: physical and chemical. **PHYSICAL PROPERTIES** are those which are measurable and can be seen without changing the chemical makeup of a substance. In contrast, **CHEMICAL PROPERTIES** are those that determine how a substance will behave in a chemical reaction. These two categories differ in that a physical property may be identified just by observing, touching, or measuring the substance in some way; however, chemical properties cannot be identified simply by observing a material. Rather, the material must be engaged in a chemical reaction in order to identify its chemical properties.

In both physical and chemical changes, matter is always conserved, meaning it can never be created or destroyed.

Table 9.4. Physical and Chemical Properties

PHYSICAL PROPERTIES	CHEMICAL PROPERTIES
temperature	heat of combustion
color	flammability
mass	toxicity
viscosity	chemical stability
density	enthalpy of formation

Mixtures

When substances are combined without a chemical reaction to bond them, the resulting substance is called a MIXTURE. Physical changes can be used to separate mixtures. For example, heating salt water until the water evaporates, leaving the salt behind, will separate a salt water solution.

In a mixture, the components can be unevenly distributed, such as in trail mix or soil. These mixtures are described at HETEROGENEOUS. Alternatively, the components can be HOMOGENEOUSLY, or uniformly, distributed, as in salt water.

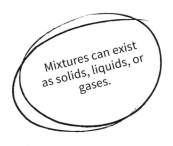
Mixtures can exist as solids, liquids, or gases.

A SOLUTION is a special type of stable homogenous mixture. The components of a solution will not separate on their own, and cannot be separated using a filter. The substance being dissolved is the SOLUTE, and the substance acting on the solute, or doing the dissolving, is the SOLVENT.

Chemical Properties of Water

Though it is one of the most common and biologically essential compounds on Earth, water is chemically abnormal. Its chemical formula is H_2O, which means that water consists of one oxygen atom bound to two hydrogen atoms. The shape of this molecule is often described as looking like Mickey Mouse, with the oxygen atom in the middle as Mickey's face and the two hydrogen atoms as his ears.

This imbalanced shape means that oxygen has a slightly positive charge localized on the two hydrogen atoms, and a slightly negative charge on the lone oxygen. Because of this polarity, water molecules attract each other and tend to clump together, a property called COHESION. Water is also extremely ADHESIVE, meaning it clings to other substances. These attractive forces account for a number of water's unique properties.

Water has a high SURFACE TENSION, meaning the bonds between water molecules on the surface of a liquid are stronger than those beneath the surface. Surface tension makes it more difficult to puncture the surface of water. Combined with adhesion, it also helps cause CAPILLARY ACTION, which is the ability of water to travel against gravity. Capillary action moves blood through vessels in the body and water from the roots to the leaves of plants.

Water is an efficient solvent for ionic compounds because of its hydrogen bonds and associated polarity. When ionic compounds like NaCl are placed in water, the individual ions are attracted to the opposite ends of the dipole moment in water. But water is stronger than the average solvent. In fact, it is known as the "universal solvent," because it is able to dissolve more substances than any other known liquid. The readiness with which ionic compounds dissolve in water is why so many minerals and nutrients are found naturally in water.

Water also has a low molecular weight. Most low-weight compounds exist in a gaseous form at room temperature, but water is a liquid at room temperature. Though water molecules have a relatively low weight, the boiling point and freezing point of water are abnormally high. This is because water's strong hydrogen bonds require high amounts of heat to break. These properties of water make it the only compound found naturally in all three phases—solid, liquid, and gas—on Earth.

Consistent with its high boiling point, water also has an unusually high specific heat index, meaning that water needs to absorb a lot of heat before it actually gets hot. This property allows the oceans to regulate global temperature, as they can absorb a large amount of energy.

Ice, or frozen water, is also abnormal. Normally molecules are tightly packed in the solid state, but water's hydrogen bonds form a crystalline lattice structure, placing molecules far apart. This extra space makes ice less dense than liquid water, which is why ice floats.

Osmosis, Diffusion, and Tonicity

Molecules and atoms have a tendency to spread out in space, moving from areas of high concentration to areas of lower concentration. This net movement is called DIFFUSION. When solutions of differing concentrations are separated from each other by a porous membrane, the solvent molecules will flow across the membrane in order to equalize these different concentrations. This net movement of solvent particles is called OSMOSIS. Osmosis is especially important in biological contexts, as cell and organelle membranes are semi-permeable. Osmosis provides the main means by which water is transported in and out of cells.

When two solutions are separated by a semipermeable membrane, their relative concentrations (which determine the direction of the movement of solute molecules) are called TONICITY. This chemical property is typically used to describe the response of a cell when placed in a solvent.

> An important characteristic of osmosis is that the solvent molecules are free to move across the membrane, but the solute cannot cross the membrane.

Three types of tonicity are relevant in biological situations. HYPER-TONIC solutions are those which have a higher concentration of a given solute than the interior of the cell. When placed in such solutions, the cell will lose solvent (water) as it travels to areas of higher solute concentration.

HYPOTONICITY refers to a solution that has a lower concentration of a given solute than the cell. Water will enter the cell, causing it to swell in response to hypotonic solutions.

ISOTONIC solutions are those in which solute concentration equals solute concentration inside the cell, and no net flux of solvent will occur between the cell and an isotonic solution.

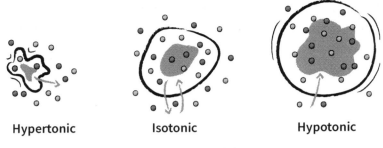

| Hypertonic | Isotonic | Hypotonic |

Figure 9.7. Tonicity

EXAMPLES

1. Which of the following is a chemical property?

   A) area

   B) boiling point

   C) solubility

   D) preferred oxidation state

   Answer:

   D) is correct. Area, boiling point, and solubility are all physical properties that can be measured without undergoing a chemical reaction. The preferred oxidation state of a metal cannot be identified in any way except through a chemical reaction, and is thus a chemical property.

2. The water glider is an insect that can walk on water. What property of water facilitates this ability?

   A) high surface tension

   B) osmosis

   C) tonicity

   D) ability of ice to float in water

   Answer:

   A) is correct. The high surface tension of water, which is a byproduct of hydrogen bonding, allows the water glider to walk on water.

States of Matter

All matter exists in one of four STATES: solid, liquid, gas, or plasma. SOLID matter has densely packed molecules and does not change volume or shape. LIQUIDS have more loosely packed molecules and can change shape but not volume. GAS molecules are widely dispersed, and gases can change both shape and volume. PLASMA is similar to a gas but contains free-moving charged particles (although its overall charge is neutral).

Particles in gases, liquids, and solids all vibrate. Those in gases vibrate and move at high speeds; those in liquids vibrate and move slightly; those in solids vibrate yet stay packed in place in their rigid structure.

Changes in temperature and pressure can cause matter to change states. Generally, adding energy (in the form of heat) changes a substance to a higher energy state (e.g., solid to liquid). Transitions from a high to lower energy state (e.g., liquid to solid) release energy. Each of these changes has a specific name:

- solid to liquid: melting
- liquid to solid: freezing
- liquid to gas: evaporation
- gas to liquid: condensation
- solid to gas: sublimation
- gas to solid: deposition

A CRYSTAL is a specific type of solid where atoms are arranged in a regular, repeating, geometric pattern known as a crystal lattice.

The occurrence of these processes depends on the amount of energy in individual molecules, rather than the collective energy of the system. For example, in a pool of water outside on a hot day, the whole pool does not evaporate at once; evaporation occurs incrementally in molecules with a high enough energy. Evaporation is also more likely to occur in conjunction with a decrease in the gas pressure around a liquid, since molecules tend to move from areas of high pressure to areas of low pressure.

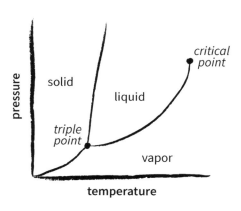

Figure 9.8. Phase Diagram

PHASE DIAGRAMS are used to indicate the phase in which a substance is found at a given pressure and temperature. Phase diagrams are constructed on an x, y-coordinate system where temperature is plotted along the x-axis and pressure is plotted along the y-axis. Phase regions are areas on a phase diagram (corresponding to specific temperature and pressure combinations) at which the substance will exist in a particular physical phase. Lines called phase boundaries separate these phase regions, representing pressure and temperature combinations at which the substance undergoes phase transitions.

Every phase diagram includes two important points. The TRIPLE POINT is the point at which the lines of equilibrium intersect and all three phases (solid, liquid, and gas) exist in equilibrium. The second special point on a phase diagram is the CRITICAL POINT. This point is found along the phase boundary between liquid and gas, and is the point at which the phase boundary terminates. This represents the fact that at very high temperature and pressure, liquid and gas phases become indistinguishable. This is known as a supercritical fluid.

EXAMPLES

1. Sublimation is the change from
   A) gas to solid
   B) liquid to solid
   C) gas to liquid
   D) solid to gas

2. The process that takes place when water reaches its boiling point is called
   A) condensation.
   B) evaporation.
   C) melting.
   D) sublimation.

Answer:

B) is correct. Evaporation is the process of conversion from liquid to gas that occurs at the boiling point.

Chemical Reactions

A CHEMICAL REACTION involves some sort of chemical change in molecules, atoms, or ions when two or more of these interact. It is important to note that chemical reactions are not the same as state changes. For example, liquid water changing to ice is not a chemical reaction because water and ice have the same chemical properties, just different physical ones. A chemical reaction occurs between two reactants (substances) that form a new substance with different chemical properties than either of the two initial reactants.

REACTANTS are the substances that are consumed or altered in the chemical reaction, while PRODUCTS are substances formed as a result of the chemical reaction. Equations are usually written with the reactants on the left, the products on the right, and an arrow between them. The state of the chemical compounds are sometimes noted using the labels s (solid), l (liquid), g (gas), or aq (aqueous, meaning a solution).

Chemical reactions generally occur in two directions. A reaction can move "forward" (from reactants to products), and in "reverse" (from products to reactants). To describe this, chemists say that the reaction occurs in two directions. Oftentimes, the arrow in a chemical equation has a head on each side, signifying that the reaction occurs in both directions.

The equilibrium point of a reaction is defined as the point where both the forward and reverse reactions are occurring at equal rates simultaneously—products are turning into reactants and reactants back into products. This produces a state in which, while the reaction is still taking place, no net change in concentration of reactants or products is occurring.

Balancing Chemical Reactions

In the equation below, H_2 and O_2 are the reactants, while water (H_2O) is the product.

$$2H_2 + O_2 \rightarrow 2H_2O$$

In this equation, the number 2 is called a coefficient, and it describes the number of atoms or molecules involved in the reaction. In this reaction, four hydrogen atoms (two molecules of H_2) react with two oxygen atoms. Note that the products also contain four hydrogen and two oxygen molecules. When chemical equations are written, they must include the same number of each atom on both the reactant and product side of the arrow. This is an important step because chemical reactions adhere to the LAW OF CONSERVATION OF MATTER, which states that matter is neither created nor destroyed in a chemical reaction.

In order to balance the equation above, first examine the initial equation without coefficients, which looks like this:

$$H_2 + O_2 \rightarrow H_2O$$

This equation is unbalanced: there are two H atoms on each side, but the reactant side has two O atoms while the product side only has one. To fix this discrepancy, a coefficient of 2 is added in front of the product, H_2O, making the number of O atoms equal on both sides of the equation:

$$H_2 + O_2 \rightarrow 2H_2O$$

Now there are four H atoms on the product side while there are only 2 on the reactant side. This means that in order to finish balancing the equation, a coefficient of 2 must be added in front of H_2, so that there are four H atoms on the reactant side as well:

$$2H_2 + O_2 \rightarrow 2H_2O$$

Remember that in a chemical reaction, only the coefficients may be changed in order to balance it; the subscripts must not be changed. This would be like changing the actual chemical in the equation.

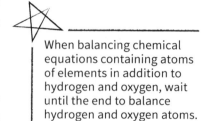

When balancing chemical equations containing atoms of elements in addition to hydrogen and oxygen, wait until the end to balance hydrogen and oxygen atoms.

Types of Reactions

There are several common types of chemical reactions, including decomposition, substitution, and combustion reactions.

DECOMPOSITION reactions are a common class of reaction, consisting of the separation of a compound into atoms or simpler molecules:

General Reaction: AB → A + B

$$2H_2O_2 \rightarrow 2H_2O + O_2$$

SINGLE REPLACEMENT reactions are those in which a part of one molecule is replaced by another atom or molecule. Reactivity in single substitutions is determined by the ACTIVITY SERIES: elements on the list will replace any element that is below it on the list.

General Reaction: AB + C → AC + B

$$CH_4 + Cl_2 \rightarrow CH_3Cl + HCl$$

Table 9.5. Activity Series

Li	Ca	Mn	Ni	Cu
K	Na	Zn	Sn	Hg
Ba	Mg	Cr	Pb	Ag
Sr	Al	Fe	H_2	Pd
Pt	Au			

In a DOUBLE REPLACEMENT reaction, two parts of two different molecules swap places:

General Reaction: $AB + CD \rightarrow CB + AD$

$$CuCl_2 + 2AgNO_3 \rightarrow Cu(NO_3)_2 + 2AgCl$$

COMBUSTION or burning reactions are high-temperature reactions in which a great deal of heat is released. In combustion reactions, oxygen is a reactant and carbon dioxide and water are produced. Because of the substantial amount of heat energy produced by combustion reactions, they have been important means of generating energy throughout human history, including combustion of fossil fuels, coal, and oil.

General Reaction: $CxHx + O_2 \rightarrow CO_2 + H_2O$

$$2C_8H_{18} + 25O_2 \rightarrow 16CO_2 + 18H_2O$$

Reaction Rates

EXOTHERMIC REACTIONS are defined as those which produce energy, whereas ENDO-THERMIC REACTIONS need energy in order to occur. Regardless of whether energy is absorbed or released overall, every chemical reaction requires a certain amount of energy in order to begin. This amount is referred to as the ACTIVATION ENERGY.

Collisions of reactant particles supply the activation energy for a reaction. The more particles collide, the more energy will be produced. Thus, the more often particles collide, the more likely a reaction is to occur. However, it is quite possible that though some particles collide, not enough energy is generated for an actual reaction to occur.

Given the variability in activation energies of a reaction, as well as variation in the frequency of reactant particle collisions, not all chemical reactions occur at the same rate. A number of variables affect the rate of reaction, including temperature, pressure, concentration, and surface area. The higher the temperature, pressure and concentration, the more likely particles are to collide and thus the reaction rate will be higher. The same is true of surface area for a reaction between a solid and a liquid in which it is immersed. The larger the surface area, the more solid reactant particles are in contact with liquid particles, and the faster the reaction occurs.

EXAMPLES

1. When the following chemical equation for the combustion of methanol (CH_3OH) is balanced, what is the coefficient of H_2O?

    $\_\_CH_3OH + \_\_O_2 \rightarrow \_\_CO_2 + \_\_H_2O$

    A) 3
    B) 2
    C) 1
    D) 4

    Answer:

    D) is correct.

The same number of C and O atoms appear on both sides, so start by balancing for H: $\_\_CH_3OH + \_\_O_2 \rightarrow \_\_CO_2 + 2H_2O$

Next, add a coefficient on the left to balance O: $2CH_3OH + \_\_O_2 \rightarrow \_\_CO_2 + 2H_2O$

Next, add or change coefficients to balance C and H: $2CH_3OH + \_\_O_2 \rightarrow 2CO_2 + 4H_2O$

Finally, add coefficients to balance O: $2CH_3OH + 3O_2 \rightarrow 2CO_2 + 4H_2O$

2. How is the following reaction classified?

$2KClO_3 \rightarrow 2KCl + 3O_2$

   A) decomposition
   B) combustion
   C) substitution
   D) double displacement

Answer:

A) is correct. This reaction has a single reactant compound and produces simpler molecules. It is therefore a decomposition reaction.

3. What is the missing product in the following combustion reaction?

$C_{10}H_8 + 12O_2 \rightarrow H_2O + \_\_\_\_$

   A) CO
   B) CH_4
   C) CO_2
   D) $C_2H_3O_2$

Answer:

C) is correct. All combustion reactions produce H_2O and CO_2, so the missing product is CO_2.

Catalysts

CATALYSTS reduce the amount of energy that a chemical reaction needs in order to happen, so that the reaction can occur more easily. However, the catalyst itself remains chemically unchanged and is not consumed at all in the reaction. A catalyst lowers the ACTIVATION ENERGY needed for a reaction to take place, and it will change the rate of both directions of the reaction.

Catalysts function by one of two main methods. The first is ADSORPTION, where particles stick to the surface of the catalyst and move around, increasing their likelihood of collision. A more complicated method is the creation of INTERMEDIATE COMPOUNDS which are unstable and then break down into other substances, leaving the catalyst in its original state. Many enzymes (proteins which function as catalysts), which are discussed below, work via the creation of intermediate compounds.

If the rate of a chemical reaction can be increased, it can also be decreased. INHIBITORS are essentially the opposite of catalysts, and they act to slow down the reaction rate or even stop the reaction altogether. Inhibitors are used for various reasons, including giving scientists more control over reactions. Both inhibitors and catalysts naturally play significant roles in the chemical reactions that occur in human bodies.

Enzymes

ENZYMES are efficient catalysts functioning in biochemical reactions. They are large, soluble protein molecules that serve to speed up chemical reactions in cells. Cellular respiration, DNA replication, digestion, protein synthesis, and photosynthesis are common processes, all essential for life, that are catalyzed with enzymes.

Enzyme inhibitors will typically function by binding to an enzyme and thereby preventing it from functioning.

Like other types of catalysts, enzymes take part in a reaction to provide an alternative pathway with a smaller activation energy, but they remain unchanged themselves. However, enzymes only alter the reaction rate; they do not actually change the equilibrium point of a reaction. Also, unlike most chemical catalysts, enzymes are very selective, which means that they only catalyze certain reactions. (Many other types of catalysts catalyze a variety of reactions.)

This particular aspect of enzyme behavior is referred to as the LOCK AND KEY MODEL. This alludes to the fact that not all keys can open all locks; most keys can only open specific locks. Similarly, the shape of any one enzyme only matches the shape of the molecule it reacts with, called a SUBSTRATE. The ACTIVE SITE is the place on the enzyme that directly contacts the substrate, or the place where the two "puzzle pieces" fit together facilitating the actual reaction.

As suggested by the lock and key model, enzymes are typically highly specific to the reaction they catalyze. In a cellular context, why would it be detrimental if enzymes universally catalyzed any reaction?

Enzymes have a characteristic optimum temperature at which they function best and require a sufficient substrate concentration. The reason for these restrictions is that variables like temperature and pH affect the shape of an enzyme's active site. In fact, if the temperature is increased too much, usually past 60 degrees Celsius, an enzyme can become DENATURED. This means that the active site has undergone a permanent change in shape, so it can no longer serve its purpose as a catalyst.

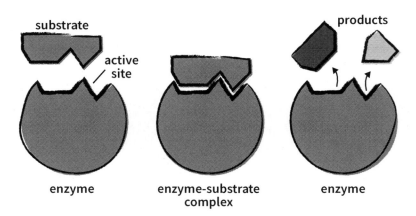

Figure 9.9. Lock and Key Model of Enzymes

Acids and Bases

Many scientists have attempted to define and differentiate the properties of acids and bases throughout the centuries. As far back as the sixteenth century, Robert Boyle noted that acids are corrosive, sour, and change the color of vegetable dyes like litmus from blue to red. On the other hand, bases, or alkaline solutions are slippery, bitter, and change the color of litmus from red to blue. The litmus test is still used today to determine whether a solution is acidic or basic.

Later, Svante Arrhenius gave an even more specific definition of acids and bases. He defined ACIDS as compounds that ionize when they dissolve in water, releasing H^+ ions along with a negative ion called a COUNTERION. For example, the well-known acid HCl (hydrochloric acid) dissolves into H^+ and Cl^- ions in water.

Similarly, Arrhenius defined bases as substances which release OH^- ions (hydroxide) and a positive ion when dissolved in water. For example, the compound NaOH dissolves into Na^+ (the counterion) and OH^- ions in water. His theory also explains why acids and bases neutralize each other. If acids have an H^+ ion and bases have an OH^- ion, when combined the ions will form water. Along with the water, the counterions usually combine to form a salt. For example, when HCl and NaOH are combined, the result is water and table salt (H_2O and NaCl).

Thomas Lowry and J.N. Bronsted later presented a revised theory of acids and bases. In the Bronsted-Lowry definition of acids and bases, acids are defined as proton donors and bases as proton acceptors. An acid and base are always paired as reactants. The base reactant produces a CONJUGATE ACID as a product, paired with a CONJUGATE BASE produced from the reactant acid. Water, often involved in these reactions, can either accept or donate a proton, meaning that it can act as either an acid or a base, depending on the particular equation.

In the example below, acetic acid (CH_3CO_2H) is dissolved in water, producing a conjugate base ($CH_3CO_2^-$). Water acts as the base, and its conjugate acid is the hydronium ion (H_3O^+).

$$CH_3CO_2H \quad + \quad H_2O \quad \rightarrow \quad CH_3CO_2^- \quad + \quad H_3O^+$$

acid	base	conjugate base	conjugate acid

This is perhaps easiest to understand when considering the definition of hydrogen cations. H⁺ is essentially a lone proton, and may act as an acid, being donated to another molecule. If it is in a solution of water, it can combine with water to form hydronium, H_3O^+, which is always an acid as it is a proton acceptor.

Any base containing a Group 1 or Group 2 metal is a strong base.

The strength of an acid or base is measured on the pH scale, which ranges from 1 – 14, with 1 being the strongest acid, 14 the strongest base, and 7 being neutral. A substance's pH value is a measure of how many hydrogen ions are in the solution. The scale is exponential, meaning an acid with a pH of 3 has ten times as many hydrogen ions as an acid with a pH of 4. Water, which separates into equal numbers of hydrogen and hydroxide ions, has a neutral pH of 7.

STRONG ACIDS AND BASES are defined as those that completely ionize in water. Other acids and bases are considered weak, which means that they only partially ionize in water.

Table 9.6. Strong Acids and Bases

STRONG ACIDS	STRONG BASES
HI	NaOH
HBr	KOH
$HClO_4$	LiOH
$HClO_3$	RbOH
HCl	CsOH
HNO_3	$Ca(OH)_2$
H_2SO_4	$Ba(OH)_2$
HIO_4	$Sr(OH)_2$

EXAMPLES

1. Which is NOT a definition of an acid?
   A) A substance that contains hydrogen and produces H+ in water.
   B) A substance that donates protons to a base.
   C) A substance that reacts with a base to form a salt and water.
   D) A substance that accepts protons.

   Answer:

   D) is correct. Acids increase the concentration of hydrogen ions in solution and do not accept protons.

2. Which of the following is NOT a strong acid?
   A. $HClO_3$
   B. $HClO_4$
   C. HNO_3
   D. HNO_2

   Answer:

   D) is correct. HNO_2 is not a strong acid. All the other choices are strong acids.

ten

SCIENTIFIC REASONING

The Scientific Method

As developed over thousands of years of painstaking inquiry, the scientific method is a mechanism by which unbiased observations are analyzed and constructed into a testable framework, which is then either confirmed or left unsupported.

Properly interpreting results obtained using the scientific method requires acknowledging that scientific endeavors approach the truth—they do not necessarily reveal an irrefutable truth. Thus, previous scientific findings that have been subsequently corrected should not be considered erroneous; rather they should be viewed as less accurate than determinations made using improved technology and methodology. Similarly, current medical views are not only subject to change but almost certain to change as medical science advances.

Utility of the scientific method is by no means restricted to professional scientists. Its principles are of particular importance to medical practitioners, who must impartially observe symptoms, form a preliminary diagnosis, and verify its accuracy. Medical practitioners must employ scientific medical knowledge to properly treat maladies and assess the effectiveness of these treatments. As such, a proper understanding of the scientific method is paramount for medical practitioners at all stages.

In brief, the scientific method involves several sequential stages, and the reliability of each stage is contingent on the reliability of the preceding stages. First, OBSERVATIONS are made in as unbiased a manner as possible. In evaluating medical treatments, this often involves "blinding" both practitioners and patients to the experimental group identity of participants (a "double-blind" experimental design). Blinding ensures that the expectations of the patients do not affect the outcomes of their treatment (potentially resulting in a placebo effect) and that the expectations of the practitioners do not bias the interpretation of the results.

The observations are then evaluated in the context of existing medical knowledge of the disease and its treatment. This will properly determine the treatment efficacy and possibly its mechanism of action in cases when the effects of the treatment are not thoroughly

1. Observation
2. Evaluating obs.
3. Hypothesis
4. Test
5. Theory

understood. These observations are then formed into a **HYPOTHESIS**, a specific testable question regarding the treatment or disease etiology. Critically, this hypothesis must be falsifiable; in other words, if a hypothesis cannot feasibly be disproven by scientifically rigorous testing, it is invalid scientifically.

The hypothesis is then **TESTED** through a carefully designed experiment or trial. It is important to eliminate confounding variables in experimental design. For example, a cardiac drug may be given to patients in a trial, while a placebo is given to healthy control individuals. If the controls are considerably older than the patients, this may artificially bias some outcome measures of the trial to make the drug seem more effective than it would otherwise appear.

Finally, the aggregate results of experiments may be constructed into a working **THEORY** relating to the etiology of a disease or its treatment. The term *theory* implies that while understanding of a concept is still developing and subject to change, it is heavily supported by multiple lines of evidence. For example, the notion that following proper sterile procedures is essential to avoid infection following medical procedures arises from the germ theory of disease. An overwhelming amount of data support this understanding of disease pathology, so using the word *theory* implies that it is very likely that germs cause infection, while still leaving room for change based on the results of future research.

Designing Experiments

Designing a medical study may entail using the scientific method itself to develop foundational knowledge for further advancement in the experimental process. For example, investigators might develop a **HYPOTHESIS-SEEKING** study for a poorly understood disease or treatment. They might predict that a treatment would induce changes to gene expression, without knowing which genes will be affected. Once some information is gleaned about a particular disease or treatment, a **HYPOTHESIS-DRIVEN** investigation might be undertaken, in which investigators test a particular hypothesis (e.g. "because we know that this treatment affects gene X, and gene X is related to the cause of this disease, we predict that regulating gene X might be essential for the treatment to be effective").

Scientists use a rigorous set of rules to design experiments. The protocols of experimental design are meant to ensure that scientists are actually testing what they set out to test. A well-designed experiment will measure the impact of a single factor on a system, thus allowing the experimenter to draw conclusions about that factor.

Every experiment includes variables, which are the factors that may impact the outcome of the experiment. **INDEPENDENT VARIABLES** are controlled by the experimenter. They are usually the factors that the experimenter has hypothesized will have an effect on the system. The **DEPENDENT VARIABLES** are factors that are influenced by the independent variable. These are the variables that are being tested or measured in the experiment.

Often, a design will include a treatment group and a **CONTROL GROUP**, which does not receive the treatment. **CONTROL VARIABLES** are variables that are held constant in all treatment groups so that they do not affect the dependent variable.

For example, in an experiment investigating which type of fertilizer has the greatest effect on plant growth, the independent variable is the type of fertilizer used. The scientist is controlling, or manipulating, the type of fertilizer. The dependent variable is plant growth because the amount of plant growth depends on the type of fertilizer. The type of plant, the amount of water, and the amount of sunlight the plants receive are control variables because those variables of the experiment are kept the same for each plant.

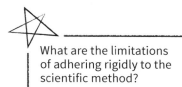

What are the limitations of adhering rigidly to the scientific method?

When designing an experiment, scientists must identify possible sources of error. These can be **CONFOUNDING VARIABLES**, which are factors that act like the independent variable and thus can make it appear that the independent variable has a greater effect than it actually does. The design may also include unknown variables that are not controlled by the scientists. Finally, scientists must be aware of human error, particularly in collecting data and making observations, and of possible equipment errors.

During the experiment, scientists collect data, which must then be analyzed and presented appropriately. This may mean running a statistical analysis on the data (e.g., finding the mean) or putting the data in graph form. Such an analysis allows scientists to see trends in the data and determine if those trends are statistically significant. From that data, scientists can draw a **CONCLUSION** about the experiment.

Scientists often use **MODELS** in their research. These models are a simplified representation of a system, and are often used to describe phenomena that cannot be directly observed or measured. For example, a mathematical equation that describes fluctuations in a population might be used to test how a certain variable is likely to affect that population. Or, a scientist might use a greenhouse to model a particular ecosystem so that she or he can more closely control the variables in the environment.

EXAMPLES

1. A chemistry student is conducting an experiment in which she tests the relationship between reactant concentration and heat produced by a reaction. In her experiment, she alters the reactant concentration and measures heat produced. The independent variable in the experiment is the

   A) reactant concentration
   B) reaction rate
   C) amount of heat produced by the reaction
   D) product concentration

   Answer:

   A) is correct. The independent variable is deliberately changed in the course of the experiment.

2. Why is the germ theory of disease considered to be a theory?

   A) There is insufficient evidence to support it.
   B) Valid alternative explanations exist.
   C) It is strongly supported by existing evidence.
   D) It has only limited clinical application.

Answer:

C) is correct. A scientific theory is typically strongly supported by evidence, despite public misunderstanding to the contrary.

3. A team of investigators wants to address the question, "which genes within the hippocampus are altered in the context of depression?" Their methods are focused around large-scale genetic screening of as many genes as possible throughout the genome. Which of the following best describes this type of investigation?

   A) hypothesis-driven
   B) hypothesis-seeking
   C) double-blind study
   D) a model

Answer:

B) is correct. This hypothetical investigation would be hypothesis-seeking, as the team hopes to generate potential target genes to guide subsequent experiments.

PART IV: ENGLISH AND LANGUAGE USE

eleven

GRAMMAR

Parts of Speech

The **PARTS OF SPEECH** are the building blocks of sentences, paragraphs, and entire texts. Grammarians have typically defined eight parts of speech—nouns, pronouns, verbs, adverbs, adjectives, conjunctions, prepositions, and interjections—all of which play unique roles in the context of a sentence. Though some words fall easily into one category or another, many words can function as different parts of speech based on their usage within a sentence.

> The ATI TEAS will ask you to identify parts of speech by name, so make sure to memorize all eight.

Nouns and Pronouns

NOUNS are the words that describe people, places, things, and ideas. Most often, nouns fill the position of subject or object within a sentence. Nouns have several subcategories: common nouns (*chair, car, house*), proper nouns (*Julie, Montana*), noncountable nouns (*money, water*), and countable nouns (*dollars, cubes*), among others. There is much crossover among these subcategories (for example, *chair* is common and countable), and other subcategories do exist.

PRONOUNS replace nouns in a sentence or paragraph, allowing a writer to achieve a smooth flow throughout a text by avoiding unnecessary repetition. The unique aspect of the pronoun as a part of speech is that the list of pronouns is finite: while there are innumerable nouns in the English language, there are only a few types of pronouns. The ones important for the TEAS follow:

> Identify the pronouns in the following sentence and the word(s) they refer back to:
> Marcus and Paula offered to pick up the cake because they live close to the bakery, but I told them I would do it myself.

PERSONAL PRONOUNS act as subjects or objects in a sentence.

> <u>She</u> received a letter; I gave the letter to <u>her</u>.

POSSESSIVE PRONOUNS indicate possession.

> The apartment is <u>hers</u>, but the furniture is <u>mine</u>.

REFLEXIVE or **INTENSIVE PRONOUNS** intensify a noun or reflect back on a noun.

I made the dessert <u>myself</u>.

INDEFINITE PRONOUNS simply replace nouns to avoid unnecessary repetition.

<u>Several</u> came to the party to see <u>both</u>.

Table 11.1. Personal, Possessive, and Reflexive Pronouns

CASE	FIRST PERSON		SECOND PERSON		THIRD PERSON	
	Singular	**Plural**	**Singular**	**Plural**	**Singular**	**Plural**
Subject	I	we	you	you (all)	he, she, it	they
Object	me	us	you	you (all)	him, her, it	them
Possessive	mine	ours	yours	yours	his, hers, its	theirs
Reflexive/ intensive	myself	ourselves	yourself	yourselves	himself, herself, itself	themselves

EXAMPLES

1) What purpose do nouns usually serve in a sentence?
   A. They indicate possession.
   B. They act as subject or object.
   C. They intensify other nouns.
   D. They clarify when an action occurs.

   Answers:
   A. Incorrect. Possessive pronouns and other conventions of Standard English indicate possession.
   B. **Correct.** Nouns are people, places, things, or ideas; they usually act as the subject or object in a sentence.
   C. Incorrect. Reflexive pronouns intensify other nouns and pronouns.
   D. Incorrect. Verb tense explains when actions occur in time.

2) _____ *baked the cookies herself and ate most of them.*
   Which pronoun best completes the sentence?
   A. she
   B. you
   C. they
   D. I

   Answer:
   A. **Correct.** The subject of the sentence is female (as shown by the reflexive pronoun *herself*), so the female subject pronoun *she* should be used.

Verbs

VERBS express action (*run, jump, play*) or state of being (*is, seems*). Verbs that describe action are ACTION VERBS, and those that describe being are LINKING VERBS.

> Action: My brother plays tennis.
>
> Linking: He is the best player on the team.

Verbs are conjugated to indicate PERSON, which refers to the point of view of the sentence. First person is the speaker (*I, we*); second person is the person being addressed (*you*); and third person is outside the conversation (*they, them*). Verbs are also conjugated to match the NUMBER (singular or plural) of their subject. HELPING VERBS (*to be, to have, to do*) are used to conjugate verbs. An unconjugated verb is called an INFINITIVE and includes the word *to* in front (*to be, to break*).

PARTICIPLES are verb forms lacking number and person. The PAST PARTICIPLE is usually formed by adding the suffix *–ed* to the verb stem (*type* becomes *typed*; *drop* becomes *dropped*). The PRESENT PARTICIPLE is always formed by adding the suffix *–ing* to the verb stem (*typing, dropping*). Participles are used in verb conjugation to indicate the state of an action (*she is going*; *we had waited*).

Participles also act in *participial phrases* that serve as descriptors in sentences:

> Seated politely, Ron listened to his friend's boring story.
>
> Maya petted the sleeping cat.

When a present participle acts as a noun, it is called a GERUND. In the following sentence, *running* is a noun and serves as the subject of the sentence:

> Running is my favorite form of exercise.

Verbs are also conjugated to indicate TENSE, or when the action has happened. Actions can happen in the past, present, or future. Tense also describes over how long a period the action took place:

- SIMPLE verbs describe something that happened once or general truths.
- CONTINUOUS verbs describe an ongoing action.
- PERFECT verbs describe repeated actions or actions that started in the past and have been completed.
- PERFECT CONTINUOUS verbs describe actions that started in the past and are continuing.

Table 11.2. Verb Conjugation (Present Tense)

PERSON	SINGULAR	PLURAL
First person	I give	we give
Second person	you give	you (all) give
Third person	he/she/it gives	they give

Table 11.3. Verb Tenses

TENSE	PAST	PRESENT	FUTURE
Simple	I <u>gave</u> her a gift yesterday.	I <u>give</u> her a gift every day.	I <u>will give</u> her a gift on her birthday.
Continuous	I <u>was giving</u> her a gift when you got here.	I <u>am giving</u> her a gift; come in!	I <u>will be giving</u> her a gift at dinner.
Perfect	I <u>had given</u> her a gift before you got there.	I <u>have given</u> her a gift already.	I <u>will have given</u> her a gift by midnight.
Perfect continuous	Her friends <u>had been giving</u> her gifts all night when I arrived.	I <u>have been giving</u> her gifts every year for nine years.	I <u>will have been giving</u> her gifts on holidays for ten years next year.

Verbs that follow the standard rules of conjugation are called REGULAR verbs. IRREGULAR verbs do not follow these rules, and their conjugations must be memorized. Some examples of irregular verbs are given in table 11.4.

Table 11.4. Irregular Verbs

PRESENT	PAST	PAST PARTICIPLE
am	was	been
do	did	done
see	saw	seen
write	wrote	written
break	broke	broken
grow	grew	grown
speak	spoke	spoken
begin	began	begun
run	ran	run
buy	bought	bought

TRANSITIVE VERBS take a DIRECT OBJECT, which receives the action of the verb. Intransitive verbs have no object. The person or thing that receives the direct object is the INDIRECT OBJECT.

Transitive: Alex <u>gave</u> his brother the ball. (*The ball* is the direct object; *his brother* is the indirect object.)

Intransitive: She <u>jumped</u> over the fence.

EXAMPLES

1) *By this time tomorrow, we _____ in New York.*
   Which verb phrase correctly completes the sentence?
   A.   have been landing
   B.   will have landed
   C.   have landed
   D.   are landing

   Answers:

   B.   **Correct.** The phrase *by this time tomorrow* indicates an action that will take place and be completed in the future at a set time. This is the future perfect tense: *will have landed.*

2) *My friends brought me a package of souvenirs from their trip to Spain.*
   Identify the direct object in the sentence.
   A.   friends
   B.   me
   C.   package
   D.   trip

   Answers:

   A.   Incorrect. *Friends* is the subject of the sentence.
   B.   Incorrect. *Me* is the recipient of the package, so it is an indirect object.
   C.   **Correct.** *Package* is the direct object of the verb *brought.*
   D.   Incorrect. *Trip* is not related to the verb in the sentence; it is part of the prepositional phrase *from their trip to Spain.*

Adjectives and Adverbs

ADJECTIVES modify or describe nouns and pronouns. In English, adjectives are usually placed before the word being modified, although they can also appear after a linking verb such as *is* or *smells*.

> The beautiful blue jade necklace will go perfectly with my dress.
>
> I think that lasagna smells delicious.

When multiple adjectives are used, they should be listed in the following order:

1.   determiners: articles (*a, an,* and *the*), possessive adjectives (e.g., *my, her*), and descriptors of quantity (e.g., *three, several*)
2.   opinions: modifiers that imply a value (e.g., *beautiful, perfect, ugly*)
3.   size: descriptions of size (e.g., *small, massive*)
4.   age: descriptions of age (e.g., *young, five-year-old*)

5. shape: descriptions of appearance or character (e.g., *smooth*, *loud*)

6. color: descriptions of color (e.g., *blue*, *dark*)

7. origin: modifiers that describe where something came from (e.g., *American*, *homemade*)

8. material: modifiers that describe what something is made from (e.g., *cotton*, *metallic*)

9. purpose: adjectives that function as part of the noun to describe its purpose (e.g., *sewing machine*, *rocking chair*)

ADVERBS, which are often formed by adding the suffix –*ly*, modify any word or set of words that is not a noun or pronoun. They can modify verbs, adjectives, other adverbs, phrases, or clauses.

> Adjectives answer the questions *what kind? how many?* or *which one?* Adverbs answer the questions *how? when? where? why?* or *to what extent?*

> He quickly ran to the house next door. (*Quickly* modifies the verb *ran*.)
>
> Her very effective speech earned her a promotion. (*Very* modifies the adjective *effective*.)
>
> Finally, the table was set and dinner was ready. (*Finally* modifies the clause *the table was set and dinner was ready*.)

COMPARATIVE adjectives and adverbs compare two items. For most one- or two-syllable words, the suffix –*er* is added to make it comparative; the word may be followed by *than*.

SUPERLATIVE adjectives and adverbs compare three or more items. Most one- or two-syllable words are made superlative by adding a suffix, –*est*.

> My brother is tall.
>
> Comparative: My brother is taller than my sister.
>
> Superlative: My brother is the tallest of all my siblings.

Longer adjectives and adverbs must be preceded by *more* to form the comparative and *most* to form the superlative.

> My bed is comfortable.
>
> Comparative: My bed at home is more comfortable than the one at the hotel.
>
> Superlative: The bed in your guestroom is the most comfortable bed I've ever slept in!

Some adjectives and adverbs form irregular comparatives and superlatives (see Table 11.5).

> The weather is bad.
>
> Comparative: The weather is worse than yesterday.
>
> Superlative: The weather was the worst on Monday when it rained.

Table 11.5. Some Irregular Comparative and Superlative Adjectives and Adverbs

ADJECTIVE/ADVERB	COMPARATIVE	SUPERLATIVE
much	more	most
bad	worse	worst
good	better	best
little	less	least
far	further/farther	furthest/farthest

EXAMPLES

1) Which of the following sentences is CORRECTLY constructed?
   A. Between my mom and dad, my father is the oldest.
   B. I ran less than usual today.
   C. Henry's cat is more fat than mine.
   D. After taking medicine, she felt worser.

Answers:
   A. Incorrect. The speaker has two parents and is comparing their father to their mother. Thus *older*, not *oldest*, should be used.
   B. **Correct.** The speaker is comparing today's run to the norm, not to any additional instances, so the comparative is acceptable here. Furthermore, the word *than* appears, a clue that the comparative is appropriate. *Less* is the irregular comparative form of *little*.
   C. Incorrect. *Fat* is a one-syllable adjective, so it should be written *fatter* in the comparative form. In general, only three-syllable adjectives (or longer) are preceded by *more* to form the comparative.
   D. Incorrect. While the comparative could be appropriate here, *worser* is not a word; *worse* is already in the comparative form.

2) *He carelessly sped around the flashing yellow light.*
   Which is the adverb in this sentence?
   A. flashing
   B. yellow
   C. around
   D. carelessly

Answer:
   A. Incorrect. *Flashing* is an adjective describing *light*.
   B. Incorrect. *Yellow* is an adjective describing *light*.
   C. Incorrect. *Around* is a preposition working with the verb *sped* to explain the relationship between the subject and the light.
   D. **Correct.** *Carelessly* is an adverb modifying *sped* and explaining *how* the driving occurred. The subject was not mindful as he drove; he raced through a yellow light when he should have exercised caution.

Conjunctions

CONJUNCTIONS join words into phrases, clauses, and sentences. The COORDINATING CONJUNCTIONS (FANBOYS) join two independent clauses: For, And, Nor, But, Or, Yet, So. They are always preceded by a comma.

> Marta went to the pool, <u>and</u> Alex decided to go shopping.
>
> Annie didn't want to eat tacos for dinner, <u>so</u> she picked up a pizza on her way home.

SUBORDINATING CONJUNCTIONS join dependent clauses to the independent clauses to which they are related.

> We chose that restaurant <u>because</u> Juan loves pizza.

Table 11.6. Subordinating Conjunctions

Time	after, as, as long as, as soon as, before, since, until, when, whenever, while
Manner	as, as if, as though
Cause	because
Condition	although, as long as, even if, even though, if, provided that, though, unless, while
Purpose	in order that, so that, that
Comparison	as, than

EXAMPLES

1) *He liked to cook and baking was his specialty.*
   The following sentence contains an error. How should it be rewritten?

   I. He liked to cook, and baking was his specialty.
   II. He liked to cook so baking was his specialty.
   III. He liked to cook, baking was his specialty.

   A. I only
   B. I and II only
   C. I and III only
   D. I, II, and IIII

   Answers:

   A. Correct. This sentence includes two independent clauses: "He liked to cook" and "baking was his specialty." They should be joined by a comma and coordinating conjunction (here, *and* is a reasonable choice).

2) *Anne and Peter drank their coffee languidly while they read the paper.*
   Which of the following parts of speech is *while* as used in the sentence?
   A. subordinating conjunction
   B. coordinating conjunction
   C. irregular verb
   D. adverb

Prepositions

PREPOSITIONS set up relationships in time (*after the party*) or space (*under the cushions*) within a sentence. A preposition will always function as part of a prepositional phrase—the preposition along with the object of the preposition.

Table 11.7. Common Prepositions

PREPOSITIONS

about	by	off	toward
among	despite	on	under
around	down	onto	underneath
at	during	out	until
before	except	outside	up
behind	for	over	upon
below	from	past	with
beneath	in	since	within
beside	into	through	
between	near	till	
beyond	of	to	

COMPOUND PREPOSITIONS

according to	because of	in place of	on account of
aside from	by means of	in respect to	out of
as of	in addition to	in spite of	prior to
as well as	in front of	instead of	with regard to

EXAMPLE

John and Carol must drive through the tunnel, but Carol is claustrophobic.

Identify the prepositional phrase in the sentence.

A. must drive

B. through the tunnel

C. drive through

D. but Carol is

Answers:

A.   Incorrect. *Must drive* is a verb phrase.

B.   Correct. "Through the tunnel" is a prepositional phrase explaining the relationship between the subjects and the tunnel using the preposition *through* and the object *the tunnel*.

C.   Incorrect. While *through* is a preposition, *drive through* is not a prepositional phrase. It does not contain an object.

D.   Incorrect. "But Carol is" is the beginning of a second independent clause connected to the first by a coordinating conjunction (*but*). The clause *Carol is* consists of a noun and verb only.

Interjections

INTERJECTIONS have no grammatical attachment to the sentence itself other than to add expressions of emotion. These parts of speech may be punctuated with commas or exclamation points and may fall anywhere within the sentence.

Ouch! He stepped on my toe.

EXAMPLE

"Come here! Look! Our team won the Super Bowl! Yay!"
Identify the interjection in the following sentence.

A.   Come here!

B.   Our team won

C.   Look!

D.   Yay!

Answers:

A.   Incorrect. *Come here* is a command; the speaker is instructing another person to perform an action using the verb *to come*. The second person *you* is the implied subject.

B.   Incorrect. *Our team won* is an independent clause and the beginning of the sentence "Our team won the Super Bowl."

C.   Incorrect. *Look* is a command; the speaker is instructing another person to perform an action using the verb *to look*. The second person *you* is the implied subject.

D.   Correct. *Yay* is an expression of emotion.

Constructing Sentences

Phrases

A PHRASE is a group of words that communicates a partial idea and lacks either a subject or a predicate. Several phrases may be strung together, one after another, to add detail and interest to a sentence.

Phrases are categorized based on the main word in the phrase. A PREPOSITIONAL PHRASE begins with a preposition and ends with an object of the preposition; a VERB PHRASE is composed of the main verb along with its helping verbs; and a NOUN PHRASE consists of a noun and its modifiers.

> Prepositional phrase: The dog is hiding under the porch.
>
> Verb phrase: The chef wanted to cook a different dish.
>
> Noun phrase: The big, red barn rests beside the vacant chicken house.

An APPOSITIVE PHRASE is a particular type of noun phrase that renames the word or group of words that precedes it. Appositive phrases usually follow the noun they describe and are set apart by commas.

> My dad, a clock maker, loved antiques.

VERBAL PHRASES begin with a word that would normally act as a verb but is instead filling another role within the sentence. These phrases can act as nouns, adjectives, or adverbs.

> Noun: To visit Europe had always been her dream.
>
> Adjective: Enjoying the stars that filled the sky, Dave lingered outside for quite a while.

A command may look like a phrase because it lacks a subject, but it's actually a complete sentence. The subject of the sentence is assumed to be you:

Try it. → (You) try it.

EXAMPLE

Dodging traffic, Rachel drove to work on back roads.

What type of phrase is underlined in the sentence?

A. prepositional phrase

B. noun phrase

C. verb phrase

D. verbal phrase

Answers:

A. Incorrect. A prepositional phrase must start with a preposition.

B. Incorrect. A noun phrase includes only the noun and its modifiers.

C. Incorrect. A verb phrase is composed of the main verb and its helping verbs, if any.

D. Correct. The phrase is a verbal phrase modifying the noun *Rachel*. It begins with the word *dodging*, derived from the verb *to dodge*.

Clauses and Types of Sentences

CLAUSES contain both a subject and a predicate. They can be either independent or dependent. An INDEPENDENT (or main) CLAUSE can stand alone as its own sentence:

> The dog ate her homework.

Dependent (or subordinate) clauses cannot stand alone as their own sentences. They start with a subordinating conjunction, relative pronoun, or relative adjective, which will make them sound incomplete:

> <u>Because</u> the dog ate her homework

Table 11.8. Words That Begin Dependent Clauses

SUBORDINATING CONJUNCTIONS	RELATIVE PRONOUNS AND ADJECTIVES
after, although, as, because, before, even if, even though, if, in order that, once, provided that, since, so, so that, than, that, though, unless, until, when, whenever, where, whereas, wherever, whether, while	how, that, when, where, which, who, whoever, whom, whomever, whose, why

Sentences can be classified based on the number and type of clauses they contain. A SIMPLE SENTENCE will have only one independent clause and no dependent clauses. The sentence may contain phrases, complements, and modifiers, but it will comprise only one independent clause, one complete idea.

> The cat ran under the porch.

Just because a sentence is simple doesn't mean it has to be short! A simple sentence has only one subject and one verb, but can have lots of modifying phrases. To help identify the type of sentence, cross out modifiers, objects, and prepositional phrases:

> ~~The new~~ car ~~that I bought with the money I earned at my summer job~~ ~~already~~ needs ~~new tires and new brake pads~~.

A COMPOUND SENTENCE has two or more independent clauses and no dependent clauses.

> The cat ran under the porch, and the dog ran after him.

A COMPLEX SENTENCE has only one independent clause and one or more dependent clauses.

> The cat, who is scared of the dog, ran under the porch.

A COMPOUND-COMPLEX SENTENCE has two or more independent clauses and one or more dependent clauses.

> The cat, who is scared of the dog, ran under the porch, and the dog ran after him.

The ATI TEAS will ask you to identify types of sentences by name, so make sure to memorize the four types and how to identify them.

Table 11.9. Sentence Structure and Clauses

SENTENCE STRUCTURE	INDEPENDENT CLAUSES	DEPENDENT CLAUSES
Simple	1	0
Compound	2 +	0
Complex	1	1 +
Compound-complex	2 +	1 +

Punctuation

Terminal punctuation marks are used to end sentences. The PERIOD (.) ends declarative (statement) and imperative (command) sentences. The QUESTION MARK (?) terminates interrogative sentences (questions). Lastly, EXCLAMATION POINTS end exclamatory sentences, in which the writer or speaker is exhibiting intense emotion or energy.

> Sarah and I are attending a concert.
>
> How many people are attending the concert?
>
> What a great show that was!

The colon and the semicolon, though often confused, each have a unique set of rules for their use. While both punctuation marks are used to join clauses, the construction of the clauses and the relationship between them is different. The SEMICOLON (;) is used to join two independent clauses (IC; IC) that are closely related. It can also be used to join items in a list when those items already include a comma.

> I need to buy a new car soon; my old car broke down last month.
>
> The guests at the party included Mrs. Green, my third-grade teacher; Mr. Doakes, my neighbor; and Dr. Kayani, our school principal.

The COLON (:) is used to introduce a list, definition, or clarification. The clause preceding the colon has to be independent, but what follows the colon can be an independent clause, a dependent clause, or a phrase.

> The buffet offers three choices: ham, turkey, or roast beef.
>
> He decided to drive instead of taking the train: he didn't think the train would arrive in time.

COMMAS show pauses in the text or set information apart from the main text. There are lots of rules for comma usage, so only the most common are summarized here.

1. Commas separate two independent clauses along with a coordinating conjunction.

> George ordered the steak, but Bruce preferred the ham.

2. Commas separate coordinate adjectives.

> She made herself a big bowl of cold, delicious ice cream.

3. Commas separate items in a series.

> The list of groceries included cream, coffee, donuts, and tea.

4. Commas separate introductory words and phrases from the rest of the sentence.

> For example, we have thirty students who demand a change.

5. Commas set off nonessential information and appositives.

> Estelle, our newly elected chairperson, will be in attendance.

6. Commas set off the day and month of a date within a text.

> I was born on February 16, 1958.

7. Commas set up numbers in a text of more than four digits.

> We expect 25,000 visitors to the new museum.

8. Commas set off the names of cities from their states, territories, or provinces.

> She lives in Houston, Texas.

QUOTATION MARKS have a number of different purposes. They enclose titles of short, or relatively short, literary works such as short stories, chapters, and poems. (The titles of longer works, like novels and anthologies, are italicized.) Additionally, quotation marks are used to enclose direct quotations within the text of a document where the quotation is integrated into the text. Writers also use quotation marks to set off dialogue.

> We will be reading the poem "Bright Star" in class today.
>
> The poem opens with the line "Bright star, would I were steadfast as thou art."

APOSTROPHES, sometimes referred to as single quotation marks, have several different purposes.

1. They show possession.

> boy's watch, John and Mary's house

2. They replace missing letters, numerals, and signs.

> do not = don't, 1989 = '89

3. They form plurals of letters, numerals, and signs.

> A's, 10's

Less commonly used punctuation marks include:

- EN DASH (–): indicates a range
- EM DASH (—): shows an abrupt break in a sentence and emphasizes the words within the em dashes
- PARENTHESES ( ): enclose nonessential information
- BRACKETS [ ]: enclose added words to a quotation and add insignificant information within parentheses
- SLASH (/): separates lines of poetry within a text or indicates interchangeable terminology
- ELLIPSES (...): indicates that information has been removed from a quotation or creates a reflective pause

---

EXAMPLES

1) Which sentence includes an improperly placed comma?

- **A.** Ella, Cassie, and Cameron drove to South Carolina together.
- **B.** Trying to impress his friends, Carl ended up totaling his car.
- **C.** Ice cream is my favorite food, it is so cold and creamy.
- **D.** Mowing the lawn, Frank discovered a family of baby rabbits.

Answers:

- A. Incorrect. The commas separate items in a series (in this case, the three friends).
- B. Incorrect. The comma correctly follows the verbal phrase "trying to impress his friends," which modifies *Carl*.
- **C. Correct.** "Ice cream...food" and "it...creamy" are two independent clauses. The writer should include a coordinating conjunction like *for* or separate the clauses with a semicolon.
- D. Incorrect. The comma correctly follows the verbal phrase "mowing the lawn," which modifies *Frank*.

2) *Oak trees—with proper care—can grow upwards of thirty feet; providing shade for people, shelter for animals, and perches for birds.*

The above sentence contains an error. How can the writer fix it?

- **A.** replace the em dashes with commas
- **B.** remove the comma after *people*
- **C.** insert an apostrophe at the end of *animals*
- **D.** replace the semicolon with a comma

Answers:

- A. Incorrect. Both em dashes and commas are appropriate here.
- B. Incorrect. The comma is properly used in a list of items.
- C. Incorrect. *Animals* is acting as a plural noun with no possession indicated.
- **D. Correct.** "Providing shade..." is not an independent clause; therefore, it cannot be preceded by a semicolon.

Capitalization

CAPITALIZATION is writing the first letter of a word in uppercase and the remaining letters in lowercase. The table below shows the most important rules for capitalization.

Table 11.10. Capitalization Rules

RULE	EXAMPLE
Words that begin sentences should be capitalized.	The patient's vitals are normal.
Proper nouns, including names of people and specific places, should be capitalized. The names of general locations (river, school) are not capitalized.	My sister Maria moved to Florida so she could live near the ocean.
The names of holidays are capitalized. Do not capitalize the word *day* unless it's part of the holiday's official name.	We will be opening presents on Christmas day; on Memorial Day we'll go to the parade.
Titles should be capitalized when used as a part of a person's name, but not when they stand alone.	Richard Atwell, the governor of Virginia, will be hosting a dinner to honor President Green.
Titles of works of art, including books, movies, and songs, should be capitalized. Do not capitalize prepositions or conjunctions.	She went to the store to buy a copy of the book *The Comfort Garden: Tales from the Trauma Unit*.
The pronoun *I* should always be capitalized.	He and I have never understood one another.

EXAMPLE

Which of the following sentences does NOT contain an error in capitalization?

A. Robert and Kelly raced across the River in their small boats.

B. ducks flying in a V-formation cross the Midwest in the fall.

C. The chairman of the board, Jessica Smith, will lead today's meeting.

D. The Senators from Virginia and Louisiana strongly favor the bill.

Answers:

A. Incorrect. *River* should not be capitalized. In this sentence, it is a common noun.

B. Incorrect. As the first word in a sentence, *ducks* should be capitalized.

C. **Correct.** *Jessica Smith*, as a proper noun, should be capitalized, but "chairman of the board" should not because it is separated from the name by a comma.

D. Incorrect. *Senators* should not be capitalized because this word replaces a name in this sentence.

Common Language Errors

Subject-Verb Agreement

Verbs must agree in number with their subjects. Common rules for subject-verb agreement are given next.

1. Single subjects agree with single verbs; plural subjects agree with plural verbs.

    > The girl walks her dog.
    >
    > The girls walk their dogs.

2. Compound subjects joined by *and* typically take a plural verb unless considered one item.

    > Correctness and precision are required for all good writing.
    >
    > Macaroni and cheese makes a great snack for children.

3. The linking verbs agree with the subject and not the subject complement (predicate nominative).

    > My favorite is strawberries and apples.
    >
    > My favorites are strawberries and apples.

4. When a relative pronoun (*who, whom, which, that*) is used as the subject of the clause, the verb will agree with the antecedent of the relative pronoun.

    > This is the student who is receiving an award.
    >
    > These are the students who are receiving awards.

5. All single, indefinite pronouns agree with single verbs.

    > Neither of the students is happy about the play.
    >
    > Each of the many cars is on the grass.
    >
    > Every one of the administrators speaks highly of Trevor.

To make conjugating verbs easier, cross out words that appear between the subject and the verb:

> The new library ~~with its many books and rooms~~ fills a long-felt need.

EXAMPLE

Which sentence in the following list is CORRECT in its subject-verb agreement?

A. My sister and my best friend lives in Chicago.

B. My parents or my brother is going to pick me up from the airport.

C. Neither of the students refuse to take the exam.

D. The team were playing a great game until the rain started.

Answers:

A. Incorrect. Because the sentence reads "My sister and my best friend," the subject is plural and needs a plural verb (*live*).

B. **Correct.** The verb agrees with the closest subject—in this case, the singular *brother*.

C. Incorrect. *Neither* is a singular, indefinite pronoun, so the agreement is singular. *Neither refuses...*

D. Incorrect. In the context of a game, the team is functioning as a singular, so it should take a singular verb. *The team was...*

Pronoun-Antecedent Agreement

Similarly, pronouns must agree with their antecedents (the words they replaced) in number; however, some pronouns also require gender agreement (*him, her*). **PRONOUN-ANTECEDENT AGREEMENT** rules can be found next:

1. Antecedents joined by *and* typically require a plural pronoun.

> The <u>children and their dogs</u> enjoyed <u>their</u> day at the beach.
>
> If the two nouns refer to the same person, a singular pronoun is preferable.
>
> My <u>best friend and confidant</u> still lives in <u>her</u> log cabin.

2. For compound antecedents joined by or, the pronoun agrees with the nearer or nearest antecedent.

> Either the resident mice <u>or the manager's cat</u> gets <u>itself</u> a meal of good leftovers.

3. When indefinite pronouns are used in a sentence, the pronoun must agree with the number of the indefinite pronoun.

> <u>Neither</u> student finished <u>his or her</u> assignment.
>
> <u>Both</u> students finished <u>their</u> assignments.

4. When collective nouns function as antecedents, the pronoun choice will be singular or plural depending on the function of the collective.

> The <u>audience</u> was cheering as <u>it</u> rose to <u>its</u> feet in unison.
>
> Our <u>family</u> are spending <u>their</u> vacations in Maine, Hawaii, and Rome.

5. When *each* and *every* precede the antecedent, the pronoun agreement will be singular.

> <u>Each and every man, woman, and child</u> brings unique qualities to <u>his or her</u> family.
>
> <u>Every creative writer, technical writer, and research writer</u> is attending <u>his or her</u> assigned lecture.

Because English does not have a nongendered singular pronoun, it's common in everyday speech to treat *they* or *their* as singular:

> Common usage: <u>Every student</u> should check <u>their</u> homework before turning it in.

Because this usage is controversial, on tests it's important to use the technically correct response:

> Technically correct: <u>Every student</u> should check <u>his or her</u> homework before turning it in.

EXAMPLES

1) Which sentence in the following list is CORRECT in its pronoun-antecedent agreement?
    A. The grandchildren and their cousins enjoyed their day at the park.
    B. Most of the grass has lost their deep color.
    C. The jury was relieved as their commitment came to a close.
    D. Every boy and girl must learn to behave themselves in school.

    Answers:

    A. **Correct.** The plural antecedents *Grandchildren* and *cousins* match the plural possessive pronoun *their*.
    B. Incorrect. The antecedent *grass* is singular; therefore its matching pronoun should also be the singular *its*, not *their*. The sentence should read, "Most of the grass has lost <u>its</u> deep color."
    C. Incorrect. Here, the collective noun *jury* is functioning as a singular body and thus takes a singular pronoun. The sentence should read, "The jury was relieved as <u>its</u> commitment came to a close."
    D. Incorrect. When *every* precedes the antecedent, the pronoun agreement is singular. The technically correct sentence should read, "Every boy and girl must learn to behave <u>himself or herself</u> in school."

2) Which sentence in the following list is CORRECT in its pronoun and antecedent agreement?
    A. Either my brother or my dad will bring their van to pick us up.
    B. The university is having their tenth fundraiser tonight.
    C. Alyssa and Jacqueline bought herself a big lunch today.
    D. Each dog, cat, and rabbit has its own bowl and blanket.

    Answers:

    A. Incorrect. In sentences with correlative conjunctions like *either...or*, pronouns (and verbs) agree with the nearest antecedent. Technically this sentence should read, "Either my brother or my dad will bring <u>his</u> van to pick us up."
    B. Incorrect. The antecedent *university* is a singular noun—an institution. Its pronoun should also be singular. The sentence should read, "The university is having <u>its</u> tenth fundraiser tomorrow night."
    C. Incorrect. Antecedents joined by *and* typically require a plural pronoun. The sentence should read, "Alyssa and Jacqueline bought <u>themselves</u> a big lunch today."
    D. **Correct.** When *each* precedes the antecedent, the pronoun agreement is singular. The pronoun *its* therefore agrees with the antecedents *Each dog, cat, and rabbit*.

Verb Tense Agreement

In any passage, verb tense should be consistent and make sense in the context of other verbs, adverbs, and general meaning.

> Incorrect: Deborah was speaking with her colleague when her boss will appear, demanding a meeting.

The first part of the sentence states that Deborah *was speaking* with her colleagues, an action occurring in the past. Thus, it would make no sense for her boss to interrupt her in the future (*will appear*). The sentence can be corrected by putting her boss's action in the past tense as well:

> Correct: Deborah was speaking with her colleague when her boss appeared, demanding a meeting.

Pay attention to how verbs are conjugated in the beginning of a sentence or passage, and look for adverbial clues to spot any errors in verb tense agreement.

EXAMPLE

Which of the following sentences has correct verb tense agreement?

A. Veronica attends cooking classes, and she went to yoga classes too.

B. Veronica attended cooking classes, and she went to yoga classes too.

C. Veronica attended cooking classes, and she goes to yoga classes too.

D. Veronica attended cooking classes, and she will go to yoga classes too.

Answer:

B. **Correct.** The use of *too* suggests that both Veronica's activities are occurring at the same time. Only choice B has the two verbs in the same tense: *attended* and *went* are both past tense.

Parallelism

Errors in **PARALLELISM** prevent a writer from creating a smooth flow, or coherence, from word to word and sentence to sentence. Writers should create parallel structure in words, phrases, and clauses wherever two or more similar and equally important ideas exist next to each other in a sentence.

> Incorrect: Amanda could program computers, repair cars, and knew how to bake croissants.
>
> Correct: Amanda could program computers, repair cars, and bake croissants.

Looking at each part of the list individually helps highlight the error: the final item reads "Amanda could knew how to make croissants." This error is fixed by writing the verbs in parallel structure: *program*, *repair*, and *bake*.

In sentences with multiple prepositional phrases in a parallel series, the preposition must be repeated unless the same preposition begins each phrase.

> Incorrect: You can park your car in the garage, the carport, or on the street.
>
> Correct: You can park your car in the garage, in the carport, or on the street.

> ## EXAMPLE
>
> *Shelly achieved more at nursing school because she was going to bed earlier, eating healthy food, and _____ home to study more.*
>
> Which word or phrase best completes the sentence?
>
> **A.** staying
>
> **B.** to stay
>
> **C.** will be staying
>
> **D.** stays
>
> **Answer:**
>
> **A. Correct.** The other verbs in the series are *going* and *eating*, so *staying* is the only verb that fits in the series.

Sentence Construction Errors

There are three main types of sentence construction errors: fragments, comma splices (comma fault), and fused sentences (run-on). A FRAGMENT occurs when a group of words is not a complete sentence but is punctuated like one. The fragment might be a phrase or a dependent clause. To fix a fragment, an independent clause needs to be created.

> Fragment (phrase): The girl in my class who asks a lot of questions.
>
> Correct: The girl in my class who asks a lot of questions sits in the back row.

> Fragment (dependent clause): Because of the big storm we had last weekend.
>
> Correct: Because of the big storm we had last weekend, the park will be closed.

A COMMA SPLICE (comma fault) occurs when two independent clauses are joined together in a paragraph with only a comma to "splice" them together. FUSED (run-on) sentences occur when two independent clauses are joined with no punctuation whatsoever. To fix a comma splice or fused sentence, add the correct punctuation and/or conjunction.

> Comma splice: My family eats turkey at Thanksgiving, we eat ham at Christmas.
>
> Correct: My family eats turkey at Thanksgiving, and we eat ham at Christmas.
>
> Correct: My family eats turkey at Thanksgiving. We eat ham at Christmas.

> Correct: My family eats turkey at Thanksgiving; we eat ham at Christmas.

> Fused sentence: I bought a chocolate pie from the bakery it was delicious.
>
> Correct: I bought a chocolate pie from the bakery. It was delicious.
>
> Correct: I bought a chocolate pie from the bakery, and it was delicious.
>
> Correct: I bought a chocolate pie from the bakery; it was delicious.

Another common error that can occur in sentence structure is a dangling modifier, which occurs when a modifying phrase is separated from the word it describes. The sentence itself is still grammatically correct but can be confusing.

> Incorrect: Discussing the state of the nation, I listened to the president's speech.

Here, the president, not the narrator, is discussing the state of the nation; the narrator is simply *listening*. However, the participial phrase "Discussing the state of the nation" is disconnected from the word it modifies, *president*. Thus it is *dangling* in the sentence, creating confusion. The sentence needs to be rewritten to move the phrase next to the word it modifies.

> Correct: I listened to the president's speech discussing the state of the nation.

EXAMPLE

Which of the following is correctly punctuated?

A. Since she went to the store.

B. The football game ended in a tie, the underdog caught up in the fourth quarter.

C. The mall is closing early today so we'll have to go shopping tomorrow.

D. When the players dropped their gloves, a fight broke out on the ice hockey rink floor.

Answers:

A. Incorrect. This is a dependent clause and needs an independent clause to be complete.

B. Incorrect. This is a comma splice.

C. Incorrect. This is a fused sentence.

D. Correct. This is a complete sentence that is punctuated properly with a comma between the dependent and independent clauses.

Easily Confused Words

A, AN: *A* precedes words beginning with consonants or consonant sounds; *an* precedes words beginning with vowels or vowel sounds.

AFFECT, EFFECT: *Affect* is most often a verb; *effect* is usually a noun. (*The experience affected me significantly* OR *The experience had a significant effect on me.*)

AMOUNT, NUMBER: *Amount* is used for noncountable sums; *number* is used with countable nouns.

CITE, SITE: The verb *cite* credits an author of a quotation, paraphrase, or summary; the noun *site* is a location.

EVERY DAY, EVERYDAY: *Every day* is an indefinite adjective modifying a noun; *everyday* is a one-word adjective implying frequent occurrence. (*Our visit to the Minnesota State Fair is an everyday activity during August.*)

FEWER, LESS: *Fewer* is used with a countable noun; *less* is used with a noncountable noun. (*Fewer parents are experiencing stress since the new teacher was hired. Parents are experiencing less stress since the new teacher was hired.*)

GOOD, WELL: *Good* is always the adjective; *well* is always the adverb except in cases of health. (*She felt well after the surgery.*)

IMPLIED, INFERRED: *Implied* is something a speaker does; *inferred* is something the listener does after assessing the speaker's message. (*The speaker implied something mysterious, but I inferred the wrong thing.*)

IRREGARDLESS, REGARDLESS: *Irregardless* is nonstandard usage and should be avoided; *regardless* is the proper usage of the transitional statement.

ITS, IT'S: *Its* is a possessive case pronoun; *it's* is a contraction for *it is*.

PRINCIPAL, PRINCIPLE: As a noun, *principal* is an authority figure, often the head of a school; as an adjective, *principal* means *main*; the noun *principle* means idea or tenet. (*The principal of the school spoke on the principal meaning of the main principles of the school.*)

QUOTE, QUOTATION: *Quote* is a verb; *quotation* is a noun.

SHOULD OF, SHOULD HAVE: *Should of* is improper usage—*of* is not a helping verb and therefore cannot complete the verb phrase; *should have* is the proper usage. (*He should have driven.*)

THAN, THEN: *Than* sets up a comparison; *then* indicates a reference to a point in time. (*When I said that I liked the hat better than the gloves, my sister laughed; then she bought both for me.*)

THEIR, THERE, THEY'RE: *Their* is the possessive case of the pronoun *they*; *there* is the demonstrative pronoun indicating location or place; *they're* is a contraction of the words *they are*.

TO LIE (TO RECLINE), TO LAY (TO PLACE): *To lie* is the intransitive verb meaning *to recline*; *to lay* is the transitive verb meaning *to place something*. (*I lie out in the sun; I lay my towel on the beach.*)

UNIQUE: *Unique* is an ultimate superlative; it should not be preceded by adverbs like *very* or *extremely*. (*The experience was unique.*)

WHO, WHOM: *Who* is the subject relative pronoun. (*My son, who is a good student, studies hard.*) Here, the son is carrying out the action of studying, so the pronoun is a subject pronoun (*who*). *Whom* is the object relative pronoun. (*My son, whom the other students admire, studies hard.*) Here, *son* is the object of the other students' admiration, so the pronoun standing in for him, *whom*, is an object pronoun.

YOUR, YOU'RE: *Your* is the possessive case of the pronoun *you*; *you're* is a contraction of the words *you are*.

EXAMPLE

My dad, who is a car fanatic, has a very unique way of celebrating the holiday season. He decorates his Ford Mustang with Christmas lights, which have a striking effect when the car cruises down the street. Then he drives to the homes of our relatives to drop off holiday gifts.

The above passage has an error. How should it be fixed?

A. change *who* to *whom*

B. delete *very* before the adjective *unique*

C. change *effect* to *affect*

D. change *Then* to *Than*

Answers:

A. Incorrect. The relative pronoun *who* is acting as the subject of the subordinate clause "who is a car fanatic," so it is correct. *Whom* is the object pronoun.

B. **Correct.** *Unique* is an ultimate superlative, meaning it cannot be modified by adverbs like *very*. If something is unique, it cannot be more or less unique than something else.

C. Incorrect. Here, *effect* is a noun meaning *impression*. It is used correctly in this passage. *Affect* is generally used as a verb meaning "to act upon."

D. Incorrect. *Then* refers to a point in time; here, when the narrator's father drives to deliver holiday gifts. It is used correctly in this passage. *Than* sets up a comparison and would not make sense here.

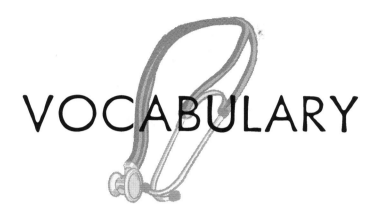

twelve

VOCABULARY

Like the Reading test, the English portion of the TEAS will ask you to identify the meaning of certain words. These words will only appear in a single sentence, not in a passage, so you'll have minimal context clues. Instead, you'll need to learn how to use the word itself to find the meaning. You'll also be asked about the common rules of spelling.

Word Structure

In addition to using the context of the sentence and passage to determine the meaning of an unfamiliar word, the word itself can give you clues about its meaning. Each word consists of distinct pieces that help determine meaning; the most familiar of these pieces are root words, prefixes, and suffixes.

Root Words

ROOT WORDS are bases from which many words take their foundational form and meaning. The most common root words are Greek and Latin, and a broad knowledge of these roots can greatly improve your ability to determine the meaning of words in context. Knowing root words cannot always provide the exact meaning of a word, but combined with an understanding of the word's place in the sentence and the context surrounding the word, it will often be enough to answer a question about meaning or relationships.

Table 12.1. List of Common Roots

Roots	Meaning	Examples
alter	other	alternate, alter ego
ambi	both	ambidextrous
ami, amic	love	amiable
amphi	both ends or all sides	amphibian
anthrop	man, human, humanity	misanthrope, anthropologist
apert	open	aperture

Table 12.1. List of Common Roots (continued)

Roots	Meaning	Examples
aqua	water	aqueduct, aquarium
aud	to hear	audience
auto	self	autobiography
bell	war	belligerent, bellicose
bene	good	benevolent
bio	life	biology
ced	yield, go	secede, intercede
cent	one hundred	century
chron	time	chronological
circum	around	circumference
contra/counter	against	contradict
crac, crat	rule, ruler	autocrat, bureacrat
crypt	hidden	cryptogram, cryptic
curr, curs, cours	to run	precursory
dict	to say	dictator, dictation
dyna	power	dynamic
dys	bad, hard, unlucky	dysfunctional
equ	equal, even	equanimity
fac	to make, to do	factory
form	shape	reform, conform
fort	strength	fortitude
fract	to break	fracture
grad, gress	step	progression
gram	thing written	epigram
graph	writing	graphic
hetero	different	heterogeneous
homo	same	homogenous
hypo	below, beneath	hypothermia
iso	identical	isolate
ject	throw	projection
logy	study of	biology
luc	light	elucidate
mal	bad	malevolent
meta, met	behind, between	metacognition-behind the thinking
meter/metr	measure	thermometer
micro	small	microbe
mis/miso	hate	misanthrope
mit	to send	transmit
mono	one	monologue
morph	form, shape	morphology
mort	death	mortal
multi	many	multiple

Roots	Meaning	Examples
phil	love	philanthropist
port	carry	transportation
pseudo	false	pseudonym
psycho	soul, spirit	psychic
rupt	to break	disruption
scope	viewing instrument	microscope
scrib/scribe	to write	inscription
sect/sec	to cut	section
sequ, secu	follow	consecutive
soph	wisdom, knowledge	philosophy
spect	to look	spectator
struct	to build	restructure
tele	far off	telephone
terr	earth	terrestrial
therm	heat	thermal
ven, vent	to come	convene
vert	turn	vertigo
voc	voice, call	vocalize, evocative

Prefixes

In addition to understanding the root of a word, it is vital to recognize common affixes that change the meaning of words and demonstrate their relationships to other words. PREFIXES are added to the beginning of a word and frequently change the meaning of the word itself by indicating an opposite or another specifically altered meaning.

Table 12.2. Examples of Prefixes

Prefixes	Meaning	Examples
a, an	without, not	anachronism, anhydrous
ab, abs, a	apart, away from	abscission, abnormal
ad	toward	adhere
agere	act	agent
amphi, ambi	round, both sides	ambivalent
ante	before	antedate, anterior
anti	against	antipathy
archos	leader, first, chief	oligarchy
bi	two	binary, bivalve
bene	well, favorable	benevolent, beneficent
caco	bad	cacophony
circum	around	circumnavigate
corpus	body	corporeal
credo	belief	credible
demos	people	demographic
di	two, double	dimorphism, diatomic

Table 12.2. Examples of Prefixes (continued)

PREFIXES	MEANING	EXAMPLES
dia	across, through	dialectic
dis	not, apart	disenfranchise
dynasthai	be able	dynamo, dynasty
ego	I, self	egomaniac, egocentric
epi	upon, over	epigram, epiphyte
ex	out	extraneous, extemporaneous
geo	earth	geocentric, geomancy
ideo	idea	ideology, ideation
in	in	induction, indigenous
im	not	immoral
inter	between	interstellar
lexis	word	lexicography
liber	free, book	liberal
locus	place	locality
macro	large	macrophage
micro	small	micron
mono	one, single	monocle, monovalent
mortis	death	moribund
olig	few	oligarchy
peri	around	peripatetic, perineum
poly	many	polygamy
pre	before	prescient
solus	alone	solitary
subter	under, secret	subterfuge
un	not	unsafe
utilis	useful	utilitarian

Suffixes

A SUFFIX, on the other hand, is added to the end of a word and generally indicates the word's relationship to other words in the sentence. Suffixes can change the part of speech or indicate if a word is plural or related to a plural.

Table 12.3. Examples of Suffixes

SUFFIXES	MEANING	EXAMPLES
able, ible	able, capable	visible
age	act of, state of, result of	wreckage
al	relating to	gradual
algia	pain	myalgia
an, ian	native of, relating to	riparian
ance, ancy	action, process, state	defiance
ary, ery, ory	relating to, quality, place	aviary
cian	processing a specific skill or art	physician

Suffixes	Meaning	Examples
cule, ling	very small	animalcule, sapling
cy	action, function	normalcy
dom	quality, realm	wisdom
ee	one who receives the action	nominee
en	made of, to make	silken
ence, ency	action, state of, quality	urgency
er, or	one who, that which	professor
escent	in the process of	adolescent, senescence
esis, osis	action, process, condition	genesis, neurosis
et, ette	small one, group	baronet, lorgnette
fic	making, causing	specific
ful	full of	frightful
hood	order, condition, quality	adulthood
ice	condition, state, quality	malice
id, ide	a thing connected with or belonging to	bromide
ile	relating to, suited for, capable of	purile, juvenile
ine	nature of	feminine
ion, sion, tion	act, result, or state of	contagion
ish	origin, nature, resembling	impish
ism	system, manner, condition, characteristic	capitalism
ist	one who, that which	artist, flautist
ite	nature of, quality of, mineral product	graphite
ity, ty	state of, quality	captivity
ive	causing, making	exhaustive
ize, ise	make	idolize, bowdlerize
ment	act of, state or, result	containment
nomy	law	autonomy, taxonomy
oid	resembling	asteroid, anthropoid
some	like, apt, tending to	gruesome
strat	cover	strata
tude	state of, condition of	aptitude
um	forms single nouns	spectrum
ure	state of, act, process, rank	rapture, rupture
ward	in the direction of	backward
y	inclined to, tend to	faulty

Homophones and Homographs

HOMOPHONES are words that sound the same but have different meanings; HOMOGRAPHS are words that are spelled the same way but have different meanings. On the TEAS, you may be asked to identify which homophone is appropriate in the given context, or you may need to identify the correct definition of a homograph as it is used in a sentence.

A good knowledge of homophones is especially important as many words applicable to medicine (*heel/heal, oral/aural*) may be homophones. Is a patient healing, or does he or she have a heel problem? Should medication be administered orally or aurally? Does the patient have a tic, or has he or she been bitten by a tick?

Examples of homophones include:

- ◆ tic/tick
- ◆ pain/pane
- ◆ gait/gate
- ◆ oral/aural
- ◆ mail/male
- ◆ heel/heal

Examples of homographs include:

- ◆ tear (to rip/liquid produced by the eye)
- ◆ compound (to mix/an enclosed area that includes a building or group of buildings)
- ◆ bank (a place to store money/the side of a river/a stockpile)
- ◆ novel (a piece of fiction/something new)

- change (to make different/money left over after a transaction)
- rose (a flower/to move upward)
- die (to pass away/a six-sided, numbered cube)

EXAMPLE

Which of the following is the best synonym for *proceeds* as used in the sentence?

The <u>proceeds</u> from the dance will be donated to a local charity.

A) entertainment

B) movement

C) profit

D) snacks

Answer:

C) is correct. *Proceeds* can mean either *profit* or *moving forward*. In this sentence, it is used to mean *profit* because *profit* can be donated to charity and thus makes sense in the context of the sentence.

Spelling

A knowledge of spelling is essential for the TEAS. Homophones, basic rules of spelling, and commonly misspelled words will be tested.

Rules of Spelling

English spelling can be complex and confusing. Fortunately, the TEAS won't test you on the more obscure or uncommon spelling rules. Instead, you'll be asked to identify misspellings related to common conjugation patterns (like pluralization) and identify commonly misspelled words.

PLURALS

There are several ways to make a word plural. Most commonly, add an *–s* to a word:

doctors
hospitals

For words that already end in an *s*, or that end in *–sh*, *–ch*, *–x*, and *–z*, add *–es*.

dresses
brushes
branches
boxes
waltzes

Generally, words that end in *y* are made plural by dropping the *y* and adding *–ies*.

> baby → babies
>
> nursery → nurseries
>
> surgery → surgeries

Generally, words that end in *f* are made plural by dropping the *f* and adding *–ves*.

> shelf → shelves
>
> scarf → scarves

In medicine, many words are derived from Latin. It is important to know their proper plural forms.

> vertebra → vertebrae
>
> bronchus → bronchi

I BEFORE E

The phrase *I before E except after C or when sounded like A as in neighbor or weigh* is helpful in order to remember the relationship between the vowels *i* and *e* in words.

> bel**ie**ve
>
> conc**ei**ve
>
> r**ei**gn

CHANGE A FINAL Y TO I

If adding a suffix to a word ending in *y*, the *y* must be changed to an *i*, unless the suffix itself begins with *i* or unless a vowel immediately precedes the final *y* in the root word.

> plenty + –ful → plentiful
>
> justify + –ing → justifying
>
> justify + –ed → justified
>
> display + –ed → displayed

DOUBLE FINAL CONSONANT

When adding a suffix like *–ed* or *–ing* to a word ending in a consonant, that final consonant is usually doubled if it is preceded by one vowel and completes a one-syllable word or accented syllable.

> refer + –ed → referred

It's doubled because the consonant ends on an accented syllable (re-FER) and is preceded by *one* vowel (ref**e**r).

> limit + –ing → limiting

It's not doubled because the consonant does not end an accented syllable (LI-mit).

seep + –ed → seeped

It's not doubled because the final *p* is preceded by more than one vowel.

consent + –ed → consented

It's not doubled because the final *t* is not preceded by a vowel.

DROP FINAL *E*

Usually, if a root ends with *e*, the *e* is dropped when adding a suffix unless the suffix begins with a consonant.

measure + ing → measuring
measure + ment → measurement

Commonly Misspelled Words

a lot	acceptable	accidentally
accommodate	acknowledgement	acquire
acquit	amateur	analysis
argument	beginning	calendar
category	changeable	column
committed	conceivable	conscientious
consensus	definitely	eighth
embarrassment	equipment	especially
exhilarate	existence	foreign
guarantee	generally	government
harass	humorous	immediate
immediately	inoculate	judgment
leisure	liaison	license
lightning	loneliness	maintenance
maneuver	medieval	millennium
minuscule	mischievous	necessary
neighbor	noticeable	occasionally
parallel	personnel	playwright
possession	proceed	profession
publicly	pursue	questionnaire
quizzes	restaurant	receive
recommend	referred	rhyme
rhythm	schedule	separate
sincerely	supersede	technique
unanimous	vacuum	weird

EXAMPLES

1. Which of the following is misspelled in the sentence below?

    Respondents were asked to complete a simple questionnaire to determine their eligability.

    A) respondents

    B) questionnaire

    C) determine

    D) eligability

    Answer:

    D) is correct. *Eligability* should be spelled *eligibility*.

2. Which of the following nouns is written in the correct plural form?

    A) monkies

    B) parties

    C) watchs

    D) sheeps

    Answer:

    B) is correct. Only *parties* has been made plural correctly.

PART V: TEST YOUR KNOWLEDGE

thirteen

PRACTICE TEST

Mathematics

Directions: Read the problem carefully, and choose the best answer.

1. A car dealership's commercials claim that this year's models are 20% off the list price, plus they will pay the first 3 monthly payments. If a car is listed for $26,580, and the monthly payments are set at $250, which of the following is the total potential savings?

   A) $1,282
   B) $5,566
   C) $6,066
   D) $20,514

2. A dry cleaner charges $3 per shirt, $6 per pair of pants, and an extra $5 per item for mending. Annie drops off 5 shirts and 4 pairs of pants, 2 of which need mending. Assuming the cleaner charges an 8% sales tax, which of the following will be the amount of Annie's total bill?

   A) $45.08
   B) $49.00
   C) $52.92
   D) $88.20

3. A sandwich shop earns $4 for every sandwich (s) it sells, $2 for every drink (d), and $1 for every cookie (c). If this is all the shop sells, which of the following equations represents what the shop's revenue (r) is over three days?

   A) $r = 4s + 2d + 1c$
   B) $r = 8s + 4d + 2c$
   C) $r = 12s + 6d + 3c$
   D) $r = 16s + 8d + 4c$

4. Which of the following is the y-intercept of the line whose equation is $7y - 42x + 7 = 0$?

   A) $(\frac{1}{6}, 0)$
   B) $(6, 0)$
   C) $(0, -1)$
   D) $(-1, 0)$

5. $4 - \frac{1}{2^2} + 24 \div (8 + 12)$
   Simplify the expression. Which of the following is correct?

   A) 1.39
   B) 2.74
   C) 4.95
   D) 15.28

6. A rectangular field has area of 1452 square feet. If the length is three times the width, which of the following is the width of the field?

    A) 22 feet
    B) 44 feet
    C) 242 feet
    D) 1452 feet

7. The owner of a newspaper has noticed that print subscriptions have gone down 40% while online subscriptions have gone up 60%. Print subscriptions once accounted for 70% of the newspaper's business, and online subscriptions accounted for 25%. Which of the following is the overall percentage growth or decline in business?

    A) 13% decline
    B) 15% decline
    C) 28% growth
    D) Business has stayed the same.

8. $(6.4)(2.8) \div 0.4$

    Simplify the expression. Which of the following is correct?

    A) 16.62
    B) 17.92
    C) 41.55
    D) 44.80

9. Bridget is repainting her rectangular bedroom. Two walls measure 15 feet by 9 feet, and the other two measure 12.5 feet by 9 feet. One gallon of paint covers an average of 32 square meters. Which of the following is the number of gallons of paint that Bridget will use? (There are 3.28 feet in 1 meter.)

    A) 0.72 gallons
    B) 1.43 gallons
    C) 4.72 gallons
    D) 15.5 gallons

10. $5\frac{2}{3} \times 1\frac{7}{8} \div \frac{1}{3}$

    Simplify the expression. Which of the following is correct?

    A. $3\frac{13}{24}$
    B. $6\frac{3}{4}$
    C. $15\frac{3}{4}$
    D. $31\frac{7}{8}$

11. Based on a favorable performance review at work, Matt receives a $\frac{3}{20}$ increase in his hourly wage. If his original hourly wage is represented by w, which of the following represents his new wage?

    A) $0.15w$
    B) $0.85w$
    C) $1.12w$
    D) $1.15w$

12. A restaurant employs servers, hosts, and managers in a ratio of 9:2:1. If there are 36 total employees, which of the following is the number of hosts at the restaurant?

    A) 3
    B) 4
    C) 6
    D) 8

13. Which statement about the following set is true?

    {60, 5, 18, 20, 37, 37, 11, 90, 72}

    A) The median and the mean are equal.
    B) The mean is less than the mode.
    C) The mode is greater than the median.
    D) The median is less than the mean.

14. A woman's dinner bill comes to $48.30. If she adds a 20% tip, which of the following will be her total bill?

A) $9.66

B) $38.64

C) $48.30

D) $57.96

0.2x
48.30
9.660 +
48.30
57.960

15. Which of the following lists is in order from least to greatest?

A) $\frac{1}{7}$, 0.125, $\frac{6}{9}$, 0.60

B) $\frac{1}{7}$, 0.125, 0.60, $\frac{6}{9}$

C) 0.125, $\frac{1}{7}$, 0.60, $\frac{6}{9}$

D) 0.125, $\frac{1}{7}$, $\frac{6}{9}$, 0.60

16. Which of the following is equivalent to 3.28?

A) $3\frac{1}{50}$

B) $3\frac{1}{25}$

C) $3\frac{7}{50}$

D) $3\frac{7}{25}$

151
50

17. $x \div 7 = x - 36$

$\frac{x}{7} = x - 36$
$\frac{x}{7} - x = -36$

Solve the equation. Which of the following is correct?

A) $x = 6$

B) $x = 42$

C) $x = 126$

D) $x = 252$

18. After taxes, a worker earned $15,036 in 7 months. Which of the following is the amount the worker earned in 2 months?

A) $2,148

B) $4,296

C) $6,444

D) $8,592

19. If m represents a car's average mileage in miles per gallon, p represents the price of gas in dollars per gallon, and d represents a distance in miles, which of the following algebraic equations represents the cost, c, of gas per mile?

A) $c = \frac{dp}{m}$

B) $c = \frac{p}{m}$

C) $c = \frac{mp}{d}$

D) $c = \frac{m}{p}$

20. Melissa is ordering fencing to enclose a square area of 5625 square feet. Which of the following is the number of feet of fencing she needs?

A) 75 feet

B) 150 feet

C) 300 feet

D) 5,625 feet

$\sqrt{5625} \times 4$

75 x
75
375
455
9 25

21. Adam is painting the outside of a 4-walled shed. The shed is 5 feet wide, 4 feet deep, and 7 feet high. Which of the following is the amount of paint Adam will need for the four walls?

A) 80 ft.²

B) 126 ft.²

C) 140 ft.²

D) 560 ft.²

5 x 4 x 7 = 140

22. A circular swimming pool has a circumference of 49 feet. Which of the following is the diameter of the pool?

A) 15.6 feet

B) 17.8 feet

C) 49 feet

D) 153.9 feet

23.

Employee Hours

EMPLOYEE	HOURS WORKED
Suzanne	42
Joe	38
Mark	25
Ellen	50
Jill	45
Rob	46
Nicole	17
Deb	41

The table above shows the number of hours worked by employees during the week. Which of the following is the median number of hours worked per week by the employees?

A) 38

B) 41

C) 42

D) 41.5

24. According to the graph, which of the following was Sam's average monthly income from January through May? (Round to the nearest hundred.)

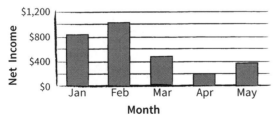

Sam's Net Income by Month

A) $200

B) $500

C) $600

D) $1,100

25. Which of the following is equivalent to 8 pounds and 8 ounces? (Round to the nearest tenth of a kilogram.)

A) 3.6 kilograms

B) 3.9 kilograms

C) 17.6 kilograms

D) 18.7 kilograms

26. $(4.71 \times 10^3) - (2.98 \times 10^2)$

Simplify the expression. Which of the following is correct?

A) 1.73×10

B) 4.412×10^2

C) 1.73×10^3

D) 4.412×10^3

27. Which of the following is not a negative value?

A) $(-3)(-1)(2)(-1)$ $3 \cdot 26 - 6$

B) $14 - 7 + (-7)$ 0

C) $7 - 10 + (-8)$ -

D) $-5(-2)(-3)$

28. $10^2 - 7(3 - 4) - 25$ $100 - 7(-1) - 25$
$= 100 - 7(-1) - 25$
$= 100 + 7 - 25 = 82$

Simplify the expression. Which of the following is correct?

A) -12

B) 2

C) 68

D) 82

29. $\dfrac{5^2(3) + 3(-2)^2}{4 + 3^2 - 2(5 - 8)}$ $= \dfrac{75 + 12}{4 + 9 + 6} = \dfrac{87}{19}$

Simplify the expression. Which of the following is correct?

A) $\dfrac{9}{8}$

B) $\dfrac{87}{19}$

C) 9

D) $\dfrac{21}{2}$

30. Anna is buying fruit at the farmers' market. She selects 1.2 kilograms of apples, 800 grams of bananas, and 300 grams of strawberries. The farmer charges her a flat rate of $4 per kilogram. Which of the following is the total cost of her produce?

A) $4.40 $1.2 +$
$.8$
$.3$
$2.3 \times$

B) $5.24 h

C) $9.20 9.2

D) $48.80

31. $\left(1\frac{1}{2}\right)\left(2\frac{2}{3}\right) \div 1\frac{1}{4}$

Simplify the expression. Which of the following is correct?

A) $3\frac{1}{12}$

B) $3\frac{1}{5}$

C) 4

D) 5

32. Which of the following lists is in order from least to greatest?

A) $2^{-1}, -\frac{4}{3}, (-1)^3, \frac{2}{5}$

B) $-\frac{4}{3}, (-1)^3, 2^{-1}, \frac{2}{5}$

C) $-\frac{4}{3}, \frac{2}{5}, 2^{-1}, (-1)^3$

D) $-\frac{4}{3}, (-1)^3, \frac{2}{5}, 2^{-1}$

33. Which of the following is 2.7834 rounded to the nearest tenth?

A) 2.7

B) 2.78

C) 2.8

D) 2.88

34. $\frac{4x-5}{3} = \frac{\frac{1}{2}(2x-6)}{5}$

Simplify the expression. Which of the following is the value of x?

A) $-\frac{2}{7}$

B) $-\frac{4}{17}$

C) $\frac{16}{17}$

D) $\frac{8}{7}$

35. $8x - 6 = 3x + 24$

Solve the equation. Which of the following is correct?

A) $x = 2.5$

B) $x = 3.6$

C) $x = 5$

D) $x = 6$

36. A student gets 42 questions out of 48 correct on a quiz. Which of the following is the percentage of questions that the student answered correctly?

A) 1.14%

B) 82.50%

C) 85.00%

D) 87.50%

Reading

Directions: Read the question, passage, or figure carefully, and choose the best answer.

The table below shows categories for systolic blood pressure.

Categories	Systolic Range
Normal	< 120
Prehypertension	120 - 139
Hypertension Stage 1	140 - 159
Hypertension Stage 2	160 - 179
Hypertensive Crisis	> 180

A patient's blood pressure reading is shown below.

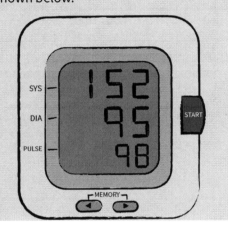

1. What category does the patient fall in?
   A) normal
   B) prehypertension
   C) hypertension stage 1
   D) hypertension stage 2

The social and political discourse of America continues to be permeated with idealism. An idealistic viewpoint asserts that the ideals of freedom, equality, justice, and human dignity are the truths that Americans must continue to aspire to. Idealists argue that truth is what should be, not necessarily what is. In general, they work to improve things and to make them as close to ideal as possible.

2. Which of the following best captures the author's purpose?
   A) to advocate for freedom, equality, justice, and human rights
   B) to explain what an idealist believes in
   C) to explain what's wrong with social and political discourse in America
   D) to persuade readers to believe in certain truths

The next four questions are based on this passage.

Skin coloration and markings have an important role to play in the world of snakes. Those intricate diamonds, stripes, and swirls help the animals hide from predators, but perhaps most importantly (for us humans, anyway), the markings can also indicate whether the snake is venomous. While it might seem counterintuitive for a venomous snake to stand out in bright red or blue, that fancy costume tells any nearby predator that approaching him would be a bad idea.

If you see a flashy-looking snake in the woods, though, those markings don't necessarily mean it's venomous: some snakes have found a way to ward off predators without the actual venom. The scarlet kingsnake, for example, has very similar markings to the venomous coral snake with whom it frequently shares a habitat. However, the kingsnake is actually nonvenomous; it's merely pretending to be dangerous to eat. A predatory hawk or eagle, usually hunting from high in the sky, can't tell the difference between the two species, and so the kingsnake gets passed over and lives another day.

3. What is the author's primary purpose in writing this essay?

   A) To explain how the markings on a snake are related to whether it's venomous.

   B) To teach readers the difference between coral snakes and kingsnakes.

   C) To illustrate why snakes are dangerous.

   D) To demonstrate how animals survive in difficult environments.

4. What can the reader conclude from the passage above?

   A) The kingsnake is dangerous to humans.

   B) The coral snake and the kingsnake are both hunted by the same predators.

   C) It's safe to handle snakes in the woods because you can easily tell whether they're poisonous.

   D) The kingsnake changes its markings when hawks or eagles are close by.

5. What is the best summary of this passage?

   A) Humans can use coloration and markings on snakes to determine whether they're venomous.

   B) Animals often use coloration to hide from predators.

   C) The scarlet kingsnake and the coral snake have nearly identical markings.

   D) Venomous snakes often have bright markings, although nonvenomous snakes can also mimic those colors.

6. Which of the following is the purpose of this passage?

   A) to inform

   B) to entertain

   C) to describe

   D) to persuade

The next two questions are based on this passage.

How to Plant Potatoes

Before Planting

Plant potatoes no later than 2 weeks after the last spring freeze.

Cut potatoes into pieces 1 to 2 days before planting.

Loosen soil using a tiller or hand trowel.

Mix fertilizer or compost into loosened soil.

Planting

Dig a 4-inch-deep trench and place potatoes 1 foot apart.

Cover potatoes loosely with soil.

After Planting

Water immediately after planting, and then regularly afterward to keep soil moist.

After 6 weeks, mound soil around the base of the plant to ensure roots stay covered.

7. Which of the following is the first step to take after planting potatoes?

   A) Mound soil around the base of the plant.

   B) Water immediately.

   C) Mix fertilizer or compost into loosened soil.

   D) Place potatoes 1 foot apart.

8. Which of the following should be done after the soil has been loosened with a tiller or trowel?

   A) Mix fertilizer or compost into loosened soil.

   B) Dig a 4-inch-deep trench.

   C) Cut potatoes into pieces.

   D) Mound soil around the base of the plant.

The next two questions are based on this email.

Alan —

   I just wanted to drop you a quick note to let you know I'll be out of the office for the next two weeks. Elizabeth and I are finally taking that trip to France we've been talking about for years. It's a bit of a last-minute decision, but since we had the vacation time available, we figured it was now or never.

   Anyway, my team's been briefed on the upcoming meeting, so they should be able to handle the presentation without any hiccups. If you have any questions or concerns, you can direct them to Joanie, who'll be handling my responsibilities while I'm out.

   Let me know if you want any special treats. I don't know if you can take chocolate and cheese on the plane, but I'm going to try!

   Best regards,

   Michael

9. Which of the following most likely describes the relationship between the author and Alan?

   A) competitive

   B) formal

   C) friendly

   D) caring

10. Which of the following best captures the author's purpose?

   A) to ask Alan if he wants any special treats from France

   B) to brag to Alan about his upcoming vacation

   C) to inform Alan that he will be out of the office

   D) to help Alan prepare for the upcoming meeting

The next three questions are based on this passage.

Carl's Car Depot is hosting its one-day-only summer sale event! All sedans, trucks, SUVs, and more are marked to move quickly. We're offering no money down and low (like, really low) monthly payments. You won't find prices like these anywhere else in the city (or the state, or anywhere else you look). No matter what you're looking for, we have the new and used cars you need. We only drop our prices this low once a year, so don't miss out on this great deal!

11. Which of the following best describes the author's purpose?

    A) The author wants to tell customers what kinds of cars are available at Carl's Car Depot.

    B) The author wants to encourage other car dealerships to lower their prices.

    C) The author wants to provide new and used cars at affordable prices.

    D) The author wants to attract customers to Carl's Car Depot.

12. Based on the context, which of the following is the meaning of the word *move* in the passage?

    A) drive

    B) sell

    C) advance forward

    D) change location

13. Which of the following is NOT mentioned by the author as a reason to visit Carl's Car Depot?

    A) They are offering lifetime warranties on new cars.

    B) The sale will only last one day.

    C) They have the lowest prices in town.

    D) They are offering no money down and low monthly payments.

14. Although Ben *said* he supported his coworkers, his actions suggested he did not condone their behavior.

Italics are used for which of the following reasons?

    A) to show a word is intentionally misspelled

    B) to indicate a word in a foreign language

    C) to emphasize a contrast

    D) to reference a footnote

The next two questions are based on this map.

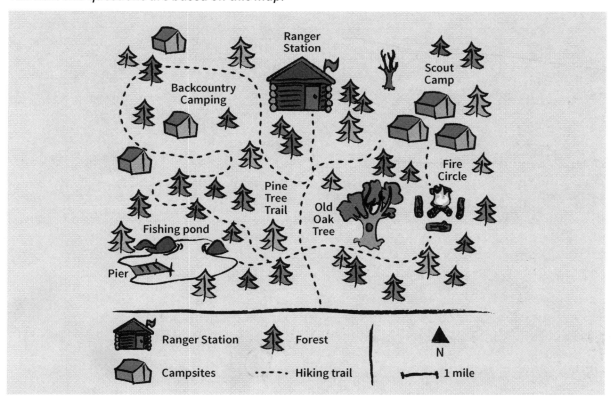

15. Which of the following is located due north of the Fire Circle?

    A) Old Oak Tree

    B) Scout Camp

    C) Fishing Pond

    D) Backcountry Camping

16. If a camper followed the trail from the Fishing Pond to the Scout Camp and passed by the Fire Circle, which of the following would she also have to pass by?

    A) Old Oak Tree

    B) Ranger Station

    C) Backcountry Camping

    D) Pier

17. Which of the following would be a primary source for an article on the Battle of Gettysburg?

    A) a letter written by a local farmer who witnessed the battle

    B) a documentary about the battle produced by a local TV station

    C) a novelization of the battle written by the great-grandson of a Union soldier

    D) a history textbook for a college-level course in American history

---

The next five questions are based on this passage.

It had been a long morning for Julia. She'd been woken up early by the sound of lawn mowers outside her window, and despite her best efforts, had been unable to get back to sleep. So, she'd reluctantly got out of bed, showered, and prepared her morning cup of coffee. At least, she tried to anyway. In the kitchen she'd discovered she was out of regular coffee and had to settle for a decaffeinated cup instead.

Once on the road, her caffeine-free mug of coffee didn't help make traffic less annoying. In fact, it seemed to Julia like the other drivers were sluggish and surly as well—it took her an extra fifteen minutes to get to work. And when she arrived, all the parking spots were full.

By the time she'd finally found a spot in the overflow lot, she was thirty minutes late for work. She'd hoped her boss would be too busy to notice, but he'd already put a pile of paperwork on her desk with a note that simply said "Rewrite." She wondered if she should point out to her boss that she hadn't been the one to write the reports in the first place, but decided against it.

When the fire alarm went off an hour later, Julia decided she'd had enough. She grabbed her purse and headed outside with her coworkers. While everyone else stood around waiting for the alarm to quiet, Julia determinedly walked to her car, fired up the engine, and set a course for home.

18. Which of the following is the most likely reason Julia did not return to work after the alarm?

    A) She was embarrassed that should could not finish the work her boss asked for.

    B) She was tired and wanted to go home.

    C) She got stuck in traffic and could not get back to her office.

    D) Her boss gave her the afternoon off.

19. Which of the following statements based on the passage should be considered an opinion?

    A) Julia's boss asked her to do work to help one of her coworkers.

    B) Julia was late to work because of traffic.

    C) It was irresponsible for Julia to leave work early.

    D) Julia was tired because she'd been woken up early.

20. Which of the following lists Julia's actions in the correct sequence?

A) Julia woke up early and found she didn't have any regular coffee. When she got to work, her boss had a lot for her to do. When the fire alarm went off, she decided to go home.

B) Julia got to work and decided she was too tired to do the work her boss asked for, so she went home to get a cup of coffee.

C) Julia woke up when the fire alarm went off and couldn't get back to sleep. She then got stuck in traffic and arrived at work thirty minutes late.

D) Julia was woken up early by a lawnmower and then got stuck in traffic on the way to her office. Once there, she found that the office was out of coffee and she had a lot of work to do. When the fire alarm went off, she decided to go home.

21. The final sentence of the passage states that Julia *set a course for home*. Which of the following is the most accurate interpretation of this sentence?

A) Julia cannot go directly home.

B) Julia is planning to drive home.

C) Julia wants to go home but will go back to work.

D) Julia is worried the fire at her office will spread to her home.

22. Which of the following conclusions is best supported by the passage?

A) Julia will find a job closer to her home.

B) Julia will lose her job.

C) Julia will feel guilty and return to work.

D) Julia will drive home and go to sleep.

Alexander Hamilton and James Madison called for the Constitutional Convention to write a constitution as the foundation of a stronger federal government. Madison and other Federalists like John Adams believed in separation of powers, republicanism, and a strong federal government. Despite the separation of powers that would be provided for in the US Constitution, anti-Federalists like Thomas Jefferson called for even more limitations on the power of the federal government.

23. In the context of the passage above, who would most likely NOT support a strong federal government?

A) Alexander Hamilton

B) James Madison

C) John Adams

D) Thomas Jefferson

Chapter 2: Amphibians of Texas

1. Frogs
   A) Tree Frogs
   B) _____
   C) True Frogs

2. Toads
   A) True Toads
   B) Narrowmouth Toads
   C) Burrowing Toads

3. Salamanders

24. Based on the pattern in the headings, which of the following is a reasonable heading to insert in the blank spot?

A) Gray Tree Frog

B) Tropical Frogs

C) Newts

D) Spadefoot Toads

25. Which of the following is an example of a secondary source that would be used in a documentary about World War I?

A) an essay by a historian about the lasting effects of the war

B) photographs of military equipment used in the war

C) a recorded interview with a veteran who fought for the US Army

D) letters written by soldiers to their families

> Victoria won easily and had plenty of time to rest before her next scheduled match.

26. Based on the context, which of the following is the meaning of the word *match* in the sentence?

A) a competitive event

B) a suitable pair

C) a slender piece of wood used to start a fire

D) a prospective marriage partner

The next two questions are based on this table.

Book Sales by Distributor

DISTRIBUTOR	COST STRUCTURE
Wholesale Books	$100 for the first 25 books; $80 for every 25 additional books
The Book Barn	$98 for every 25 books
Books and More	$3.99 per book
Quarter Price Books	$3.99 per book for the first 25 books; $2.99 for each additional book

27. A school wants to buy seventy-five textbooks. Based on the pricing chart, which of the following distributors would offer the cheapest price for the books?

A) Wholesale Books

B) The Book Barn

C) Books and More

D) Quarter Price Books

28. A teacher wants to buy an additional twenty-five books for her classroom. If she orders her books separately, which distributor would offer the cheapest price?

A) Wholesale Books

B) The Book Barn

C) Books and More

D) Quarter Price Books

The next two questions are based on this passage.

The study showed that private tutoring is providing a significant advantage to those students who are able to afford it. Researchers looked at the grades of students who had received free tutoring through the school versus those whose parents had paid for private tutors. The study included 2,500 students in three high schools across four grade levels. The study found that private tutoring corresponded with a rise in grade point average (GPA) of 0.5 compared to students who used the school's free tutor service and 0.7 compared to students who used no tutoring. After reviewing the study, the board is recommending that the school restructure its free tutor service to provide a more equitable education for all students.

29. Which of the following would weaken the author's argument?

- **A)** a report stating that the cited study was funded by a company that provides discounted tutoring through schools
- **B)** a study showing differences in standardized test scores among students at schools in different neighborhoods
- **C)** a statement signed by local teachers stating that they do not provide preferential treatment in the classroom or when grading
- **D)** a study showing that GPA does not strongly correlate with success in college

30. Which of the following types of arguments is used in the passage?

- **A)** emotional argument
- **B)** appeal to authority
- **C)** specific evidence
- **D)** rhetorical questioning

Start with the shapes shown below. Follow the directions.

| A | B | C | D | E | F |

1. Remove block C.
2. Remove block E.
3. Place block A immediately after block D.
4. Add block C after block A.

31. Which of the following shows the order in which the shapes now appear?

- **A)** | B | D | A | F |
- **B)** | B | D | A | E | F |
- **C)** | B | D | A | C | F |
- **D)** | B | D | F | A | C |

The next two questions are based on this passage.

After looking at five houses, Robert and I have decided to buy the one on Forest Road. The first two homes we visited didn't have the space we need—the first had only one bathroom, and the second did not have a guest bedroom. The third house, on Pine Street, had enough space inside but didn't have a big enough yard for our three dogs. The fourth house we looked at, on Rice Avenue, was stunning but well above our price range. The last home, on Forest Road, wasn't in the neighborhood we wanted to live in. However, it had the right amount of space for the right price.

32. Which of the following lists the author's actions in the correct sequence?

- **A)** The author looked at the house on Forest Road, then at a house with a yard that was too small, then at two houses that were too small, and then finally at a house that was too expensive.
- **B)** The author looked at the house on Forest Road, then at two houses that were too small, then at a house with a yard that was too small, and then finally at a house that was too expensive.
- **C)** The author looked at two homes with yards that were too small, then a house with only one bathroom, then a house that was too expensive, and then finally the house on Forest Road.
- **D)** The author looked at two homes that were too small, then a house with a yard that was too small, then a house that was too expensive, and then finally at the house on Forest Road.

33. What is the author's conclusion about the house on Pine Street?

   A) The house did not have enough bedrooms.

   B) The house did not have a big enough yard.

   C) The house was not in the right neighborhood.

   D) The house was too expensive.

34. A voter wants to find out the locations of polling places for an upcoming state election. Which of the following sources should the voter use?

   A) a website run by the state's board of elections

   B) an endorsement of a candidate from a local newspaper

   C) a blog run by a local radio personality

   D) a book on the history of elections

The next two questions are based on this passage.

Mr. Tim Morgan —

This letter is to inform Mr. Morgan that his application for the position of Lead Technician has been received by our Human Resources team. We have been pleased to receive a higher-than-expected number of applications for this position, and we are glad that Mr. Morgan is among the many who find our company an attractive place to build a career. Due to the influx of applications, our Human Resources team will be taking longer than previously stated to review candidates and schedule interviews. Please look for further communication from our Human Resources team in the next two to three weeks.

Regards,

Allison Wakefield

Head of Human Resources

35. Which of the following best describes the purpose of the passage?

   A) to let Mr. Morgan know that he will likely not receive an offer for the job of Lead Technician due to the high number of applicants

   B) to express to Mr. Morgan how pleased the Human Resources team was to receive his application

   C) to offer Mr. Morgan the position of Lead Technician

   D) to inform Mr. Morgan that the review of candidates will take longer than expected

36. Which of the following conclusions is well supported by the passage?

   A) The Human Resources team had previously informed Mr. Morgan that he would receive feedback on his application in less than two weeks.

   B) Mr. Morgan is well qualified for the position of Lead Technician and will be offered an interview.

   C) The Human Resources team will have trouble finding a qualified candidate for the position of Lead Technician.

   D) Mr. Morgan will respond to this communication by removing himself from consideration for the positon of Lead Technician.

The next three questions are based on this passage.

The greatest changes in sensory, motor, and perceptual development happen in the first two years of life. When babies are first born, most of their senses operate in a similar way to those of adults. For example, babies are able to hear before they are born; studies show that babies turn toward the sound of their mothers' voices just minutes after being born, indicating they recognize the mother's voice from their time in the womb.

The exception to this rule is vision. A baby's vision changes significantly in its first year of life; initially it has a range of vision of only 8 – 12 inches and no depth perception. As a result, infants rely primarily on hearing; vision does not become the dominant sense until around the age of 12 months. Babies also prefer faces to other objects. This preference, along with their limited vision range, means that their sight is initially focused on their caregiver.

37. Which of the following is a concise summary of the passage?

    A) Babies have no depth perception until 12 months, which is why they focus only on their caregivers' faces.

    B) Babies can recognize their mothers' voices when born, so they initially rely primarily on their sense of hearing.

    C) Babies have senses similar to those of adults except for their sense of sight, which doesn't fully develop until 12 months.

    D) Babies' senses go through many changes in the first year of their lives.

38. Which of the following senses do babies primarily rely on?

    A) vision

    B) hearing

    C) touch

    D) smell

39. Which of the following best describes the mode of the passage?

    A) expository

    B) narrative

    C) persuasive

    D) descriptive

The next two questions are based on this passage.

In Greek mythology, two gods, Epimetheus and Prometheus, were given the work of creating living things. Epimetheus gave good powers to the different animals. To the lion he gave strength; to the bird, swiftness; to the fox, sagacity; and so on. Eventually, all of the good gifts had been bestowed, and there was nothing left for humans. As a result, Prometheus returned to heaven and brought down fire, which he gave to humans. With fire, human beings could protect themselves by making weapons. Over time, humans developed civilization.

40. Which of the following is the meaning of the word *bestowed* as it is used in the passage?

    A) purchased

    B) forgotten

    C) accepted

    D) given

41. Which of the following provides the best summary of the passage?

A) Epimetheus was asked to assign all the good traits to the animals, which upset Prometheus. In retaliation, Prometheus brought fire to humans, which allowed them to reign over the other animals.

B) Epimetheus and Prometheus were both asked to create living things and assign traits to living creatures. Epimetheus gave all of the positive traits to the other animals and left nothing for humans, so Prometheus brought humans fire. This fire allowed human beings to thrive.

C) Epimetheus and Prometheus were given the job of assigning traits to the animals. They decided to give strength to lions, swiftness to birds, sagacity to the fox, and fire to humans. This fire has helped humans grow to be superior to other animals.

D) Prometheus decided that humans needed fire to protect themselves from the other animals. He brought fire down from heaven and taught humans how to make weapons, which allowed humans to hunt animals.

---

3. Balanced Nutrition
   A. Sources of Iron
      1) Animal-Based Sources
         a. Beef
         b. Pork
         c. _____
      2) Plant-Based Sources
         a. Leafy Greens
         b. Nuts and Seeds
   B. Sources of Calcium
   C. Sources of Omega-3 Fatty Acids

Spring: artichokes, broccoli, chives, collard greens, peas, spinach, watercress

Summer: beets, bell peppers, corn, eggplant, green beans, okra, tomatoes, zucchini

Fall: acorn squash, brussels sprouts, cauliflower, endive, ginger, sweet potatoes

Winter: Belgian endive, buttercup squash, kale, leeks, turnips, winter squash

42. Based on the pattern in the headings, which of the following is a reasonable subheading to insert in the blank spot?

A) Dairy

B) Lamb

C) Legumes

D) Vitamins

43. According to the guide, in which of the following seasons would ginger be harvested?

A) spring

B) summer

C) fall

D) winter

The next two questions are based on this passage.

The odds of success for any new restaurant are slim. Competition in the city is fierce, and the low margin of return means that aspiring restaurateurs must be exact and ruthless with their budget and pricing. The fact that The Hot Dog has lasted as long as it has is a testament to its owners' skills.

44. Which of the following conclusions is well supported by the passage?

A) The Hot Dog offers the best casual dining in town.

B) The Hot Dog has a well-managed budget and prices items on its menu appropriately.

C) The popularity of The Hot Dog will likely fall as new restaurants open in the city.

D) The Hot Dog has a larger margin of return than other restaurants in the city.

45. Which of the following is the meaning of *testament* as used in the sentence?

A) story

B) surprise

C) artifact

D) evidence

The next two questions are based on this excerpt.

46. A student wants to find information on the Italian painter Sandro Botticelli. On which of the following pages will the student most likely find this information?

A) 55

B) 71

C) 95

D) 114

47. A student wants to find information on a church built in 1518. On which of the following pages should the student begin to look for this information?

A) 59

B) 105

C) 153

D) 179

The next two questions are based on this passage.

As you can see from the graph, my babysitting business has been really successful. The year started with a busy couple of months—several snows combined with a large number of requests for Valentine's Day services boosted our sales quite a bit. The spring months have admittedly been a bit slow, but we're hoping for a big summer once school gets out. Several clients have already put in requests for our services!

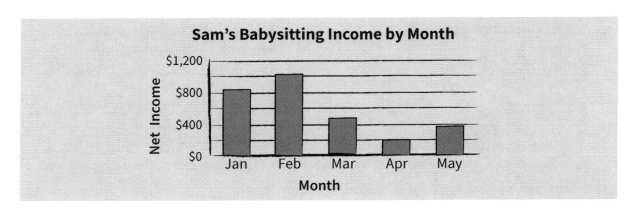

Sam's Babysitting Income by Month

48. Based on the information in the graph, how much more did Sam's Babysitting Service bring in during February than during April?

   A) $200
   B) $900
   C) $1100
   D) $1300

49. Which of the following best describes the tone of the passage?

   A) professional
   B) casual
   C) concerned
   D) neutral

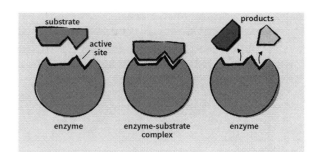

50. The diagram represents the lock-and-key model of enzymes. According to the figure, the products are formed from which of the following?

   A) the enzyme
   B) the enzyme-substrate complex
   C) the substrate
   D) the active site

51. Which of the following sentences indicates the end of a sequence?

   A) Our ultimate objective was to find a quality coat at an affordable price.
   B) We chose this particular restaurant because of its outdoor seating.
   C) Finally, we were able to settle in to enjoy the movie.
   D) Initially, it seemed unlikely that we'd be able to keep the puppy.

Battle of Sidi Barrani	115 – 6
Battle of Someri	203 – 205
Battle of Stalingrad	306 – 310
Battle of Studzianki	311 – 312
Battle of the Scheldt	110 – 2, 207

52. A student wants to find information on the Battle of the Scheldt. According to the index for a history textbook, where should the student look?

   A) 110
   B) 115
   C) 203
   D) 307

53. Which of the following sentences indicates the end of a sequence?

   A) Unfortunately, the stock did not perform as well as we had hoped.
   B) The next day, we were able to find a band we liked that also fit our budget.
   C) Overall, my friends and I found the experience rewarding.
   D) Before we go to the restaurant,

let's look at the menu.

Science

Directions: Read the question carefully, and choose the best answer.

1. Which of the following describes the primary function of the respiratory system?

   A) to create sound and speech

   B) to take oxygen into the body while removing carbon dioxide

   C) to transport nutrients to the cells and tissue of the body

   D) to act as a barrier between the body's organs and outside influences

2. Which of the following is the first step of the scientific method?

   A) construct a hypothesis

   B) make observations

   C) analyze data

   D) form a question

3. The process of organisms with an advantageous trait surviving more often and producing more offspring than organisms without the advantageous trait describes which of the following basic mechanisms of evolution?

   A) gene flow

   B) genetic drift

   C) mutation

   D) natural selection

4. Oxygen is exchanged between blood and tissues at which of the following areas?

   A) capillaries

   B) veins

   C) ventricles

   D) arteries

5. Which of the following containins a single immature egg cell that is released during ovulation?

   A) oocytes   *is the egg*

   B) follicles   *contain a sac w/ 1 egg*

   C) ovaries

   D) fallopian tubes

6. Which of the following describes the muscular organ that processes food material into increasingly smaller pieces, mixes it with saliva to create a bolus, and creates a barrier to transport food into the esophagus?

   A) pharynx

   B) tongue

   C) diaphragm

   D) stomach

7. Which of the following chambers of the heart receives blood returning from the lungs during pulmonary circulation?

   A) left atrium

   B) right atrium

   C) left ventricle

   D) right ventricle

8. Which of the following is the lobe in the cerebral cortex primarily responsible for processing and integrating sensory information received from the rest of the body?

   A) frontal lobe

   B) occipital lobe

   C) parietal lobe   *primary sensory processing*

   D) temporal lobe

9. Which of the following is an example of adaptive immunity?

    A) inflammation

    B) fever

    C) antibodies

    D) phagocytosis

10. Which of the following describes a situation in which research results are consistent with every subsequent experiment, but the test used in the experiment does not measure what it claims to measure?

    A) reliable, but not valid

    B) valid, but not reliable

    C) neither reliable nor valid

    D) both reliable and valid

11. Which of the following Mendellian laws describes how pairs of alleles within genes separate and recombine separately from other genes?

    A) law of segregation

    B) law of dominance

    C) law of independent assortment

    D) law of predictive traits

12. Which of the following describes how atomic radius varies across the periodic table?

    A) Atomic radius increases from top to bottom and left to right on the periodic table.

    B) Atomic radius increases from top to bottom and right to left on the periodic table.

    C) Atomic radius increases from top to bottom and toward the halogens on the periodic table.

    D) Atomic radius increases from top to bottom and toward the noble gases on the periodic table.

13. Which of the following is NOT a tissue layer found in skeletal bone?

    A) periosteum

    B) bone marrow

    C) enamel

    D) cancellous bone

14. Which of the following sets of valves is primarily responsible for preventing blood flow from major blood vessels to the heart?

    A) atrioventricular valves

    B) semilunar valves

    C) tricuspid valves

    D) bicuspid valves

15. Which of the following is the connective area where nerve impulses send neurotransmitters across a synapse to a muscle cell to stimulate muscle contraction?

    A) sarcomere

    B) tendon

    C) myelin sheath

    D) neuromuscular junction

16. Bone is composed primarily of which of the following inorganic materials?

    A) calcium

    B) magnesium

    C) collagen

    D) potassium

17. Which of the following is the region of the brain that controls and regulates autonomic functions such as respiration, digestion, and heart rate?

    A) cerebellum

    B) medulla oblongata

    C) temporal lobe

    D) cerebral cortex

18. Which of the following is the primary physical barrier the body uses to prevent infection?

    A) mucus membranes

    B) stomach acid

    C) skin

    D) urine

19. Which of the following describes the primary function of the pyloric sphincter?

    A) to regulate the movement of food material from the stomach to the duodenum

    B) to neutralize stomach acid

    C) to prevent digested food materials and stomach acid from entering the esophagus

    D) to begin the process of chemical digestion

20. Which of the following is the location of fertilization in the female?

    A) uterus

    B) fallopian tube

    C) endometrium

    D) ovary

21. The pineal gland is located in which of the following areas in the body?

    A) below the larynx

    B) above the kidney

    C) at the center of the brain hemispheres

    D) at the base of the brain

22. How many neutrons are in an atom of the element $_{38}^{88}$Sr?

    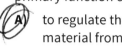 *Element mass. nr.*

    A) 38

    B) 88

    C) 50

    D) 126

23. Which of the following biological macromolecules is non-soluble, composed of hydrocarbons, and acts as an important source of energy storage for the body?

    A) carbohydrates

    B) nucleic acids

    C) lipids

    D) proteins

24. Which of the following is specialized tissue in the right atrium that acts as the heart's natural pacemaker by generating the electrical signal for the heartbeat?

    A) sinus venosus

    B) sinoatrial node

    C) atrioventricular node

    D) tricuspid valve

25. Which of the following is a dense, interconnected mass of nerve cells located outside of the central nervous system?

    A) ganglion

    B) dendrite

    C) cranial nerve

    D) pons

26. Which of the following is a true statement about dominance in genetics?

    A) All genes follow Mendel's law of dominance.

    B) A dominant allele will always be expressed.

    C) When two dominant alleles are present, the resulting phenotype will express both traits.

    D) There are three or more alleles possible for all genes.

27. Two mice are both heterozygous for two traits: white fur (Ww) and short fur (Ss). Their offspring are most likely to have which of the following genotypes for these traits?

A) wwss

B) WWSS

C) WwSs

D) WWSs

28. Which of the following describes the general function of cytokines in the immune system?

A) They communicate between cells to instigate an immune response.

B) They inhibit blood clotting during inflammation responses.

C) They bind to specific pathogens to increase pathogen mass.

D) They transport pathogens trapped in mucus to be destroyed in the stomach.

29. Which of the following describes the path through which air moves during inhalation?

A) mouth/nose > pharynx > larynx > trachea > bronchi > bronchioles > alveoli

B) bronchioles > alveoli > bronchi > larynx > pharynx > lungs

C) mouth/nose > bronchi > bronchioles > alveoli > lungs > trachea

D) alveoli > bronchioles > lungs > bronchi > trachea > larynx > pharynx > mouth/nose

30. Which of the following cell organelles are the site of lipid synthesis?

A) smooth endoplasmic reticulum

B) ribosome

C) rough endoplasmic reticulum

D) Golgi apparatus

31. Which of the following is NOT a function of progesterone in the female reproductive system?

A) expression of secondary sexual characteristics, such as enlarged breasts

B) stimulation of milk production in the breasts

C) regulation and preparation of the endometrial lining of the uterus for potential pregnancy

D) inhibition of contractions of the uterus as the ovum is released

32. Which of the following layers of skin acts as an energy reserve by storing adipocytes and releasing them into circulation when energy is needed?

A) epidermis

B) dermis

C) hypodermis

D) stratum basale

33. Neurotransmitters send chemical messages across the gap between one neuron and another through which of the following structures?

A) Schwann cell

B) ganglion

C) synapse

D) axon

34. Muscle tissues will often require quick bursts of energy. As a result, which of the following organelles would be most likely to be found in higher than normal amounts in muscle cells?

A) ribosomes

B) chloroplasts

C) vacuoles

D) mitochondria

The next three questions are based on the following passage.

A scientist designs an experiment to test the hypothesis that exposure to more sunlight will increase the growth rate of elodea, a type of aquatic plant. The scientist has accumulated data from previous experiments that identify the average growth rate of elodea exposed to natural sunlight in the wild.

In the experiment set up, there are three tanks housing ten elodea each. Tank A is positioned in front of a window to receive natural sunlight similar to what elodea are exposed to; tank B is positioned in front of the same window but has an additional sunlight-replicating lamp affixed to it; and tank C is positioned in a dark corner with no exposure to natural sunlight.

35. When setting up the above experiment, the scientist has the option of using a separate water filter for each of the three tanks or using a single filtration system that attaches all three and affects them simultaneously. Which of the following filter set ups makes a more valid experiment and why?

   A) separate filters for each of the three tanks, because this ensures a higher quality of water for each tank

   B) one filtration system for all three tanks, because this makes filtration a controlled variable

   C) one filtration system for all three tanks, because this reduces the workload for the researcher

   D) separate filters for each of the three tanks, because this adds another variable to be tested and analyzed for inclusion in the experiment's results

36. The above experimental design description is an example of which of the following types of experiments?

   A) field experiment
   B) natural experiment
   C) controlled experiment
   D) observational study

37. Which of the following is the control group in the above experiment?

   A) tank A
   B) tank B
   C) tank C
   D) There is no control group in this experiment.

38. Which of the following is a type of white blood cell that plays a key role in adaptive immunity by seeking out, attacking, and destroying targeted pathogens?

   A) memory B cells
   B) neutrophils
   C) antibodies
   D) cytotoxic T cells

39. Which of the following are the blood vessels that transport blood to the heart?

   A) arteries
   B) capillaries
   C) venules
   D) veins

40. Which of the following is the primary function of the large intestine?

   A) absorbing digested material into the blood
   B) nutrient processing and metabolizing
   C) absorbing water and compacting material into solid waste
   D) bile production and storage

41. Water is capable of dissolving many substances that organisms need to carry on life functions. Which of the properties of water listed below is responsible for its ability to dissolve important nutrients like ionic salt compounds?

A) adhesion

B) cohesion

C) high specific heat

D) high polarity

42. Chromatids divide into identical chromosomes and migrate to opposite ends of the cell in which of the following phases of mitosis?

A) metaphase

B) anaphase

C) prophase

D) telophase

43. A series of muscle contractions that transports food down the digestive tract in a wave-like fashion describes which of the following?

A) digestion

B) deglutition

C) defecation

D) peristalsis

44. Which of the following is NOT a function of the liver?

A) nutrient processing

B) blood filtration and detoxification

C) cholesterol and lipoprotein production

D) insulin production and blood sugar regulation

45. $2C_6H_{14} + 19O_2 \rightarrow 12CO_2 + 14H_2O$

The reaction above is an example of which of the following?

A) substitution reaction

B) acid-base reaction

C) enzyme reaction

D) combustion reaction

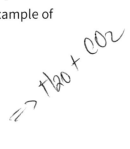

46. Which of the following are regions of the digestive system in which amylase is produced?

A) pancreas and salivary glands

B) gall bladder and salivary glands

C) gall bladder and liver

D) pancreas and liver

47. Which of the following describes a cell's reaction to being placed in a hypertonic solution?

A) The cell will shrink as water is pulled out of the cell to equalize the concentrations inside and outside of the cell.

B) The cell will swell as water is pulled into the cell to equalize the concentrations inside and outside of the cell.

C) The cell will remain the same size since the concentrations inside and outside the cell are equal to begin with.

D) The pH inside the cell will drop in order to equalize the pH inside and outside the cell.

48. Which of the following are the two major zones of the respiratory system?

A) left bronchus and right bronchus

B) nose and mouth

C) larynx and pharynx

D) conducting and respiratory

49. Which of the following choices would contain the code for making a protein?

A) mRNA

B) tRNA

C) rRNA

D) DNA polymerase

50. Which of the following distinguishes the isotopes of an element?

A) Isotopes are atoms of the same element that have different ionic charges.

B) Isotopes are atoms of elements within the same group on the periodic table.

C) Isotopes are atoms of the same element that have different numbers of neutrons.

D) Isotopes are atoms of the same element with different electron configurations.

51. Which of the following is the cartilaginous flap that protects the larynx from water or food while still allowing the flow of air?

A) epiglottis

B) bronchioles

C) epithelium

D) tongue

52. Which of the following describes the function of the fascia in muscle tissue?

A) to enclose, protect, support, and separate muscle tissue

B) to connect muscle tissue to bone

C) to serve as the contractile unit of muscle

D) to slide past the actin protein cells in muscle to create contraction

53. Which of the following correctly describes a strong acid?

A) A strong acid completely ionizes in water.

B) A strong acid donates more than one proton.

C) A strong acid contains at least one metal atom.

D) A strong acid will not decompose.

English and Language Usage

Directions: Read the question carefully, and choose the best answer.

1. Which of the following sentences follows the rules of capitalization?

   A) As juveniles, african white-backed vultures are darkly colored, developing their white feathers only as they grow into adulthood.

   B) Ukrainians celebrate a holiday called *Malanka* during which men dress in costumes and masks and play tricks on their neighbors.

   C) Because of its distance from the sun, the planet neptune has seasons that last the equivalent of forty-one earth years.

   D) Edward Jenner, considered the Father of immunology, invented the world's first vaccine.

> First and foremost, they receive an <u>annual pension payment. The amount of the pension</u> has been reviewed and changed a number of times, most recently to reflect the salary of a high-level government executive.

2. Which of the following would NOT be an acceptable way to revise and combine the underlined portion of the sentences above?

   A) annual pension payment, the amount of which

   B) annual pension payment; the amount of the pension

   C) annual pension payment; over the years since 1958, the amount of the pension

   D) annual pension payment, the amount of the pension

3. Which of the following sentences has the correct subject-verb agreement?

   A) The Akhal-Teke horse breed, originally from Turkmenistan, have long enjoyed a reputation for bravery and fortitude.

   B) The employer decided that he could not, due to the high cost of health care, afford to offer other benefits to his employees.

   C) Though Puerto Rico is known popularly for its beaches, its landscape also include mountains, which play home to many of the island's rural villages.

   D) Each of the storm chasers decide whether or not to go out when rain makes visibility low.

4. Which of the following is a compound sentence?

   A) Plague, generally not a major public health concern, actually continues to spread among rodent populations today, and it even occasionally makes its way into a human host.

   B) Modern archeology, which seeks answers to humanity's questions about its past, is helped significantly by new technologies.

   C) In the fight against obesity, countries around the world are imposing taxes on sodas and other sugary drinks in an effort to curb unhealthy habits.

   D) Because the assassination of President John F. Kennedy continues to haunt and fascinate Americans, new movies, books, and television series about it are being released every year.

[handwritten note: Compound sentence = 2 independent clauses, separated by comma and (and, or, ...)]

5. Which of the following would most likely be found in an academic research paper on the world's food supply?

   A) It's ridiculous that so many people in the world are hungry while others just throw away tons of uneaten food.

   B) I've always believed that it's our moral duty as a people to provide food and clean water to those who do not have access to it, which is why I have made research of the food supply my life's work.

   C) Advances in agricultural technology over the past five decades have led to a steady increase in the global food supply, and the populations of many countries around the world are benefitting.

   D) Poor people should appeal to their governments for help feeding their families.

Sandra's principal reason for choosing the job was that it would be full-time and would offer benefits.

6. Which of the following is the complete subject in the sentence?

   A) Sandra's principal reason for choosing the job

   B) Sandra's principal reason

   C) Sandra's principal

   D) Sandra

7. After a twelve-hour workday _____ James was exhausted when he heard the news.

   A) .

   B) ;

   C) ,

   D) —

Parrots, among the most intelligent birds in the world, have been prized pets for many centuries; in fact, the first recorded instance of parrot training was written in the thirteenth century.

8. Which of the following is a synonym for *prized* as used in the sentence?

   A) unlikely

   B) misunderstood

   C) rewarded

   D) valued

9. Which of the following prefixes would be used to indicate that something is *inside* or *within*?

   A) intra–

   B) trans–

   C) anti–

   D) hyper–

10. Which of the following is correctly punctuated?

   A) The artist Prince, whose death shocked America in April of 2016; was one of the most successful musical artists of the last century.

   B) The artist Prince, whose death shocked America in April of 2016, was one of the most successful musical artists of the last century.

   C) The artist Prince—whose death shocked America in April of 2016, was one of the most successful musical artists of the last century.

   D) The artist Prince, whose death shocked America in April of 2016: was one of the most successful musical artists of the last century.

> Everyday items like potatos, bread, onions, and even saliva are the tools of art conservators, who work to clean and restore works of art.

11. Which of the following is misspelled in the sentence below?

    (A)) potatos *potatoes*
    B) saliva
    C) conservators
    D) restore

> The American Academy of Arts and Sciences includes members whose topics of study span many disciplines such as math, science, arts, humanities, public affairs, and business.

12. Which of the following is an appropriate synonym for *disciplines* as it is used in the sentence?

    A) locations
    B) regions
    C) punishments
    (D)) fields

> Today, astrophysicists study the same stars that were observed by the astronemers of the ancient world, though today's techniques and technology are much more advanced.

13. Which of the following is misspelled in the sentence?

    A) astrophysicists *astrophysicists*
    B) astronemers *astronomers*
    C) techniques *techniques*
    D) technology *technology*

14. Which of the following nouns is written in the correct plural form?

    A) vertebraes
    B) gooses
    C) octopusses
    (D)) potatoes

Complex sentence = independent clause + depending sentence (+ because)

15. Which of the following is a complex sentence?

    A) When skywriting, a pilot flies a small aircraft in specific, particular formations, creating large letters visible from the ground.
    B) The public defense attorney was able to maintain her optimism despite her dearth of courtroom wins, her lack of free time, and her growing list of clients.
    (C)) Because the distance between stars in the galaxy is far greater than the distance between planets, interstellar travel is expected to be an even bigger challenge than interplanetary exploration.
    D) Invented in France in the early nineteenth century, the stethoscope underwent a number of reiterations before the emergence of the modern form of the instrument in the 1850s.

16. Which of the following sentences is irrelevant as part of a paragraph composed of these sentences?

    (A)) Traffic around the arena was heavy, so we were worried we'd miss the opening pitch.
    B) My brother and I won tickets in a radio station contest to see his favorite team play on opening day.
    (C)) To win the contest, you had to be the 395th caller and know the answer to a trivia question; we waited anxiously by the phone for the contest to begin.
    D) My brother has followed the team since childhood, so we knew he'd be able to answer the trivia question correctly.

I. Types of Engines
    A. Heat Engines
        i. Combustion Engines *H₂0 + CO₂*
        ii. Non-Combustion Heat Engines
    B. Electric Engines
    C. Physically Powered Motors
        i. Pneumatic Motors
        ii Hydraulic Motors

17. Which of the following statements about the outline is true?

A) Heat engines are the most common type of engine.

B) Pneumatic and hydraulic motors are both types of electric engines.

C) The three types of engines are heat engines, electric engines, and pneumatic motors.

D) Heat engines can be broken down into combustion and non-combustion engines.

The patient's preoperative evaluation is scheduled for next Wednesday.

18. In the sentence, the prefix *pre–* indicates that the evaluation will take place at which of the following times?

A) before the operation

B) after the operation

C) during the operation

D) outside of the operation

19. Which of the following root words would be used in a word related to the body?

A) corp

B) auto

C) man

D) bio

Unlike a traditional comic book, a graphic novel is released as one single publication, either in the form of one long story or an anthology.

20. Which of the following is an appropriate synonym for *traditional* as it is used in the sentence?

A) old-fashioned

B) conventional

C) expensive

D) popular

Her new tennis racket cost her a hundred bucks, but it was worth the steep price tag.

21. Which of the following words from the sentence is slang?

A) cost

B) bucks

C) steep

D) tag

Though professional dental care is widely available in the developed world, the prevalence of cavities is much higher there.

22. Which of the following parts of speech is *widely* as used in the sentence?

A) adjective

B) noun

C) adverb

D) verb

Typically, water that has evaporated remains in the sky in cloud form for less than ten days before falling to Earth again as precipitation.

23. Which of the following parts of speech is *remains* as used in the sentence?

A) noun

B) verb

C) adjective

D) adverb

> Though the term *nomad* is often associated with early populations, nomadic cultures exist today, especially in the mountain's of Europe and Asia.

24. Which of the following punctuation marks is used incorrectly?

    A) the comma after *populations*

    B) the comma after *today*

    C) the apostrophe in *mountain's*

    D) the period after *Asia*

> On Parents' Day, a public holiday in the Democratic Republic of Congo, families celebrate parents' both living and deceased.

25. Which of the following punctuation marks is used incorrectly?

    A) the apostrophe in *Parents' Day*

    B) the comma following *Day*

    C) the comma following *Congo*

    D) the apostrophe in *parents'*

> Unfortunately, the belief that change-lings could be convinced to leave was not just <u>an innocuous superstition. On some occasions,</u> harm came to the individual who was thought to be a changeling.

26. Which is the best way to revise and combine the underlined portion of the sentences?

    A) an innocuous superstition, on some occasions,

    B) an innocuous superstition, but on some occasions,

    C) an innocuous superstition; however, on some occasions,

    D) an innocuous superstition: on some occasions,

27. Which of the following phrases follows the rules of capitalization?

    A) President Carter and his advisors

    B) Robert Jones, the senior Senator from California

    C) my Aunt and Uncle who live out west

    D) the party on New Year's eve

28. Which of the following sentences has correct pronoun-antecedent agreement?

    A) The storm, which included three days of rain, was very strong, and they left half the city flooded.

    B) Each of the cars needs to be examined for damage by a mechanic; he may need repairs.

    C) The number of people who had to evacuate hasn't been confirmed, but it is small.

    D) Many people were able to take advantage of shelters, where he or she was kept safe from the storm.

ANSWER KEY

Mathematics

1. **C)**

    First calculate 20% of the list price:

    0.20 × $26,580 = $5,316

    Next calculate the savings over the first 3 months of payments:

    3 months × $250/month = $750

    Find the total savings:

    $5,316 + $750 = **$6,066**

2. **C)**

    First find the total cost before tax:

    5 shirts × $3/shirt + 4 pants × $6/pants + 2 items mended × $5/item mended = $49

    Now multiply this amount by 1.08 to account for the added 8% sales tax:

    $49 × 1.08 = **$52.92**

3. **A)**

    Let s be the number of sandwiches sold. Each sandwich earns $4, so selling s sandwiches at $4 each results in revenue of $4s$. Similarly, d drinks at $2 each gives $2d$ of income and cookies bring in $1c$. Summing these values gives a total of revenue = **4s + 2d + 1c**.

4. **C)**

    The y-intercept will have an x value of 0. This eliminates choices A), B) and D).

    Plug $x = 0$ into the equation and solve for y to find the y-intercept:

    $7y - 42(0) + 7 = 0$, so $7y = -7$ and therefore $y = -1$. The correct answer is **(0, −1)**.

5. **C)**

    First complete the operations in parentheses: $4 - \frac{1}{2^2} + 24 \div (8 + 12) = 4 - \frac{1}{2^2} + 24 \div (20)$

    Next simplify the exponents: $4 - \frac{1}{2^2} + 24 \div (20) = 4 - \frac{1}{4} + 24 \div (20)$

    Then complete multiplication and division operations: $4 - \frac{1}{4} + 24 \div (20) = 4 - 0.25 + 1.2$

    Finally complete addition and subtraction operations:

    $4 - 0.25 + 1.2 = $ **4.95**

6. **A)**

    The area of a rectangle is *length × width*, so $A = 3w(w)$. The area was given, so $1452 = 3w^2$

    Solving for w: $484 = w^2$ and $L = \pm 22$.

    Since width must be positive, $w = $ **22 feet**.

7. **A)**

    Calculate the decline:

    40% decline in 70% of the business = $0.40 \times 0.70 = 0.28 = 28\%$ decline

Calculate the growth:

60% growth in 25% of the business =
0.60 × 0.25 = 0.15 = 15% growth

Find the net change:

28% decline + 15% growth = −0.28 + 0.15
= −0.13 = **13% decline**

8. **D)**

The first step is to multiply (resulting in 17.92); then divide the result by 0.4, making **44.80** the solution.

9. **B)**

First convert the dimensions to meters:

$15 \text{ ft.} \times \frac{1 \text{ m}}{3.28 \text{ ft.}} = 4.57 \text{ m}$

$9 \text{ ft.} \times \frac{1 \text{ m}}{3.28 \text{ ft.}} = 2.74 \text{ m}$

$12.5 \text{ ft.} \times \frac{1 \text{ m}}{3.28 \text{ ft.}} = 3.81 \text{ m}$

Next find the total area in square meters:

total area = 2(4.57 m × 2.74 m) + 2(3.81 m × 2.74 m) = 45.9 m²

Finally convert the area to gallons of paint:

$45.9 \text{ m}^2 \times \frac{1 \text{ gallon}}{32 \text{ m}^2} = \textbf{1.43 gallons}$

10. **D)**

First convert mixed fractions to improper fractions:

$5\frac{2}{3} \times 1\frac{7}{8} \div \frac{1}{3} = \frac{17}{3} \times \frac{15}{8} \div \frac{1}{3}$

Next flip the divisor fraction and multiply:

$\frac{17}{3} \times \frac{15}{8} \div \frac{1}{3} = \frac{17}{3} \times \frac{15}{8} \times \frac{3}{1} =$
$\frac{17 \times 15 \times 3}{3 \times 8 \times 1} = \frac{765}{24}$

Now divide the numerator by the denominator to convert back to a mixed fraction:

$\frac{765}{24} = 31\frac{21}{24}$

Finally find the greatest common factor to reduce the fraction:

$31\frac{21}{24} = 31\frac{21 \div 3}{24 \div 3} = \textbf{31}\frac{\textbf{7}}{\textbf{8}}$

11. **D)**

A $\frac{3}{20}$ increase means the new wage is
$w + w\left(\frac{3}{20}\right)$, or $w\left(1 + \frac{3}{20}\right)$.

Convert the fraction to decimal form:

$\frac{3}{20} = \frac{3}{20}\left(\frac{5}{5}\right) = \frac{15}{100} = 0.15$

The new wage is:

$w(1 + 0.15) = \textbf{1.15w}$

12. **C)**

In algebraic terms, the ratio can be expressed with the following equation:

$9x + 2x + 1x = 36$

Here, x represents some common factor by which each number of employees was divided to reduce the ratio. Solve for x, then find $2x$ to solve for the number of hosts:

$9x + 2x + 1x = 36$

$12x = 36$

$x = 3$

$2x = 2 \times 3 = \textbf{6}$

13. **D)**

{5, 11, 18, 20, **37**, 37, 60, 72, 90}

median = 37

mode = 37

mean = $\frac{60 + 5 + 18 + 20 + 37 + 37 + 11 + 90 + 72}{9}$

= 38.89

The median is less than the mean.

14. **D)**

Adding 20% is equivalent to paying 120% of the bill:

$\$48.30 \times \frac{120}{100} = \textbf{\$57.96}$

15. **C)**

Convert the fractions to decimals:

$\frac{6}{9} \approx 0.67$

$\frac{1}{7} \approx 0.14$

Now order the numbers from smallest to largest:

0.125 < 0.14 < 0.60 < 0.67

Write the decimals as fractions to find the correct answer:

0.125, $\frac{1}{7}$, 0.60, $\frac{6}{9}$

16. **D)**

Because the last decimal digit is in the hundredths place, the decimal part of the number is written as a fraction over 100. The fraction of $\frac{28}{100}$ reduces to $\frac{7}{25}$.

17. **B)**

Start by multiplying both sides by 7:

$7(x \div 7) = 7(x - 36)$

$x = 7x - 252$

Now subtract $7x$ from both sides:

$x - 7x = 7x - 252 - 7x$

$-6x = -252$

Finally divide both sides by −6:

$\frac{-6x}{-6} = \frac{-252}{-6}$

$x = \mathbf{42}$

18. **B)**

A proportion is written using two ratios relating amount earned to months, with x representing the unknown amount:

$\frac{15,036}{7} = \frac{x}{2}$.

The proportion is solved by cross-multiplying and dividing: $7x = 30,072$, $x = 4,296$. The solution is **$4,296**.

19. **B)**

The cost c of gas has units dollars per mile. Construct an expression that yields these units:

$\frac{p}{m} = \frac{\left(\frac{\$}{\text{gal.}}\right)}{\left(\frac{\text{mi.}}{\text{gal.}}\right)} = \frac{(\$)(\text{gal.})}{(\text{mi.})(\text{gal.})} = \mathbf{\frac{\$}{\text{mi.}}}$

20. **C)**

Use the area to find the length of one side of the square:

$A = s^2$

$5,625 \text{ ft.}^2 = s^2$

$s = \sqrt{5,625 \text{ ft.}^2} = 75 \text{ ft.}$

Now multiply the side length by 4 to find the perimeter:

$P = 4s$

$P = 4(75 \text{ ft.}) = \mathbf{300 \text{ ft.}}$

21. **B)**

Find the area of all of the sides of the shed. Two walls measure 5 feet by 7 feet; the other two walls measure 4 feet by 7 feet:

$A = 2l_1 w_1 + 2l_2 w_2$

$A = 2(5 \text{ ft.})(7 \text{ ft.}) + 2(4 \text{ ft.})(7 \text{ ft.})$

$A = 70 \text{ ft.}^2 + 56 \text{ ft.}^2 = \mathbf{126 \text{ ft.}^2}$

22. **A)**

The formula for the circumference of a circle is:

$C = 2\pi r$

Because $d = 2r$, this formula can be rewritten:

$C = \pi d$

$49 \text{ ft.} = \pi d$

$d = \frac{49 \text{ ft.}}{\pi} = \mathbf{15.6 \text{ ft.}}$

23. **D)**

To find the median, first order the data points from smallest to largest:

17, 25, 38, 41, 42, 45, 46, 50

There is an even number of data points. Locate the middle two points and take the average:

17, 25, 38, 41, 42, 45, 46, 50

$(41 + 42) \div 2 = \mathbf{41.5}$

24. **C)**

Find Sam's income for each month:

January: $900

February: $1100

March: $500

April: $200

May: $400   Now find the average by adding those values and dividing by 5. Then round to the nearest 100:

$\frac{900 + 1100 + 500 + 200 + 400}{5} = 620 \approx \mathbf{600}$

25. **B)**

Since there are 16 ounces in a pound, 8 ounces = 0.5 pounds. The conversion factor for pounds to kilograms is therefore multiplied by 8.5 pounds. The calculation is:

$8.5 \text{ lb.} \left(\frac{1 \text{ kg}}{2.2 \text{ lb.}}\right) = \frac{8.5}{2.2} = \mathbf{3.9 \text{ kg.}}$

Notice that the 1 is on top in this conversion factor so that pounds cancel. The unit that the quantity is being converted to must always be in the numerator.

26. **D)**

To add or subtract numbers in scientific notation, the exponents of the base of 10 must be the same. The first number can be rewritten as $4.71 \times 10 \times 10^2 = 47.1 \times 10^2$. The values in front of 10^2 are subtracted, and the power of 10 stays the same, with a result of 44.12×10^2. The solution is then rewritten in proper scientific notation as **4.412×10^3**.

27. **B)**

The answer choices simplify to –6, 0, –11, and –30. Answer choice B), **0, is the only response that is not negative**.

28. **D)**

The algebraic expression can be simplified using PEMDAS.

$10^2 - 7(3 - 4) - 25$

$= 10^2 - 7(-1) - 25$

$= 100 + 7 - 25$

$= 107 - 25$

$= \mathbf{82}$

29. **B)**

The algebraic expression can be simplified using PEMDAS.

$$\frac{5^2(3) + 3(-2)^2}{4 + 3^2 - 2(5 - 8)} = \frac{5^2(3) + 3(-2)^2}{4 + 3^2 - 2(-3)} \rightarrow$$

$$\frac{25(3) + 3(4)}{4 + 9 - 2(-3)} = \frac{75 + 12}{13 + 6} = \frac{\mathbf{87}}{\mathbf{19}}$$

30. **C)**

First convert everything to kilograms:

$800 \text{ g} \times \dfrac{1 \text{ kg}}{1000 \text{ g}} = 0.8 \text{ kg}$

$300 \text{ g} \times \dfrac{1 \text{ kg}}{1000 \text{ g}} = 0.3 \text{ kg}$

Next find the total weight:

$1.2 \text{ kg} + 0.8 \text{ kg} + 0.3 \text{ kg} = 2.3 \text{ kg}$

Now find the total cost by multiplying by \$4/kg:

$2.3 \text{ kg} \times \dfrac{\$4}{1 \text{ kg}} = \mathbf{\$9.20}$

31. **B)**

Each fraction is changed to an improper fraction: $\left(\frac{3}{2}\right)\left(\frac{8}{3}\right) \div \frac{5}{4}$.

Using PEMDAS and working left to right:

$\left(\frac{3}{2}\right)\left(\frac{8}{3}\right) \div \frac{5}{4} = \frac{24}{6} \div \frac{5}{4} = \frac{4}{1} \div \frac{5}{4}$.

To divide the fractions, the second fraction is flipped and then multiplied

by the first fraction, giving $\left(\frac{4}{1}\right)\left(\frac{4}{5}\right) = \frac{16}{5}$

This can be written as $\mathbf{3\frac{1}{5}}$.

32. **D)**

First, simplify the exponents:

$2^{-1} = \frac{1}{2^1} = \frac{1}{2}$

$(-1)^3 = -1$

Now, order the quantities from most negative to most positive:

$-\frac{4}{3}, -1, \frac{2}{5}, \frac{1}{2}$

33. **C)**

The digit in the tenths place is 7 and is rounded up to 8 because the digit in the hundredths place is 8, which is greater than or equal to 5. So the number is rounded up to **2.8**.

34. **C)**

A proportion is solved by cross-multiplying:

$5(4x - 5) = \frac{3}{2}(2x - 6)$

Then, the linear equation is solved for x:

$20x - 25 = 3x - 9$; $17x = 16$; $x = \frac{16}{17}$.

35. **D)**

Start by adding 6 to both sides:

$8x - 6 + 6 = 3x + 24 + 6$

$8x = 3x + 30$

Next subtract $3x$ from both sides:

$8x - 3x = 3x + 30 - 3x$

$5x = 30$

Finally divide both sides by 5 to solve for x:

$5x \div 5 = 30 \div 5$

$x = \mathbf{6}$

36. **D)**

The solution can be written as a fraction by dividing the number of correct questions by the total number of questions:

$\frac{42}{48} = 0.875$

Then, the result is multiplied by 100 for a grade of **87.5%**.

Reading

1. **C) is correct.** A 152 systolic blood pressure reading of 152 places the patient in the hypertension stage 1 category.

2. **B) is correct.** The purpose of the passage is to explain what an idealist believes in. The author does not offer any opinions or try to persuade readers about the importance of certain values.

3. **A) is correct.** The passage states that a snakes' "intricate diamonds, stripes, and swirls help the animals hide from predators, but perhaps most importantly (for us humans, anyway), the markings can also indicate whether the snake is venomous."

4. **B) is correct.** The final paragraph of the passage states that the two species "frequently [share] a habitat" and that "[a] predatory hawk or eagle, usually hunting from high in the sky, can't tell the difference between the two species, and so the kingsnake gets passed over and lives another day."

5. **D) is correct.** This summary captures the main ideas of each paragraph.

6. **A) is correct.** The author is informing readers about how skin coloration in snakes relates to whether a snake is venomous.

7. **B) is correct.** The first step in the *After Planting* section is to water the plants immediately.

8. **A) is correct.** In the *Before Planting* section, the directions say to mix in fertilizer or compost after the soil has been loosened.

9. **C) is correct.** The author and Alan have a friendly relationship, as evidenced by the author's casual tone and his offer to bring Alan a gift from his vacation.

10. **C) is correct.** The author is writing to tell Alan that he will be out of the office. The details about his trip and the meeting support this idea.

11. **D) is correct.** The author wants to bring customers into Carl's Car Depot, doing so by highlighting the low prices and range of cars available.

12. **B) is correct.** The word *sell* best describes the author's implication that the cars are priced to be sold quickly.

13. **A) is correct.** The passage does not mention warranties.

14. **C) is correct.** The word *said* is italicized to provide emphasis and contrast with the word *actions*.

15. **B) is correct.** The Scout Camp is due north of the Fire Circle.

16. **A) is correct.** The Old Oak Tree lies on the trail between the Fishing Pond and the Fire Circle.

17. **A) is correct.** A primary source is produced by someone with firsthand knowledge of the events being described. Of the choices, only the letter writer was a witness to the Battle of Gettysburg.

18. **B) is correct.** The passage describes how Julia had an exhausting morning, and it can be assumed that when "she'd had enough" she decided to go home.

19. **C) is correct.** Whether it was irresponsible for Julia to leave work is a matter of opinion. Some readers may agree, and others may disagree. The other statements are facts that can be proven from the passage.

20. **A) is correct.** Choice A describes the order of Julia's actions that matches the chronological order of the passage.

21. **B) is correct.** The phrase "set a course for home" is an idiom that means to

head in a certain direction, so Julia is planning to go home.

22. **D) is correct.** The passage emphasizes that Julia is tired, so she's most likely to drive home and go to sleep.

23. **D) is correct.** In the passage, Thomas Jefferson is defined as an anti-Federalist, in contrast with Federalists who believe in a strong federal government.

24. **B) is correct.** *Tropical Frogs* belongs under the heading *Frogs* with the other types of frogs. The blank spot should not include a specific species of frog or refer to amphibians other than frogs.

25. **A) is correct.** Only Choice A is a source produced by someone who does not have first-hand experience of World War I.

26. **A) is correct.** Victoria's win implies that she played in a competitive event.

27. **D) is correct.** Quarter Price Books has the lowest price: (3.99 × 25) + (2.99 × 50) = 249.25

28. **B) is correct.** The Book Barn would offer the lowest price: $98 for twenty-five books.

29. **A) is correct.** A company that profits from private tutoring might introduce bias into a study on the effects of private tutoring in schools.

30. **C) is correct.** The author cites specific evidence—data from a study—to support his or her argument.

31. **C) is correct.** Choice C shows the correct order of the blocks after following the directions.

32. **D) is correct.** Choice D correctly lists the houses the author visited as listed chronologically in the passage.

33. **B) is correct.** The author says that the house on Pine Street "had enough

space inside but didn't have a big enough yard for our three dogs."

34. **A) is correct.** The website of a state's board of elections will have current information about polling places, voting hours, and issues on the ballot. Other resources could be incorrect, out of date, or biased.

35. **D) is correct.** The passage concludes with the statement "our Human Resources team will be taking longer than previously stated to review candidates and schedule interviews" and a time window in which Mr. Morgan can expect to receive feedback.

36. **A) is correct.** The author of the passage states that the team will be taking "longer than previously stated," implying that she had previously told Mr. Morgan that the process would take less than two weeks.

37. **C) is correct.** The passage states that babies' senses are much like those of their adult counterparts with the exception of their vision, which develops later.

38. **B) is correct.** The passage states that "infants rely primarily on hearing."

39. **A) is correct.** The passage explains how a baby's senses develop and allow it to interact with the world.

40. **D) is correct.** The word *given* best describes the idea that the gifts have been handed out.

41. **B) is correct.** Only Choice B includes the fact that both Epimetheus and Prometheus were assigned to create living things; it then clarifies that Epimetheus gave positive traits to animals, while Prometheus gave fire to humans. This choice includes all the important parts of the passage without adding other emotions or details.

42. **B) is correct.** *Lamb* fits best with the pattern of subheadings naming specific types of meat.

43. **C) is correct.** Ginger appears on the list for fall.

44. **B) is correct.** The passage states that restaurateurs must be "exact and ruthless with their budget and pricing." The success of The Hot Dog implies that its owners have done that.

45. **D) is correct.** *Evidence* best describes the idea that The Hot Dog's longevity is proof of its owners' skills.

46. **A) is correct.** Page 55 is included in the section on Italian painters.

47. **C) is correct.** Page 153 is the beginning of the section on High Renaissance architecture, which includes the year 1518.

48. **B) is correct.** In February the service earned $1100, and in April it earned $200. The difference between the two months is $900.

49. **B) is correct.** The author uses several markers of casual writing, including the first person, exclamation marks, and informal language.

50. **C) is correct.** The diagram indicates that products are formed when the substrate is broken apart.

51. **C) is correct.** The transition word *finally* indicates the end of a sequence.

52. **A) is correct.** The index shows that the Battle of the Scheldt appears on page 110.

53. **C) is correct.** The transition word *overall* is used to indicate a conclusion or summary.

Science

1. **B) is correct.** Oxygen intake and carbon dioxide disposal are the primary functions of the respiratory system.

2. **B) is correct.** Making observations is the first step of the scientific method; observations enable the researcher to form a question and begin the research process.

3. **D) is correct.** The mechanism of natural selection is rooted in the idea that there is variation in inherited traits among a population of organisms, and that there is differential reproduction as a result.

4. **A) is correct.** Capillaries are very small blood vessels found where veins and arteries meet. They are the site of material exchange.

5. **B) is correct.** Ovarian follicles each contain a sac with an immature egg, or oocyte. During the female reproductive cycle, several oocytes will mature into a mature ovum. Eventually, one ovum is released per cycle during ovulation.

6. **B) is correct.** The tongue is a muscle that plays a primary role in digestion and, in conjunction with teeth, prepares food for swallowing.

7. **A) is correct.** The left atrium receives oxygenated blood, then moves it downward into the left ventricle.

8. **C) is correct.** The parietal lobe is considered the primary sensory processing and integrating center of the brain.

9. **C) is correct.** Antibodies are activated by antigens and only destroy cells infected by specific pathogens.

10. **A) is correct.** Data is considered reliable if similar results are found after repeated experiments following consistent conditions; however, if data does not accurately measure the variable it is intended to measure, it is not considered valid.

11. **C) is correct.** Mendel's law of independent assortment, his second law of heredity, expands on the law of segregation by stipulating that alleles which separate in the gamete stage do so independently of other genes.

12. **B) is correct.** Proceeding top to bottom on the periodic table, atoms gain more and more layers of electrons in their orbitals, increasing radius. Proceeding right to left on the periodic table, atoms have fewer valence electrons and the attraction between nucleus and electrons decreases. Both of these effects cause a trend of increasing radius down and to the left on the periodic table.

13. **C) is correct.** Enamel is a tissue found in teeth, but not skeletal bones.

14. **B) is correct.** Semilunar valves are present in the pulmonary trunk and the aortic trunk; they allow blood to enter the vessels and prevent its return back to the heart.

15. **D) is correct.** Neuromuscular junctions are the location in which the nervous system communicates with the muscular system to create muscle contraction and movement.

16. **A) is correct.** Calcium is the most abundant mineral found in bones, as well as the entire body.

17. **B) is correct.** The medulla oblongata, along with the pons, is a portion of the brain stem that regulates critical body functions.

18. **C) is correct.** The skin, which provides a seamless layer of cells around the entire body, is the primary physical barrier that prevents pathogens from entering the body.

19. **A) is correct.** The pyloric sphincter acts as a valve at the connection of the stomach and small intestine.

20. **B) is correct.** A released ovum stays in the fallopian tube for approximately 24 hours. If sperm have not migrated up the tubes to fertilize the egg, then it moves through the uterus; if fertilization does occur, it stays in the tube for several more days as it moves to the uterus for implantation.

21. **C) is correct.** The pineal gland is located in the epithalamus and is a gland involved in the production of melatonin.

22. **C) is correct.** Subtracting the atomic number from the mass number gives the number of protons: 88 – 38 = 50.

23. **C) is correct.** Lipids, which include but are not limited to fats, are an efficient source of energy storage due to their ability to store nearly twice as much energy as carbohydrates and proteins.

24. **B) is correct.** The sinoatrial (SA) node is an area of specialized muscle tissue in the right atrium that generates an electrical signal which spreads from cell to cell to generate the heartbeat.

25. **A) is correct.** Ganglions are dense clusters of nerve cells responsible for processing sensory information and coordinating motor activity.

26. **C) is correct.** Codominance occurs when two dominant alleles are both expressed.

27. **C) is correct.** There is a $\frac{1}{4}$ chance that the resulting offspring will have a WwSs genotype.

	WS	Ws	wS	ws
WS	WWSS	WWSs	WwSS	WwSs
Ws	WWSs	WWSs	WwSs	Wwss
wS	WwSS	WwSs	wwSS	wwSs
ws	WwSs	Wsss	wwSs	wwss

28. **A) is correct.** Cytokines are small proteins released by cells that have a role in cell communication and behavior. In the immune system, some cytokines play a critical role in immune response activation by triggering inflammation, fever, and other responses.

29. **A) is correct.** This is the path air follows through the respiratory system during gas exchange.

30. **A) is correct.** The smooth endoplasmic reticulum is a series of membranes attached to the cell nucleus and plays an important role in the production and storage of lipids.

31. **A) is correct.** Expression of secondary sexual characteristics is regulated by estrogen.

32. **C) is correct.** The hypodermis is the thickest layer of skin and is the site of much of the stored fat in the human body.

33. **C) is correct.** Synapses are connections between two neurons. Nerve signals trigger the release of neurotransmitters, which carry the nerve impulse across the synaptic cleft, or gap, between cells, to be received by the receptor site of the next cell.

34. **D) is correct.** The mitochondria found in cells are what power the cell and provide it with the energy it needs to carry out its life functions. Muscle cells need a lot of ATP in order to provide the energy needed for movement and exercise.

35. **B) is correct.** Using one filtration system for all three tanks keeps the water quality across all three tanks constant and eliminates experimental bias for this variable.

36. **C) is correct.** A controlled experiment requires researchers to compare an experimental group with a control group while controlling all variables except for the independent variable, which the researcher manipulates to test the hypothesis.

37. **A) is correct.** Tank A is the control group because the sunlight variable is unchanged from the sunlight the elodea are exposed to in their natural environment.

38. **D) is correct.** Cytotoxic T cells are a part of the adaptive immune system that attack and destroy pathogens displaying specific antigens.

39. **D) is correct.** Veins are blood vessels that move blood to the heart using a series of valves.

40. **C) is correct.** The large intestine, or colon, is an s-shaped organ that dehydrates food material as it travels through the organ and is eliminated at the rectum.

41. **D) is correct.** Water is a polar molecule and as a result is able to dissolve polar substances. The polar ends of water attract the polar ends of other polar or ionic molecules, causing the substance to dissolve.

42. **B) is correct.** The sister chromatids of each chromosome are pulled apart by the spindle and pulled to opposite centrosomes during anaphase, elongating the cell in the process.

43. **D) is correct.** Peristalsis begins in the esophagus, where the bolus of food material is swallowed, and continues to transport food to the stomach, the small intestine, and the large intestine.

44. **D) is correct.** Insulin production and blood sugar regulation are performed by the pancreas.

45. **D) is correct.** Combustion is defined as a reaction with O_2 in order to produce CO_2 and H_2O.

46. **A) is correct.** Both the pancreas and salivary glands produce amylase, which is an enzyme that helps digest carbohydrates.

47. **A) is correct.** A hypertonic solution has a higher concentration than the interior of the cell, and water will rush out of the cell to equalize the concentrations, causing the cell to shrink.

48. **D) is correct.** The conducting zone consists of the upper respiratory tract from the nose and mouth through the trachea; it filters and conducts air into the lungs. The respiratory zone consists of the lower respiratory tract from the bronchioles to the alveoli and serves as a site of gas exchange.

49. **A) is correct.** mRNA is a sequence of nucleotides in which each triplet codes for a particular amino acid. The sequence of triplets in the mRNA would translate into the sequence of amino acids that make up a protein.

50. **C) is correct.** Isotopes are atoms that differ in their number of neutrons but are otherwise identical.

51. **A) is correct.** The epiglottis is the protective flap at the entrance of the larynx.

52. **A) is correct.** Fascia is connective tissue that encloses individual muscle fibers.

53. **A) is correct.** Strong acids break apart into their constituent ions immediately when placed in water.

English and Language Usage

1. **B) is correct.** Both *Ukrainians* and *Malanka* must be capitalized; both are proper nouns, and *Ukrainians* begins a sentence.

2. **D) is correct.** This choice creates a comma splice.

3. **B) is correct.** The verb is the singular *afford*, and its subject is the singular *employer*.

4. **A) is correct.** Here, two independent clauses are connected by a comma plus the coordinating conjunction *and*.

5. **C) is correct.** This choice uses formal language, the third-person perspective, and nonjudgmental language.

6. **A) is correct.** The complete subject includes the main noun (*reason*) and all its accompanying modifying phrases.

7. **C) is correct.** The introductory phrase *After a twelve-hour workday* is followed by a comma.

8. **D) is correct.** If these intelligent birds have been kept as pets for so long, and if people have taken the time to train them, it is most likely that parrots are *valued* animals.

9. **A) is correct.** The prefix *intra–* means *inside* or *within*.

10. **B) is correct.** The inessential appositive phrase *whose death shocked America in April of 2016* is correctly set apart from the rest of the sentence by commas. Choices A and D use the semicolon and colon incorrectly, and Choice C incorrectly pairs an em dash with a comma.

11. **A) is correct.** *Potatos* should be spelled *potatoes*.

12. **D) is correct.** *Fields* best describes the idea that members study many different areas of knowledge; furthermore, the word *field* may refer to something intangible. There are many topics of study in many *fields*, or disciplines.

13. **B) is correct.** *Astronemers* should be spelled *astronomers*.

14. **D) is correct.** The noun *potato* ends with the letter *o*, so it is made plural by adding *-es*.

15. **C) is correct.** This sentence includes an independent clause (*interstellar travel is expected to be an even bigger challenge than interplanetary exploration*) and a dependent clause introduced by the subordinating conjuction *because* (*Because the distance between stars in the galaxy is far greater than the distance between planets*).

16. **A) is correct.** This sentence does not relate to the flow of information provided by the other three, which tell the story of the siblings' experience with the radio contest. It only discusses the siblings' experience attending the game itself.

17. **D) is correct.** The two subheadings under "Heat Engines" are "Combustion Engines" and "Non-Combustion Engines."

18. **A) is correct.** The prefix *pre–* means *before*.

19. **A) is correct.** The root word *corp* means *body*.

20. **B) is correct.** *Conventional* best describes the idea that comic books have an established narrative framework, a main point in the sentence.

21. **B) is correct.** *Bucks* is a slang term for *dollars*.

22. **C) is correct.** *Widely* is an adverb modifying the adjective *available*.

23. **B) is correct.** *Remains* is a verb in the sentence.

24. **C) is correct.** *Mountain's* is not possessive in this sentence, so it does not require an apostrophe.

25. **D) is correct.** The second *parents'* is plural, not possessive, so it does not require an apostrophe.

26. **D) is correct.** The colon correctly signifies that the second clause builds on the first. Choice A is a comma splice. While choices B and C are grammatically correct, they create a nonsensical contrast in the passage by using the words *but* and *however*.

27. **A) is correct.** *President* is a title and should be capitalized when it precedes a name.

28. **C) is correct.** *Number* is singular, so it agrees with the singular pronoun *it*.

Follow the link below to take your second ATI TEAS practice test and to access other online study resources:

www.acceptedinc.com/ati-teas-online-resources

Made in the USA
Columbia, SC
13 January 2018